Dr Simon Forman

DR SIMON FORMAN

A Most Notorious Physician

Judith Cook

Chatto & Windus
LONDON

Published by Chatto & Windus 2001

2 4 6 8 10 9 7 5 3 1

Copyright © Judith Cook 2001

Judith Cook has asserted her right under the
Copyright, Designs and Patents Act 1988 to be identified
as the author of this work

First published in Great Britain in 2001 by
Chatto & Windus
Random House, 20 Vauxhall Bridge Road,
London SW1V 2SA

Random House Australia (Pty) Limited
20 Alfred Street, Milsons Point, Sydney,
New South Wales 2061, Australia

Random House New Zealand Limited
18 Poland Road, Glenfield,
Auckland 10, New Zealand

Random House (Pty) Limited
Endulini, 5A Jubilee Road, Parktown 2193, South Africa

The Random House Group Limited Reg. No. 954009

www.randomhouse.co.uk

A CIP catalogue record for this book
is available from the British Library

ISBN 0 7011 6899 4

Papers used by Random House are natural,
recyclable products made from wood grown in sustainable forests;
the manufacturing processes conform to the environmental
regulations of the country of origin.

Typeset by Deltatype Ltd, Wirral

Printed and bound in Great Britain by
Mackays of Chatham PLC

Contents

Illustrations

Acknowledgements

A great many people helped make this book possible, not least in various libraries. My grateful thanks therefore to Steven Tomlinson, Assistant Librarian at the Bodleian Library, Oxford, and the long-suffering staff of that institution's Duke Humphrey Library; Geoffrey Davenport, Librarian of the Royal College of Physicians; Peter Jones, Fellow and Librarian of King's College, Cambridge; Marian Pringle, Librarian at the Shakespeare Birthplace Trust; Jim Shaw, Librarian at the University of Birmingham's Shakespeare Institute, Stratford-upon-Avon; Elaine Pierce-Jones, Chester Record Office; and the British Library and London Library. In retrospect, to the late Dr A. L. Rowse, who chivvied me for years to write the book, to Anne Reynolds for putting up with me during my stints at the Bodleian and, last but hardly least, to my splendid editor, Jenny Uglow, for her help and advice.

Foreword

The time is the summer of 1611. In a fine house in Lambeth a small, middle-aged, sandy-haired man sits writing beside an open window, through which the tide, running fast up the river, brings with it the smell of the sea. There are also other scents, from the great bank of roses he has planted close to the house, others – more pungent – from his herb garden. Sunshine from outside lights up the contents of the room, picking out a shelf containing books on current medical practice, the histories and teachings of the masters of the past such as Galen and Paracelsus, and volume after volume of patients' case notes. More shelves are crowded with bottles and phials, pillboxes and jars of ingredients for medicines and salves. There are also other, stranger, objects. A stuffed crocodile sits on a side table, beside it a box of small male and female figurines, rings and oddly shaped stones with strange markings, while suspended from a cord above is what is said to be a unicorn's horn. Around the walls there are charts representing the movement of the planets, and mystical symbols and a pentacle have been painted on the floor.

The man is working on a set of calculations from which he is drawing up an astrological chart. He looks out of the window again, where the young and pretty maid is hanging the laundry over the bushes in the middle of the garden. He told her not to put it on the outside hedges after seeing a play at the Globe Theatre, *The Winter's Tale* by Will Shakespeare, in which a thief called Autolycus stole washing off just such a hedge. The sight of her bending over the bushes brings a smile to his face, reminding him of their recent romp while his wife was away visiting her relatives. He returns to his work, only to be disturbed by a knock on the door. He starts up – obviously apprehensive. But who is he? What is he so anxious about?

Some years ago I picked up a second-hand paperback in an antiquarian bookshop in Stratford-upon-Avon which specialises in Shakespeare and the age in which he lived. It was called *The Casebooks of Simon Forman* and was edited, with a commentary, by A. L. Rowse. I became so fascinated that half an hour later I was still reading it and, needless to say, bought it. Until then I knew nothing of Simon Forman, and Rowse himself, I discovered, had not actually set out in search of him but of a woman called Emilia Lanier, with whom Forman had had an affair and whom Rowse was convinced was Shakespeare's Dark Lady of the Sonnets.

Intrigued, I began seeking out other sources that might tell me more. The entry in the *Dictionary of National Biography*, written by a nineteenth-century academic, was to set the scene for the rest. Simon Forman, I learned, was nothing but a quack and a charlatan, an astrologer who purported to practise medicine, a fellow of bad repute especially where women were concerned. Other glimpses of him appeared in books on such diverse subjects as the Elizabethan underworld, the murder of Christopher Marlowe and, most striking of all, the Overbury poisoning case, in which the young Countess of Essex was charged with murder. In almost all instances the same slurs on Forman's probity were repeated.

Having got that far, more pressing matters intervened and I put the subject to one side. But later, when researching the background for a book and play about Christopher Marlowe, my interest in the elusive Simon Forman was rekindled and afterwards I set out to discover more about him. Slowly, a somewhat different picture began to emerge. He did indeed practise astrology, as did almost all the physicians of his day, but by the standards of his time he was also a careful practitioner of medicine. Only he and his friend and colleague, the distinguished Richard Napier, kept such comprehensive and immaculate case notes on their patients.[1] Rowse published only a fraction of these, but while his views on the identity of the Dark Lady have raised the hackles of academics ever since, his book is a useful guide to the massive amount of material still awaiting the scholar prepared to spend years deciphering it.

It is not easy to pin Simon Forman down, to cut through the layers of myth which have accrued to his reputation over the centuries and place him in the context of his time, but, fortunately, what makes him unique is the sheer amount of manuscript material. He left behind not only case notes but also an enormous number of papers, including a brief autobiography, a substantial diary and personal jottings recording almost every aspect of his life, his childhood experiences, his dreams and fears, his hopes and ambitions, his struggle to achieve recognition and his relationships with a wide variety of women. From these we also know of his battles to achieve professional recognition, the kind of people who consulted him and his wide range of interests.

He enjoyed poetry and tried to write it himself, loved the theatre and gave us our first accounts of Shakespeare's plays in performance. His was a curious and ever-questing mind, fascinated by the new sciences and discoveries of the late sixteenth and early seventeenth centuries, from the recent understanding of the cosmos and the place of the earth in the solar system to the wonders reported by explorers returning from America, the 'new found land'. Because of the nature of his profession he crossed the lives of both rich and poor, the famous and infamous, the noble countess and the Bankside whore, the merchant venturers and the players at the Rose and Globe theatres. And, increasingly throughout his life, he was to find himself caught up on the fringes of great events.

His diary[2] is a maddening document. It was clearly not intended to be read by others, but its content varies from fragments of texts and the briefest of entries to whole chapters of his life. Moreover, he shares with young children, when they tell of a day's happenings, an inability to differentiate between what is important and what is not; everything receives the same significance so that entries about waking up with a sore throat or mislaying a pair of hose jostle for space with serious emotional concerns and major events.

There is also a very real dichotomy between the Simon Forman of the autobiography (which ends in his early twenties) and the writings designed for publication, in which he comes across as an extremely sober, serious and somewhat pompous individual, and the writer of the diary and personal notes, where there is a glimpse of someone very different, endlessly restless, searching, game for adventure, and dabbling in dangerous pastimes.

On his death a large proportion of his papers and books, including his diary, autobiography, the casebooks, his treatises on a variety of subjects, his *Book of Plaies* and many pages of unrelated notes, passed first into the hands of Richard Napier, then from him to Elias Ashmole and so to the Ashmolean Museum in Oxford, before ending up in the Bodleian Library. At some stage when they were in the Ashmolean they were bound into volumes but in little or no date order or continuity of subject matter. Only the casebooks are in sequence. The effort to make some kind of logical order out of the rest is not helped by the fact that Forman himself would often go back to a page he had used years earlier and add more notes, few of which are relevant to the former material; but then such fine, handmade paper was expensive and it made economic sense to write in previously unused spaces.

Added to this confusion, Forman's handwriting is notoriously difficult to decipher, especially for those who are not experts in transcribing sixteenth-century script. Except on the rare occasions when he wrote for others to read, he either scrawled his letters or made notes in the most minute, abbreviated hand. The difference in clarity between his own handwriting and that of some of his contemporaries is clearly shown in the examples of letters written to him by Frances Howard, later Countess of Hertford, and Richard Napier. As to the casebooks, these are largely in abbreviated dog Latin, but fortunately he appended to them notes of the outcomes in English, along with personal details. From time to time, on really sensitive matters such as the state of his married mistress's pregnancy, he also used cipher.

One helpful detail, however, is that, most unusually, he did not use the old method of calculating the calendar. His year ran as ours does from January to December, even though most of those with whom he had dealings still used the old calendar, in which the new year began on 25 March, Lady Day. (This explains some apparent discrepancies in dating between his accounts of an event and those of others.)

So who was the man who as well as being labelled a charlatan has also been variously described over the centuries as 'a wayward genius', 'that devil, Forman', 'a most notorious physician' and, most comprehensively, as 'an unforgettable personality: mercurial, mesmerising, combative, sexually rapacious and, that rare thing, a paranoid with platoons of real enemies'?[3] What follows is his story told, whenever possible, in his own words.[4]

1

Childhood and Apprenticeship

Simon Forman was born in 'the year from the nativity of our Lord Jesus Christ 1552, the 31st December, being a Saturday and New Year's Eve at 45 minutes after nine of the clock at night'.[1] He recorded this information in the brief autobiography written about 1600, which takes him from birth to the age of twenty-one. He gave the exact time because this was a matter of great importance for an astrologer when making the calculations required for a horoscope and he always noted it if possible when recording information about his clients, although it is unlikely such information was ever more than roughly accurate.

His father was William Forman and his mother was Mary, daughter 'of John Foster': Simon was 'born of her body' in the 'village called Quidhampton in the county of Wiltshire', 'situate in the valley on the north side of the river between Wilton and Salisbury. Whose parents were well descended and of good reputation and fame, having many children and they disposed diversely.'

The 'fame' and supposed good descent of his parents are largely wishful thinking, as are the two fantasy genealogies he later invented for himself and his family. In the first of these[2] he began with a brief history of the great 'King Cimbelin' and then launched into an explanation of how the first 'Forman' acquired his name after being commended by the king for his brave, valiant and courageous service and for being 'the foremost' of men. Before long he had promoted his ancestor to 'Lord Forman', drawing an elaborate family tree (he was a good draftsman), which showed a female descendant marrying 'Malcolm, King of the Scots'. However, this fantasy line peters out after the Norman Conquest.

A second version claimed that the original family name was 'Foxson', that 'William Foxson was born in Millom Castle in Cumbria' and, as previously, that the name was changed, 'for his forwardness and valour', when he became 'Lord Forman'. He then drew up another elaborate but different family tree, in which one descendant, George, was supposed to have been on the battlefield at Bosworth Field when 'King Henry was crowned' and another was 'standard bearer to James, King of the Scots, and was slaine in that great battell of 1525'. (Presumably he meant Flodden Field in 1513.) Beside this one he put an elaborate and equally mythical coat of arms, beautifully drawn and painted and outlined in gold leaf.[3] Amusing as they are, there may be some truth in his belief that his family originated much further north, for 'Forman' is a name which is still found on the Scottish side of the border, where it can be seen in some of the older graveyards.

The facts, however, are more mundane. William Forman was a small farmer, one of fifteen similar 'free tenants' in the straggle of houses which was sixteenth-century Quidhampton. On the whole most of the material in the autobiography rings true, although Forman affords his father a higher status than he actually had, casting him in the role of a stalwart yeoman standing up against the aristocracy in the shape of the Herbert family, the Earls of Pembroke, who owned nearby Wilton Park.

According to him, the Herberts rented land off the Forman family (which seems highly dubious) and William Forman spent much time in contention with them over money for rents which he claimed were owed to him. The matter was to remain unresolved, for on the death of his father, Simon wrote, his mother did not proceed with it 'because she, being a woman, knew not how to help herself on that behalf'. In reality it was highly unlikely William Forman had much time to spare for litigation with his noble neighbour, since life was a clearly a continual struggle to make ends meet.

Mary Forman was already a widow with two children when she married William and she subsequently had a further six sons and two daughters, so William found himself with a dozen mouths to feed. Although Forman's childhood was far from idyllic and he later recalled how from his earliest years he yearned for something better, throughout his life he looked back with nostalgia on the Quidhampton of his infancy and boyhood, dreaming often of its water-meadows and marshes and gentle beauty. In spite of hardship, until the death of his father his early years were relatively happy. He writes (always referring to himself in the third person) that 'Simon' was the favourite of his father, who 'had so much affection for him that he would always have him lie at his bed's foot in a little bed for the nonce'.

He was a highly imaginative child, given to vivid dreams and nightmares: often when he went to sleep he dreamed that 'mighty mountains and hills come rolling against him' which would overrun him and bruise him, yet he 'always got up on top of them and went over them'. At other times he would dream of 'great waters like to drown him, boiling and raging as though they would swallow him up, yet he thought he did overpass them'. God, he felt, showed him these visions in his youth to signify the troubles that would beset him 'in his riper years', the mountains representing 'the great and mighty potentates that he had controversy with afterwards' and the waters 'the great counsels that were holden to overthrow him'. But, thanks be to God, he was able to 'overpass all with credit'.

When he was about seven his parents sent him to the little free school in the nearby village of Wilton, where both boys and girls learned their letters and numbers from hornbooks. Hornbooks were the universal educational aid for all small children fortunate enough to be sent to school and were flat squares usually made of horn (hence the name), often with a handle designed so that it could hang at the child's belt or girdle. The first line of the 'book', which began with a cross, was known as the criss-cross row and was followed by the letters of the alphabet, rows of numbers and the Lord's Prayer. Chalk and slates were used for any written work.

His Wilton schoolmaster was a minister called William Rydout or Rydar. By trade he was a cobbler and married with a family, but after the death of Queen Mary in 1558 'when the law did turn' and married priests were again acceptable, he took Holy Orders and so became 'a schoolmaster and teacher of children'. He could read English well, 'but had little Latin' and that he had picked up from his own sons at school in Salisbury.

Forman learned his alphabet and numbers easily enough, along with the Lord's Prayer, but for some time he had difficulty coming to grips both with reading 'and the mystery of spelling'. He was always to have a freewheeling approach to that latter 'mystery', but then at the time he was hardly alone in that nor was there any set standard. So disheartened did he become with his failure to learn to read and write that he begged his master to send him back home, as it was clear he was never going to make any progress. Rydout's solution, the accepted convention of the day, was to beat him soundly, 'which made me more diligent to my book', indeed it was apparently so effective that within a very short while he found he had learned the skills so well that he was 'never so beat for his book again' and within a year he had mastered almost all the schoolmaster could teach him.

Although Wilton was no great distance from Quidhampton, his father decided it was too far for a child to walk in the depths of winter and so arranged for him to board with the Rydouts. Forman later made a strange comment about this, which gives pause for thought: 'Boarding with this priest in the winter time he would make him [Simon] lie always naked with him, which kept him in great fear.' (With the brief return of Catholicism in 1553, Forman spent most of the first six years of his life as a practising Catholic and for the rest of it he always referred to the parish parson or vicar as a 'priest'.)

After a couple of years at a free or dame school, those boys whose fathers were members of the professions, successful merchants or forward-looking craftsmen, were likely to be sent to one of the new grammar schools, though no such opportunities were afforded to girls unless their parents were rich enough to hire tutors. However, although money was so short, Forman showed such promise by the time he reached the age of nine that his father decided, much against his mother's wishes, that he should go to the grammar school in the Close of Salisbury Cathedral. The school's headmaster was a Dr John Bowles, 'a most furious man', who had been instructed by the dean and chapter that it must be run as a free school so that no suitable boy would be refused.

The same daily pattern was followed and the same subjects taught in grammar schools throughout the land. School began at seven a.m. in winter and six a.m. in summer, and for Forman, as for Shakespeare attending King Edward VI's school in Stratford-upon-Avon and Christopher Marlowe at the King's School in Canterbury, the day opened and closed with Bible readings, psalms and prayers. The entire syllabus was in

Latin: the pupils worked from Latin grammars and phrase books, which led on to their reading *Aesop's Fables* and the works of Cato.

Shakespeare and Marlowe lived close to their respective schools and so were able to stay at home, but Forman had to board 'at one Mr. Hawknight's, that sometime was Registrar to the Bishop'. It seems Hawknight took his responsibilities lightly and much of the time Forman was sent over to the house of a canon called Mintern, who used the boy as a servant, causing him to complain that 'this canon seldom or never kept any fire in his house; but he had some load of faggots lying in his house. Always when he was a-cold he would go and carry his faggots up into the loft until he was hot; when he had carried them all up, he would fetch them down again and burn none. So he made this Simon do many a time and oft to catch a heat, saying it was better to heat himself so than to sit by the fire.'

However, whatever future hopes William Forman might have had for his bright son, possibly even sending him up to university on a scholarship, within two years they were to come to nothing. The year 1563 was bad in every way. Harvests were poor and Simon Forman noted that it was then 'the soldiers came from Newhaven and the Plague began in Salisbury'. The troops had been part of the Earl of Warwick's force, sent to France in 1563 to stiffen the resistance of the Huguenots to the ruling Guises, but all that particular adventure had achieved was to make both French factions join forces, united by their desire to throw the English out. Warwick found himself cut off in Le Havre and even though his troops were already falling victim to the plague epidemic now sweeping through northern France, he was forced to evacuate his garrison with all possible speed. The soldiers arrived on the south coast bringing the disease with them. It ravaged the southern counties before spreading north to London.

At the end of the year, the school having so far escaped the plague, Forman came home for the Christmas holidays and to celebrate his eleventh birthday. The family had 'kept a great Christmas' in spite of everything and on New Year's Eve, Simon's birthday, William Forman walked over to his piece of land 'with one of his men'. Here, according to Simon, a strange thing happened: a dove flew down and alighted on the ground in front of William, and he and his man made several attempts to catch it, but 'it would always rise up and fall again. So they followed it until it ran into a neighbour's woodbine' but without success. Having told the story to the family, William thought no more of it and the celebration of the twelve days of Christmas continued that evening with 'music, dancing and sport'. Shortly after midnight he felt tired, however, decided it was time he went to bed and made his way upstairs, where he complained that he felt as if someone had struck him on the neck.

He died between midnight and one the next morning and was buried the same day, 1 January 1564. Although the burial seems remarkably quick there is no suggestion that he died of the plague. No sooner was the burial over than Forman's mother (who, he bleakly recorded, had never loved him) informed him that she was not going to allow him to go back to school in Salisbury, there was no question of it. As it was, she 'grudged him houseroom', for it was time he earned his keep, and she sent him to look after the sheep, plough the fields, gather sticks and saw logs for the fire, 'and what fault soever was committed by the rest, he [Simon] was beaten for it'.

Writing of the death of his mother in 1604, Forman recalled that his father was only thirty-nine years old when he died, but that she had lived on as a widow for a further forty years. With a certain amount of reluctant admiration, he said that when she finally died 'she had lived then ninety-seven years and had her eyesight, limbs and memory very well – but a fortnight before she deceased she could walk alone two miles, thanks be to God'.

However, back in 1564 his resentment at seeing his chance of a decent education vanish is palpable across the divide of over four hundred years. Obviously the loss of the father must have had a tremendous economic effect on the family, but it is impossible to know whether Mary Forman simply would not allow him to continue at school because she did not believe it was right for boys of his station, or whether she really was unable to afford it, even though the three older boys were now capable of working the land. What is without doubt is that he never forgave her for it and blamed her for the years he spent struggling to learn what, when and where he could.

For nearly two years he stayed home and did as he was told, growing ever more hostile towards his mother, whom he also blamed for setting the rest of the family against him because he was 'nimble-spirited and up to anything'. Finally, accepting that he was never going to be allowed 'to follow his book' and unable to 'be quiet' at home, he had himself apprenticed to a Matthew Commin in Salisbury.

From accounts of the lives of craftsmen in Tudor England and plays such as Dekker's *The Shoemakers' Holiday* and Shakespeare's *The Merry Wives of Windsor*, we know something of the kind of households into which young lads were apprenticed. House and business usually shared the same premises, the whole presided over by the capable and practical wives of the master craftsman. Women also had the care of the children, servants, maids and journeymen and, quite often, helped their husbands to run the business as well. Apprentices, young lads often away from home and free of their parents for the first time, no doubt posed many problems and in general had a reputation for rowdy and disruptive behaviour, particularly in London, where the City fathers regularly railed against them spending their holiday time drinking and fighting. There are plenty of examples of their being banned from the playhouses for spoiling the show. As the old shepherd puts it in *The Winter's Tale*:[4] 'I would there were no age between sixteen and three-and-twenty, or that youth would sleep out the rest; for there is nothing in the between but getting wenches with child, wronging the ancientry, stealing, fighting.'

Into such a society came the country lad with ideas above his station. Most apprenticeships were to men with a specific craft, silversmiths, shoemakers, clothiers, weavers, wheelwrights and so on, but Forman discovered that Matthew Commin 'used many occupations. First he was a hosier, and thereby learned to sew and make hose. Then he was a merchant of cloth and all small wares, and sold hops, salt, oil, pitch, rosin, raisins, groceries and all apothecary drugs. Whereby Simon learned the knowledge of all wares and drugs and how to buy and sell; and grew so apt and had such good fortune that in short time his master committed all to his charge.'

It sounds too good to be true and so it proved, not least because from the first he crossed Mistress Commin; the next five years saw a running battle between them. This in itself was unfortunate, but in another way Matthew Commin's attitude towards him was worse. While the legal term of an apprenticeship was seven years he had bound himself for ten, on Commin's promise that he would allow him to attend the grammar school in Salisbury for the first three. Almost at once Commin reneged on the bargain and yet again Simon was thwarted in his attempts to study.

7

Also, as he was the youngest of the four apprentices, he was made to do the worst and most menial work, 'being little and small of stature and young of years, so [that] everyone did triumph over him. Especially a kitchen-maid named Mary Roberts; oftentimes she would knock him that the blood should run about his ears.' Gradually, however, the older apprentices left or became journeymen until finally Forman himself became the chief apprentice and one day was able to turn the tables on Mary Roberts in an incident to which he devotes many lines of his autobiography.

It being a fine day, Master and Mistress Commin, with some of their relatives, went off on a jaunt to 'the gardens', which, as they were some distance from their place of business, meant that they would be away all day. Forman and Mary were therefore left behind, he to mind the business and she to see to household tasks, with the proviso that if he became very busy she must help him in the shop.

Within a short time 'so many customers came for wares that Simon could not attend them all' and so he called to Mary to come and help him, but she refused to do so, telling him in no uncertain terms (and with bad language) that he would have to manage on his own and that if he tried to force her into the shop, she would box his ears. Faced with roomful of folk of demanding to be served, he did the best he could, after which, when finally they had all gone, he bolted the shop door, took from the counter 'the yard' used for measuring cloth and strode into the house in search of Mary. As good as her word, she immediately attempted to box his ears, whereupon he fetched her a crack across the knuckles with the yard 'and bruised her head and hands and laid her along, so crying and roaring like a bull'. He beat her so hard, he told her, to pay her back for all the years he had suffered at her hands.

Satisfaction at getting his own back soon vanished with the prospect of what would happen next. If Mistress Commin came into the house first, he had no doubt she would take Mary's part and he would get a beating from Commin. His hope lay in Commin returning before his wife so he could waylay him and explain what had happened. As luck would have it, it was the master who arrived first, to find himself confronted by an angry Forman and his maidservant 'crying and howling'. Asked the cause of this display of emotion, she replied that 'Simon' had beaten her:

"'That's well like," said he, "but, if he had, he had served thee well enough, for thou has beaten him full oft."' With that he asked his apprentice the cause.

'Sir,' Forman told him, 'here came so many customers that I could not serve them and look to the shop too; where I called Mary to help attend in the shop and see to things. She came forth and scolded me, went in again and would not do it, [saying] that people might steal what they would for her. And because thereof, I did give her three or four lambskins with the yard.'

'Thou servest her well enough,' commented Commin, 'and if she be so obstinate, serve her so again.'

Their master's words, said Forman, made 'the maid stark mad' and brought Mistress Commin on to the scene, an intervention which ended with Commin having physically to prevent his wife from beating his apprentice. This made the relationship between mistress and apprentice even worse, but it it had the reverse effect on Mary and afterwards the two young people 'agreed so well that they were never at square again, and Mary would do for him all that she could. Many a pound of butter she yielded for Simon's breakfast which before that she would never do.'

Shortly afterwards he found himself in a confrontation of another kind. Commin had taken a stall at the Lady Day Fair in Salisbury and had sent his journeyman, Richard King, and the apprentice to man it. A group of boys began throwing stones at the stalls and King sent Forman across to see who they were. Among them he recognised the two sons of Master Godfrey, keeper of the Swan Inn, who jeered at him and challenged him to a fight. While he was standing there wondering what to do next, King arrived and urged him to stand up to them. Thus emboldened, he took them on, beat them both, 'and would not after shrink for a bloody nose with any boy, for I was thoroughly fleshed by means of King'.

But despite Forman's growing confidence and assertiveness, Commin still refused to allow him to pursue any sort of further education, which was a matter of real concern. He was also kept so busy that it was almost impossible to find time to read and when one night his master discovered him doing so, he confiscated all his books, including those in Latin. By sheer luck, salvation came in the shape of a Devonshire wool man from Crediton who decided to send his son to Salisbury grammar school. He arranged for the lad to board with the Commin family and, as he shared Forman's room and bed, he brought his books home each night and agreed

9

to teach him what he had learned in his lessons during the day. This at least worked well enough for Simon to recall some of what he had learned earlier and helped him to build on it.

Romance too entered his life in the shape of Anne Young, 'a proper fine maiden', referred to then and afterwards always as 'A.Y.', the only daughter of a man of substance who lived nearby. The girl, 'being younger than Simon, loved him wonderful well and would surely see him once every day or else she would be sick'. The object of her affection was very flattered. A.Y. was the kind of girl described by Shakespeare as being 'of a coming-on disposition' and would arrive on holidays and beg Matthew Commin's permission to allow Forman to attend 'pastimes' with her.

She loved him so well, he boasted, that if 'forty youths were at play before the door in a spacious place that there was, if Simon were not among them she would not be there'. Her pursuit made everyone laugh and Commin would regularly tease him about it. As for Forman, he confided that he 'loved her not but in kindness. But because she was so kind to him, he would do anything he could do for her. And this love on her side lasted long as shall hereafter be showed . . .'

Anne Young was later destined to play a major role in his life and despite his many affairs and his marriage he never forgot her, but in these early days there was little prospect of the relationship developing. It was not unknown for even a respectable young woman to anticipate marriage if the couple were contracted to each other before witnesses and the lover had every intention of wedding her; but it was unlikely that Anne's father would have looked kindly on a penniless young apprentice as a suitable husband for his only daughter.

Within a year his apprenticeship came to an abrupt end, thanks to Mistress Commin. She now had a stall in the town on market days and on one occasion lost an amount of flax from it. Although Forman had not left his master's shop and so could not possibly be responsible for what had happened at the market, when she returned home from paying a visit she blamed him for the loss. When he hotly disputed this, pointing out that he had been nowhere near the stall all day, she hurled herself at him, grasping in her hand a similar yard (if not the same) as that with which he had beaten Mary Roberts and began to belabour him with it. Furious, he wrenched it off her, turned her out of the shop and locked the door on her, whereupon she went straight to her husband, told him Forman had attacked her and ordered Commin to beat him.

What comes across clearly from the writings of Simon Forman and others is how easily the Elizabethans resorted to violence. Masters beat their journeymen, who in turn beat the apprentices; goodwives regularly beat their maids; schoolmasters beat their pupils, who then went out and beat and bullied smaller boys; husbands beat wives and wives (more rarely) beat husbands. At a stage further, lads pulled knives on each other, while wealthier young men settled quarrels with rapiers. On one famous occasion, some years later, two of Forman's patients drew their daggers on each other while waiting to consult him. The activities of the Montagues and Capulets in *Romeo and Juliet* were not far removed from everyday life in Tudor England.

While Forman's view that Mistress Commin was 'wicked, headstrong, proud, fantastical and a consumer and spender of her husband's wealth' was hardly objective, she does seem to have been a difficult woman and the marriage an increasingly desperate one. On one occasion, Forman saw her attack her husband with her fists, whereupon Commin threw a pair of tailor's shears at her as she was going through the door, which 'nailed her clothes and her smock and her buttocks to the door. The points of the shears went clear through the door and she hung fast by the tail.' Many times when Simon and his master were visiting his land two miles out in the country, Commin would tell him sadly that there was nothing to be done but to suffer his wife's behaviour. 'Thou see'est we cannot remedy it as yet but God will send a remedy one day.'

At first Commin was reluctant to carry out his wife's order to beat Forman, but as was all too often the case when faced with one of her rages, he finally gave in. Such unfair treatment proved the last straw and Forman told his master bluntly that as he had not kept to his obligations under the terms of the apprenticeship agreement, he would leave at once and see if he could find some way to continue with his studies. It seems Commin saw the truth of this and not only agreed to let him go but gave him his full indentures for completing his apprenticeship, much to the annoyance of his wife.

Free at last, Simon went back to the grammar school and, old as he was, asked if he could again become a pupil. This was agreed and he set about studying hard, rapidly catching up with what he had missed. As the weeks went by, he found it increasingly difficult to survive and was 'driven to great extremity and hunger'. An appeal to his mother for help with food and money, in view of the fact that he had kept himself without recourse to the farm for six whole years, fell on deaf ears. So with extreme reluctance he had to 'give off to be a scholar for lack of maintenance', turning his back yet again on what he wanted most, the education which would enable him to acquire academic status and so give him a chance of a professional career. It was with a heavy heart that he set about finding some other way to make a living.

2

The Student Physician

Forman was saved from tramping the roads by the offer of a teaching post at the free school in Wilton, which he now raised in status to 'the school of the priory of St. Giles'. This was true in part since until the dissolution of the monasteries the building had been a chantry of the lepers' hospital of St Giles's Priory. While he constantly bemoaned his lack of education, his ability to read and write fluently in both English and Latin was considered sufficient qualification for the job. He taught some thirty boys and their parents provided him with most of his food, while his wages were forty shillings a half year.[1]

And half a year was all he spent at the Wilton school for, as he notes with pride, at the end of that time 'I went to Oxford for to get more learning and so left off being a schoolmaster'. Grand as it sounds, he did not 'go up' in the conventional sense. At some stage while he was teaching in 1573 he met up with an old schoolfellow, Thomas Rydar (possibly the son of his old schoolmaster), with whom he says he had been as close as with a brother, the two lads having been drawn together by the fact that Rydar's stepfather 'was as much against him as Simon's mother was against *him* [my italics]'. Both desperately wanted to pursue further learning, though without the means to support it, and were determined that some way or another they would get themselves to Oxford. Finally, having exhausted every other avenue, they discovered that two local 'gentlemen' Bachelors of Arts, John Thornborough of Magdalen College and Robert

Pinckney of Lady Mary Hall, were returning to Oxford that September to take their Masters' degrees and required servants. Forman and Rydar offered their services and so became poor scholars, Forman at Magdalen College and Rydar at Lady Mary Hall.

In fact Forman attended Magdalen School, not the college, but it was soon obvious to the two friends that what had looked like a splendid idea was not going to work in practice. The two young 'gentlemen' were feckless wasters: in their eyes servants were servants and expected to wait on them hand and foot. 'These two loved him [Simon] nothing well,' Forman wrote later, 'and many times would make him go forth to Loes, the keeper of Shotover, for his hounds to go on hunting from morning to night. They never studied nor gave themselves to their books but go to schools of fencing, to the dancing schools, to steal deer and conies, to hunt the hare, and to the wooing of wenches [and] to Dr. Lawrence of Cowley, for he had two fair daughters, Bess and Martha.'[2] Lawrence was not a doctor of medicine but a wealthy Fellow of All Souls, Regius Professor of Greek and the archdeacon of Wiltshire. 'Sir Thornborough woo'd Bess,' he continues, 'Sir Pinckney, he woo'd Martha and in the end married her. But Thornborough, he deceived Bess – as the mayor's daughter of Brackley, of which Ephues writes, deceived him. This was their ordinary haunt and thither must run Simon with the bottle and bag early and late to the great loss of his time.'

Matters went from bad to worse as the two young blades made more and more demands on Simon's time, leaving him sitting around to cool his heels for hours when he might have been studying, while they hunted, drank and pursued Lawrence's daughters.

In spite of their behaviour and lack of study, both the wealthy young men, from 'good' families, went into Holy Orders and gained almost immediate preferment. After marrying one of Lawrence's daughter, Pinckney became rector of Lydiard Millicent in 1577 and within three years had added two other rich parishes to his tally, thus ensuring himself a good income. Thornborough's career was more spectacular: after jilting the other Lawrence daughter, he became chaplain to the Earl of Pembroke at Wilton Park and was given a whole clutch of livings, after which, in quick succession, he became chaplain to the queen, then Dean of York, Bishop of Limerick, Bishop of Bristol and finally Bishop of Worcester, one of the wealthiest sees in the country. He died at the age of ninety just before the start of the Civil War.[3]

No such ladder of opportunity was available to Forman. There was little point in his remaining in Oxford[4] and at the age of twenty-one he went back to teaching at Wilton free school. Perhaps it was because he was feeling so disheartened that he, who rarely let pass an opportunity to sing his own praises, alluded only briefly to what was a rare event. In 1574 the queen came on a progress to stay with the Earl and Countess of Pembroke and 'on the 22nd day of September I came from Oxford to Quidhampton to make an oration before the Queen, [she] being at Wilton'. To be able to give such an oration, which would have been in Latin, he must certainly have been the brightest local scholar.[5]

During his stay in Oxford Forman had bought a book which was to determine the course of his life. He never explained when or why he resolved to become a physician: if he decided first and then purchased the medical text. Either way he had a mountain to climb. To understand what his decision entailed and the status of the medical profession it is useful to take a moment to survey the state of medical knowledge and accepted beliefs in England, and most of Western Europe, towards the end of the sixteenth century. This was a period when almost every form of learning was in a state of flux as the old lore, philosophies and teachings came under assault from the new sciences and discoveries, which were steadily gaining ground. However, in Forman's day, the prime source of information used for conventional medical training in England was still the second-century physician and writer on medical matters, Galen.

Born in AD 192 in what is now Turkey, Galen studied first in Alexandria and then travelled widely, learning about drugs in India and Africa before returning home to be physician to the local team of gladiators. His view of medicine dominated its practice for nearly fifteen hundred years. He believed with Plato in a three-part soul, situated in the brain, heart and liver. He developed this idea by formulating models of 'concealed body structures' (such as the liver), positing that each part functioned only when its basic elements were properly adapted and any change would result in functional failure or disease. Student physicians, he said, should study philosophy, logic, physics and ethics. In order to effect a cure it was necessary to gain the trust of a patient through a courteous bedside manner and by patiently explaining the nature of his or her disease. He practised dissection on animals since the use of human cadavers was forbidden, leading him to make assumptions which in turn led to long-lasting errors: on discovering that calves had a network of nerves and vessels at the base of the brain, for example, he deduced that this must also apply to human beings and declared that this was the site of the vital spirits. He also described the liver as 'grasping the stomach with its lobes as if by fingers', an image derived from pigs and apes.[6]

He was a strong advocate of bloodletting to relieve the body of surplus humours, excesses of blood or bile and to relieve fever. He saw knowledge of the pulse as an essential diagnostic aid and taught that blood was made in the liver and then moved to the extremities, carrying 'natural spirits' which supported the functions of growth and nutrition. The dark venous blood passed from the liver to the right ventricle of the heart, then divided into two streams. One passed to the lungs through the pulmonary artery, while the other crossed the heart through 'interseptal pores' in the left ventricle, where it mixed with *pneuma* (air), became heated and moved from there to the left ventricle of the aorta before passing onwards. His theory that the veins originated in the liver while the arteries originated in the heart, was one of the errors of his model of the circulatory system, which dominated medicine for well over a millennium until it was finally challenged by Renaissance anatomy.[7]

Galen also described 473 drugs of vegetable, animal and mineral origin, as well as compound drugs. Two were particularly celebrated: a formula of aloes, spices and herbs which had to be made into an electuary for use against body heats, obstructions and 'phlegmatic humours'; and tablets of clay from the Greek islands, containing several minerals supposedly useful against poison. Fear of poison played a major role both in medical matters and in plots of sixteenth- and early seventeenth-century drama. One famous recipe for an antidote contains nearly 150 ingredients, including half an ounce of unicorn's horn, a stag's pizzle and unlimited quantities of Orient pearls and shards of emeralds. (In actual fact it is far more likely that many supposed victims died of food poisoning rather than from subtle Italian poisons or the wearing of poisoned rings.)

A more up-to-date influence, though one regarded with suspicion by the medical establishment in England, was that of Theophrastus von Hohenheim, who was born in Switzerland in 1493 and chose the name

'Paracelsus', to signify that he surpassed the Roman second-century philosoper Celsus. From the beginning he was a radical iconoclast. The son of a physician, who taught him elementary botany, medicine and natural philosophy, he studied medicine briefly in Italy but openly boasted that he had gained most of his knowledge elsewhere: 'In my time, there were no doctors who could cure a toothache, never mind severe disease. I sought widely the certain and experienced knowledge of the art of medicine. I did not seek it only from doctors but from sheep-shearers, barbers and humble people, wise men and women, exorcisers [he studied alchemy with the Bishop of Würzburg], monks and noblemen.'

Paracelsus cut a flamboyant figure as he rode around with his potions, ointments, elixirs, precious stones and surgical instruments, a double-handed Eastern sword at his belt, and declaiming that he kept the elixir of life in his saddle pommel. He was a great proselytiser for the use of opium, which he saw as a panacea for everything from resisting poison to curing headaches, deafness, epilepsy and apoplexy, jaundice, menstrual and urinary problems, and much more. 'I possess a secret remedy which I call laudanum,' he wrote, 'which is superior to all other heroic remedies.' Its alleged ingredients were 25 per cent opium mixed with henbane, crushed pearls, mummi (an Arabic drug), amber, musk, essential oils, the dried heart of a stag and powdered unicorn's horn. He also held opium-soaked sponges over a patient's nose during operations, remoistened when necessary, although unfortunately he had no idea of the amount that was safe enough to kill pain without killing the patient.

He posited the sovereignty of nature and believed that the healer's task was to know how she operated and then obey 'her'. He pioneered a philosophy based on chemical principles, with salt, sulphur and mercury as the primary substances, and declared that all diseases were associated with the 'spirits' of particular minerals and metals, meaning spirits in the ghostly sense, advising a frightening array of metals in medical practice, including antimony, mercury, arsenic, lead and sulphur. His chemical principles explained living processes by saying they embodied spiritual and 'vital' forces. Some were dependent on the *archei*, internal living properties controlling such things as the digestion, and others on *semina*, or seeds derived from God, the Great Magus who orchestrated nature. Agents of disease might well come from emanations from the stars or minerals from the airs, especially salts. But although he held that there were 'as many diseases as pears, apples and nuts', and that each disease had a specific external cause, he still believed that the essence of disease was spiritual. Galen and others had taught the importance of studying a patient's urine in diagnosis, but Paracelsus dismissed this in favour of chemical analysis.

Not surprisingly, he condemned the acquisition of knowledge purely by book learning instead of by experience and reading of the 'Book of Nature'. However, dogmatic, controversial and difficult as he might be, with his commitment to discovering truth by observation and experiment (what we might call hands-on experience), Paracelsus was a breath of fresh air, the forerunner of men like William Harvey, who, in 1615, gave his revolutionary lecture on the circulation of the blood.

Other beliefs in Forman's day included sympathetic magic and the 'signatures' of things: for instance, the orchid looked like a testicle to show it healed venereal disease, and the blue flower of the herb borage was good for eyes because it resembled one.

Almost all Tudor physicians, including Forman, also believed in the use of astrology to diagnose an illness and chart its progress, although few relied only on the casting of horoscopes. Many, convinced of their skills in this field, also offered to cast horoscopes on an enormous range of general subjects – such as who would make a suitable husband/wife, whether or not people should embark on a certain venture, or how to discover the whereabouts of missing property. The most notable astrologer of the day was the famous Dr Dee, at one time patronised and favoured by the queen herself.

Practising astrologers believed there were rules governing the planets which, to those observing them, appeared to move in perfect harmony and regularity, whereas life on earth, by comparison, was chaotic. By plotting the positions of the planets at any given time it was possible to predict their influence on happenings here below. Ancient astrological lore set out which planets in which situations were favourable or unfavourable in given circumstances, thus offering a sense of security to those seeking help.

The planets were also held to affect agriculture, sending down heat and cold, moisture and dryness, the qualities associated with the four elements of earth, air, fire and water which formed the basis of the human body. The body itself was thought to be subject to the four principal humours, phlegm, blood, choler and bile. If any one of these became dominant, it determined the temper of mind and body. A just balance produces a good humour, a preponderance of any one an ill or evil humour, hence the adjectives phlegmatic, sanguine, choleric and bilious.

Each planet had an influence on a specific part of the body. How this worked was set out in a note by 'a student in astrologie and physicke', Gabriel Frend, in 1599:

> Aries the Head; Taurus the Necke doth guyde,
> Gemini th'armes; Cancer, stomache and Brest,
> Leo the Hart; Virgo the Belly Syde.
> Reins [kidneys], Navel and Buttocks, Libra loves best,
> Scorpio keepes Secretes sure in his neste.
> Sagittarius the Thyghes; the Goate knees doth crave,
> Legges Acquarius; Pisces Feete wyl have.

'Were we not born under Taurus?' enquires Sir Toby Belch in Shakespeare's *Twelfth Night*. 'Taurus?' responds his friend, Sir Andrew Aguecheek, 'That's sides and heart.' 'No, sir,' says Sir Toby, 'it's legs and thighs. Let me see thee caper.' In fact both were wrong by the knowledge of the day (they had been drinking for hours), which Shakespeare presumably would have expected his audience to know.

The horoscopes or 'figures' so widely used by Simon Forman were calculated with the aid of astronomical tables such as almanacs (or *ephues*) and were charts of the heavens showing the positions of the planets, sun and moon at a particular time and place. This was why, for a consultation on a personal matter, it was necessary to know the exact time, date and place of birth of the person asking for advice. Hundreds and hundreds of pages of Forman's folios are covered with such charts and drawings, with column upon column of calculations.

Forman's use of astrology was not considered quackery (one of its foremost practitioners was Elias Ashmole, the revered founder of the Ashmolean Museum), yet astrologers too had had their world turned upside down when Copernicus posited the astounding notion that the earth was not the centre of God's universe but that, along with the rest of the planets, it circled around the sun. This, coupled with Sir Francis Drake's circumnavigation of the world which proved to the nation in 1581 that the earth was not flat, made even astrologers look again at some at their philosophy.

One of the greatest hurdles Forman or any other Elizabethan medical practitioner had to overcome was to be licensed by the College of Physicians. The college, whose fine headquarters were in Knightrider Street near Blackfriars, had been founded in 1512 as a professional body to set standards and regulate those calling themselves physicians. Under a president, council and committee of censors, it took its responsibilities very seriously, but there were genuine difficulties. The recognised way to become a physician was to follow the orthodox medical curriculum at the universities of Oxford and Cambridge, or those in Scotland, and acquire a degree in medicine. Those completing the course then became 'MD', easily obtaining a licence to practise either from one of the universities, the college itself, or from both, but this was an option only for a select number of young men whose families could afford to support them through long years of study. Since there were relatively few such qualified physicians, they could demand large fees from patients and so were doctors almost solely to the wealthy.

Another route to a medical qualification of some kind was for a young man to become apprenticed to a surgeon, 'barber surgeon' or an apothecary, which at least guaranteed that the pupil had spent seven years learning his trade. But in the country at large there was a great range of other practitioners: wise women and 'white witches', skilled herbalists and bonesetters and the midwives. Others generally recognised as 'doctors' had learned their skills, like Paracelsus, from reading widely, and learning and working, as it were, on the coalface, and were good medical practitioners despite not having a university degree. There is no proof, for example, that 'Doctor' John Hall, who married Shakespeare's daughter Susannah and was considered to be one of the most respected physicians of his day, ever had any formal medical training.

But to be fair to the College of Physicians there were also a large number of quacks and charlatans skilled only in parting people from their money, necromancers who claimed to foretell the future by raising the spirits of the dead and alchemists offering to turn base metal into gold – for a price. So there was good reason for trying to bring some discipline into the practice of medicine. Unfortunately the college did not always succeed and at times, in its determination to resist the new or unconventional, it fined and imprisoned some of those who were most knowledgeable and had genuine skills.

*

This was the world in which Simon Forman set out to seek his fortune. On his return from Oxford, looking for those who might help him to learn something of the mystery of medicine, he came across the highly dubious Francis Cox, an astrologer who also dabbled in necromancy and magic and was widely considered a charlatan. Forman's naïve choice of mentor was highly unfortunate and contributed largely to his own doubtful reputation.

This has arisen in part because the mass of papers held in the Bodleian Library, splendid and informative as they are, give an unbalanced picture of his learning. They have led to the common assumption that he had little knowledge of real medicine and relied almost entirely on astrological calculations to diagnose and treat illness.[8] In 1977, however, the then librarian at King's College, Cambridge, asked historian Mary Edmund to examine a large volume once owned by Simon Forman: what she discovered changes the picture entirely. For this is no other than the 'book' Forman bought when he was in Oxford. In fact it is two books of medical texts, both in Latin, bound into one volume along with other material and with the addition of 150 interleaved folios in his own hand. One book is a compendium of medicinal herbs and simples arranged in alphabetical order, possibly written by a Franciscan called William Holm around 1415.[9] The second text, and much the more interesting, is the reason for the confusion which has obtained over the years. It consists of lectures on medical practice compiled by the Oxford master, John Cockys; indeed when you press the leaves of the book together 'Io. Cockis' is clearly to be seen in black letters three inches high. It is handwritten and very fine, with the beginning of each parchment page decorated with beautiful capital letters in red, blue and gold with trailing peacocks' feathers, while each paragraph commences with an ornate letter in blue or red.

Quite simply therefore for hundreds of years, beginning with the College of Physicians, Simon Forman's admitted and publicised reliance on the unimpeachable academic works of Cockys has been confused with his early relationship with Francis Cox.[10] There is no doubt that the copy held in King's College Library in Cambridge today belonged to Simon Forman, for he has clearly written on the inside on the front page that he bought it at 'Candlemas, Anno Domini 1574 Simonn Formann februari 2 day'.

In its margins he wrote down his own comments on the outcome of cases after following the various procedures set out in the book, adding the

21

folios detailing his own medical practices, remedies and observations on such subjects as the use of bloodletting and the way to take a pulse. He also incorporated into the manuscript large parts of another text, *The Breviary of Health*, a further collection of remedies set out in alphabetical order of disease, compiled by Andrew Boorde and first published in printed form in London in 1574. Boorde's book was one of the staples of popular medical publishing in Tudor England. To complete the picture of Forman's ownership, on one folio he drew a picture of a naked man with each part of the body marked with the appropriate planetary sign, as in the verse by Frend, and on another an elaborate doodle around his name, 'Simon'.

His brief autobiography ends when he leaves Oxford, but for the next thirty-eight years he kept a diary by which it is possible, through cross-references to his other writings, to chart his progress. The next three or four years were deeply frustrating, his poverty forcing him to take up a whole series of unsatisfactory posts. He stayed on as a teacher at Wilton free school until 19 May 1575, when he left to become personal schoolmaster to the children of the Dukes, a family of wealthy clothiers. He did not enjoy being buried in the country although they treated him reasonably well.

He was still in touch with Francis Cox, but at some point during 1575 he had a serious quarrel with him. Cox had caused him 'much trouble' (though he never specified what it was) and had even brought a 'Parson Bref to see my books and himself was like to kill me'. He does not enlarge on what brought about the dispute or why Cox of all people, with his reputation for dabbling in black magic, should have brought a parson along to see his books or which books they were, let alone why he threatened violence.

After a year with the Dukes, he cut loose again, wandering from place to place, unsettled and miserable, possibly picking up some knowledge of country medicine during his odyssey, teaching whenever the opportunity arose and, if it did not, prepared to earn his bread by labouring or hedging. From the Dukes he went on to a Master Combe at Ashmore on the borders of Wiltshire and Dorset, where he taught from June until Michaelmas; then he was off again, taking another post as a local schoolmaster, this time at Iwerne Minster, where he lodged with the vicar. 'I kept school at Iwerne Minister,' he writes, 'and had much ado with the priest, living poorly, but did hunt much privily.' One wonders if the latter refers to a little light poaching. February 1578 found him back again at the school in the Close at Salisbury, this time as a master, but by midsummer he had moved on to Oxford to stay with a friend called 'Anthony' for a few months.

Then, quite suddenly, in 1579 his unsatisfying and peripatetic existence came to an end. At least some of his time during the previous years must have been spent in studying, for he decided that he now had sufficient knowledge of both medicine and astrology to set up in practice on his own account and so took a lease on the old parsonage at Fisherton Anger, collecting the key to it 'promptly at noon on the 17 January of that year'. In spite of his inexperience (or more likely because they were blissfully ignorant of it), patients came to him straight away.[11]

Within two days of hanging out his sign he was venturing on his first bloodletting. The patient was a John Waller of Wickham and before embarking on it Forman cast a horoscope and made all the relevant calculations. Then he describes how he set about it. First he bound up Waller's arm tightly above the elbow 'with a garter', then he chafed it with his hand to 'make the blood come down until the vein appeared full', after which he took his penknife and quickly 'pekt into the vein and made a little houlle [hole]'. When he considered he had drawn off sufficient blood, about a pint or more, he loosened the garter and when the arm had stopped bleeding put fine bombast (cotton or cotton wool) on the little hole, pressed it firmly with his finger, then laid on small cloths dipped in water. Finally he wrapped a cloth round it and tied up the patient's arm 'with a towel and so gave him charge not to strain himself'. He adds that sugar is very good for staunching a flow of blood.[12]

He ended the year on a high note. 'I did prophesy the truth of many things which afterwards came to pass. The very spirits were subject unto me,' he brags, which suggests that something at least of Francis Cox had rubbed off on him, 'and I had a great name, yet could I do nothing but at adventure.' For the next six months he was kept busy learning his trade as he went along and, as the consultations increased, he saw, for the first time in his life, the possibility of a better future.

But he sold himself too well and as patients and money continued to flow in, he attracted a good deal of attention, not all of it welcome. The censors of the College of Physicians were not the only people on the lookout for unlicensed medical practitioners. In June 1579 Simon crossed the path of the man who was to be his arch enemy for a number of years. Giles Estcourt, a barrister of Lincoln's Inn, was the city clerk of Salisbury and a Justice of the Peace, and lived right in the city in a fine house in Bedwyn Street which had once belonged to St Edmund's College for priests. After continually hearing news of the popular new young 'doctor' practising on the outskirts of Salisbury, Estcourt looked into the matter and duly had him arrested for practising medicine without a licence and so 'I was robbed and spoiled of all my goods and books'. The loss of the books, if only temporary, must have been devastating not only because of their cost but because he was so reliant on them.

Determined to make an example of this upstart from the farmyard, Estcourt had him committed to prison for sixty weeks. There was no recourse or appeal to the law, for Estcourt was the law. 'I could have no justice nor law until a year was past,' writes Simon, 'during which time I suffered much trouble and defamation without desert by that cursed villain, Giles Estcourt.'

3

Love and Litigation

It was twelve months before Forman was allowed to petition the queen and Privy Council for his release from gaol, though he became sufficiently friendly with his gaolers for them to permit him to 'walk abroad' from time to time so long as he was accompanied by one of them. Not surprisingly, given the conditions in the prisons of the day, he was often ill during this time and lamented that 'I could have no justice nor law, nor could not be heard, till a whole year was past, 'til I sent to the [Privy] Council. All this year [1580] I was in prison till the 14th day of July, the which day I was delivered on bail, where now I had been sixty weeks before, and now by means of the Council's letters was so delivered. The next day after I was out of prison.'

The brush with Estcourt was to become part of a pattern over the next few years, one moment he would be in practice and comparatively well off, the next bound over or back in gaol. However, on this first occasion, uneasy about what Estcourt might do next, he made a major decision: he would go to London and see what the prospects might be for him there, even though he was, he says, 'poor, bare and with little money', his books still confiscated.

Without a horse of his own or funds to hire one, the business of getting to London was a considerable undertaking, the options being to walk there (carrying his clothes and books) or pay a few pence for lifts in carriers' carts: either way it took some time. The approach to the City from the south and west was through countryside; fields and orchards reached as far as the outskirts of Lambeth and Southwark, then suddenly the traveller was plunged into the sprawl of the Bankside. For the newly arrived Simon it was neither its stink and bustle nor the wonders of the great buildings across the river that he first thought worthy of note, but the fact that immediately on arrival he was solicited by 'a cozening quean [slut]' pretending to be his sister. He stoutly refused her advances, though it must have been the last time he ever turned down such an offer.

The cozening quean was just the start, for the streets of the City and the Bankside seethed with the streetwise on the lookout for the 'country gull', the innocent up from the sticks with money in his pocket. For any young man coming up from the country for the first time, London was a bewildering and daunting place. The City proper, on the north bank of the Thames, was by this time bursting out of its walls as more and more people from the provinces were sucked into its orbit. Foreign visitors marvelled at the fine houses and conspicuous wealth of the goldsmiths, silversmiths, skilled craftsmen and city merchants with their grand houses on Cheapside, at the entrepreneurial spirit of the growing numbers of merchant venturers and the splendour of the queen's court and her many palaces. Yet outside those same City walls were acres of ramshackle, squalid dwellings, where the poor scratched a living as best they could in narrow, filthy lanes which were incubators of epidemics and rife with crime. For those without apprenticeships, indentures of their craft, professions or other employment, life was bleak. Gaol, branding, even hanging, awaited those caught breaking the law.

Dominating the north bank of the Thames was the mighty church of St Paul's with its great square tower and its aisles full of stallholders selling souvenirs, perfumes, clothes, jewellery, books, more like an indoor market than a place of worship. The middle aisle, known as 'the Mediterranean', was where one went to meet friends, show off fashionable clothes, to see and be seen. Tourists jostled each other to pay a penny, which enabled them to climb up the great tower and, if no one in authority was about, carve their names on the wooden rail at the top alongside the hundreds of others eager to show that once in their lives they had been to London and stood in St Paul's. Around the church clustered the printers, bookshops, inns, taverns and 'ordinaries' which served the population. The ordinary was the nearest thing the Elizabethans had to a fast-food restaurant, a place where the hungry could go at dinnertime (our lunchtime) and have a bowl of soup or the dish of the day, washed down with ale.

Outside the City boundaries there were now two theatres specifically designed for drama. The first, called simply the Theatre, was built by James Burbage in 1576 on the outskirts of Finsbury Fields, and was followed a year later by the Curtain on the edge of Shoreditch, which was almost certainly built by Burbage's great rival, the entrepreneur Philip Henslowe. By the time Simon Forman reached London in 1580 going to the playhouse was rapidly becoming very popular, much to the fury of the City fathers, who were concerned for the people's morals. They used every possible opportunity to close theatres down and Henslowe was already considering the possibility of building another playhouse outside their jurisdiction, across the river on the Bankside. New dramatists were in demand and if they were looking for subject-matter for plays, then they could do worse than purchase, if they could afford it, a recently published book, Holinshed's *Chronicles of the Kings of England*.

Yet in spite of its increasingly dirty streets and fetid alleyways and the sprawling slums outside its walls, the lanes of the City going north, like those south of the Thames, still ran out into fields, common land and countryside. Housewives, maids and laundresses carried their washing up through the lanes, trying to avoid the stinking kennels which ran down the middle of them, to dry it on the hedges and bushes of Finsbury Fields, the hills above topped by windmills, while those living close to the river could still find wild radishes growing above the tideline, even close by London Bridge with its houses and shops.[1]

That single London crossing of the Thames, the marvel and magnet for country visitors, was crowded all day and until well into the night. Drawings made at the time show it packed with shops and houses, with a series of strange little projections at the back of each building. These were the lavatories: sewage went straight down into the river and if you were passing underneath when they were in use, then that was your bad luck. The shops themselves offered goods of every conceivable kind to attract customers, while from time to time users of the bridge would be gruesomely entertained by the heads of traitors stuck on pikes at the northern entry. The construction of the bridge was quite novel, for its supports were set into boat-shaped foundations, known as starlings, to protect them from the fast-running tides and currents. But the most usual way to cross the

Thames was by ferry or in one of the hundreds of wherries plying for hire. John Taylor, waterman, diarist, would-be poet and a contemporary of Forman, claimed there were no less than 40,000 ferrymen and watermen working between the mouth of the Thames and Windsor at the end of the sixteenth century. Their craft were used like today's taxis, and their owners were renowned for their toughness, use of bad language and competitiveness. They were also a useful source of gossip for those wanting information.

The south bank, where the boroughs of Lambeth and Southwark came down to the water's edge, was a different world from that of the rapidly up-and-coming area of Blackfriars opposite, not to mention the grand mansions of the nobility lining the Strand. The Bankside also had a substantial church, St Mary Overy, its share of prisons (of which the Clink was the most notorious), the great Bear Pit – which would eventually become another Henslowe enterprise – and to the west, the Paris Gardens, which were popular for recreation and assignations. However, it was also notorious for its proliferation of taverns, gambling dens, brothels and the bathhouses known as 'the stews'.

Most of the land belonged to the see of Winchester and successive bishops had been happy to turn a blind eye to what went on so long as the money from the rents and leases continued to roll in. While whores operated widely on the north side of the river, plying for trade right outside St Paul's as well as around the inns and playhouses (inside the latter too, if they could get away with it), their busiest area of operation was the Bankside, where they were popularly known as 'Winchester Geese'. Although the warren of narrow alleys and streets had its share of respectable traders, craftsmen and those importing and exporting goods (Philip Henslowe being one of the last), the income of a substantial proportion of its inhabitants was derived from a wide variety of crimes. The Bankside was the heart of the Elizabethan underworld, whose denizens even had their own slang, which was largely unintelligible to outsiders.

Two Elizabethan writers, Robert Greene, as famous for his lifestyle as for his work, and the dramatist/journalist Thomas Dekker, both wrote pamphlets warning the gullible of the hazards facing them on the streets of London. In Greene's pamphlet, *The Notable Art of Cosenage*, he describes many of the scams of the day, writing at length of the picklocks, cardsharpers, gamesters, pimps and highway robbers with whom he drank, and warning of the dangers of the brothels he regularly patronised. All this was described, he solemnly asserted, solely to warn those reading his work to avoid vice and keep to the path of virtue, for such lax behaviour could lead only to the gallows. He wrote this particular pamphlet and its sequel while living off the earnings of a prostitute called Emma Ball, having left his wife and child behind in Norfolk after running through the poor woman's money.

Suddenly set down in this great melting pot it is hardly surprising that Forman felt confused. He had no money, and even if this had not been the case he would have been hard pressed to know how to set himself up as a medical practitioner, being shabbily dressed, poorly shod, unlicensed and without the means or knowledge to find suitable accommodation from which to practise. He spent the first few days wandering about, at a loss to know how to earn his bread. Begging was not an option, 'sturdie beggars' were soon picked up by the Watch or the local constable and whipped out of the parish. Finally, having failed to find any work, he left London proper and took lodgings in Greenwich, where for a few weeks he was employed by a local carpenter.

While he was working for him, Forman claimed to have 'cured' a young man called Henry Johnson 'of a consumption', although, unusually, he did not explain how. There are, however, records of a number of remedies and supposed cures. Dr John Hall, for instance, prescribed different remedies and treatments for people depending on their humours. For one woman it was a variety of spices and drugs in wine including 'galangal', an aromatic bitter root from China, accompanied by an enema to relieve the body of ill humours and a syrup, the main ingredients of which were cinnamon bark and *Calamus aromaticus*, the dried root of the flag iris. For a young girl in whom the disease was further advanced, he prescribed a *ptysan* (tisane) made from barley, a restorative cordial composed of purslane and borage, and an enema of cooling herbs. He also recommended for her a light diet of snails, frogs and river crabs, all of a 'cooling nature'. Unhappily, the patient, Mary Wilson, died within the year. 'She sleeps now with God', noted Dr Hall.[2] Culpeper suggests a host of herbal remedies including plantain, pine nuts and 'Imperial Water', a distillation of orange, nutmegs and other spices, along with the petals of fresh damask roses and the flowers of sage, mint and thyme.

Happily, either Forman's treatment was effective or Henry Johnson had a more robust constitution which enabled him to throw off the disease. Maybe he was suffering from something else all together. Whatever the truth of the matter, he was so grateful that he paid for them both to go off and spend a few weeks in Holland. They did not stay as long as they had expected to, but it is possible that Forman took the opportunity to learn what he could of Dutch medicine in the little time available to him, for the University of Leyden was becoming famous for its teaching. The time was brief of necessity because the two young men were forced to cut their trip short when it became evident to them that Holland was in imminent danger of invasion by Spain. A few weeks later the 'the Spanish Fury', led by the Duke of Parma, swept into that wealthy and peaceful country, driving all before it. Those who opposed the Spaniards, like the people of Maastricht, were put to the sword, every man, woman and child; nor did any unfortunate visiting foreigner escape.

By the beginning of October Simon was back in London. Nothing had changed and there was no prospect of his being able to make a living. After spending a month with a friend in Newbury, he returned to his old home in Quidhampton, where he tried to re-establish himself 'and stayed there a year until the 23rd October 1581, curing sick and lame folk in the which time I cured a fellow of Chillhampton of the King's Evil, which had twenty-four holes in his throat and neck. Out of which one morning I got eighty-six worms at one time like maggots.'[3]

Scrofula, tuberculosis of the glands of the neck and the top of the spine, was known popularly as King's Evil since until as late as the eighteenth century it was believed that it could be cured by a sovereign laying his or her hands on the sick person, with the result that on any occasion when a king or queen appeared in public they would be besieged by those pleading to be restored to health. It manifested itself in symptoms which include abscesses and lumps, and Simon made a particular study of it.[4]

During the year he was again taken to court in Salisbury, this time at the Lent Assizes, where he was bound over for practising medicine without a licence. After that, in order to get by, 'he did many times thresh and dig and hedge for my living', but as soon as the term of his binding over ended he returned to Salisbury and rented a house next door to 'the skinner's on the Ditch' which ran along the eastern side of the city, hardly a salubrious or fashionable address, and advertised himself as practising both physic and, somewhat mysteriously 'surgery', a skill he never laid claim to again. His determination and persistence paid off and the number of patients consulting him increased steadily, along with their fees, so much so that he soon had sufficient funds to take the leases on two houses in Culver Street in a more superior part of the city.

He was not a believer in all work and no play and, in spite of complaining about how being hard up restricted his activities, he would not hesitate to go on any jaunt which took his fancy. On 19 August 1582 he and a friend, Robin Grey, set off for the south coast, proposing 'to go to sea and travel a little', a trip which had unfortunate consequences.

The queen and the government, looking across the water at events in the Low Countries, rightly considered that England would be next in line for a Spanish invasion, one moreover which would carry with it the blessing of the Pope. Given the dreadful conditions in the navy of the day, finding sufficient seamen to volunteer for the English fleet was a difficult task. Impressment was necessary, with the result that press-gangs were active all along the coast. Forman and Grey were staying in Studland when they ran into a naval patrol, were hauled away and spent several days locked up. Forman never explained exactly how they managed to avoid passing the next few years on one of Her Majesty's men o'war, but the most likely explanation is that they managed to bribe their way out. Not surprisingly, after this setback they decided against attempting any kind of sea voyage and spent a few days recovering on the Isle of Purbeck, before quickly returning to the safety of Salisbury.

Shortly afterwards Forman was offered an opportunity to add to his earnings from medicine and astrology by tutoring the children of the Penruddock family. Sir John Penruddock, a lawyer of Gray's Inn and later MP for Wilton, had a fine estate on the outskirts of Salisbury as well as a London house, an arrangement which was to prove very useful to Forman, although he grumbled that he 'took infinite pain and trouble but had little profit'. His own account of his employment undermines this view, for the Penruddocks looked after him well, treating him as one of the household, and on a number of occasions when Lady Penruddock and the children visited Sir John in London, she took Simon with them, which gave him an excellent opportunity to explore the city and gain some knowledge of its ways while living in comfort and security.

On the whole, the year turned out better than the previous one. A complaint against him for 'using physic' by the bishop of Salisbury had not resulted in any further action, and to enable him to take time off from his practice whenever he wished, he taught Robin Grey, the friend of the press-gang incident, how to dress wounds so that Grey could do it for him when he was away, a move which seemed sensible at the time. Between tutoring the Penruddock children and consultancy fees Forman was now living well enough to have a fine ring made for himself with 'an eagle's stone'.

But what really made 1582 a red-letter year was that it was then, at the extremely ripe old age of twenty-nine, that he finally lost his virginity. Given his insatiable sexual appetite throughout the rest of his life, it is hard to see why this took him so long. Years later he blamed this on his rejection by a woman, whom he had decided would make him a suitable wife, because of his looks: he described himself as being of less than middle height, with auburn, reddish hair, yellowish beard and freckles. However, later his appearance did not seem to diminish his ability to attract and successfully bed women outside marriage. It was with triumph that he announced at the end of the year that 'this was the first year in sum that ever I did halek cum woman . . .'. 'Halek' was Forman's personal code word for sexual intercourse and academics and other interested readers have pondered for years over its origins and roots, being unable to find anything remotely similar in Anglo-Saxon, Middle English, the Latin languages or even the Gaelic. The most likely explanation is that he simply made it up.[5]

He was obviously considered amusing company since that Christmas he was appointed Lord of the Revels, or Lord of Misrule. This must have been at the Pendruddocks' country estate, for the custom was followed only by the Court, the nobility and those landowners with houses sufficiently large to celebrate the twelve days of Christmas in style. The Lord of the Revels organised the entertainments, parties, games and amusements of the festive season, ending on Twelfth Night with a topsy-turvy day when everything was turned upside down and the Lord of the Revels ruled over the household. During his period of office Forman nearly killed himself falling off a tower trying to catch pigeons, upset some people, was 'intimate' with several women, dined well, drank much and thoroughly enjoyed himself.

For sometime he combined practising in the city with tutoring the Penruddock children. Throughout 1582 and 1583 he moved constantly to different houses to hold his consultations, finally taking a lease on one in New Street in a fashionable part of Salisbury. This was a provocative step as it brought him into closer contact with 'his enemies', though he notes that for the time being at least he managed to overcome them 'with much ado even though they gave me an ill name'. It was, he grumbled, a time of 'great expense but I had profit by my pen and I thrived reasonably well'. Emboldened by the success of his recent sexual adventures, in February 1583 he wrote that 'I did halek cum [with] two women . . . we went to London and lay there until we had spent all'. Whether the 'we' referred to himself and two local women going up to London together or he and a friend adventuring in the capital and picking up a couple of 'queans' is not clear.

But soon there was to be an entirely new and compelling emotional interest in his life, for he met up again with Anne Young, who, as a bold young girl, had set her cap at him when they were both in their teens and he was still an apprentice. She first called him in as a doctor on 23 January 1584 'to sweat her leg and cure her' and within a month they were involved in a full-scale love affair, for on 'the 29th February was the first time that ever I did halekekeros harescum cum A.Y.' By this time she must have been at least in her mid-twenties, late for marriage by Elizabethan standards, and as the daughter of a respectable family she must have received a number of offers.

In a note in the King's College manuscript, Forman defines 'youth' as being between the ages of fourteen and twenty-five, 'middle age' from twenty-five to forty-five, 'aged' as forty-five to fifty-six' and 'old-aged' fifty-six years of age until death. Anyone over fifty was an 'old bodie'.[6] By that reckoning his lover was already middle-aged and would have had no need to ask her parents' permission to marry, supposing they were still alive. She was certainly more than old enough to know that by embarking on a physical affair she ran an almost inevitable risk. It was his first serious relationship, so why did he not marry her since he could now afford to do so?

'This year,' he wrote, 'I had many things given me, [made] many new friends, and had much good of the woman I loved. I thrived reasonably well. There [was] profit by a woman's friendship in meat, money, and apparel, for healing the sick. A reasonable good and quiet year. But I had certain brawls and slanders against me about the detecting of one that stole certain things; where I was like to have been spoiled. Certain women became my enemies.'

At Michaelmas he parted on amicable terms from the Penruddocks 'of my own accord'. He had certainly taken a step up in the world, for he was able to buy a horse of his own, purchase a new sword, which he had engraved, and move into a smart property by St Thomas's churchyard. He even had sufficient funds to enable him to 'redeem' his friend, Robin Grey, from the local gaol. This does not necessarily mean that Grey had committed a serious offence, he could easily have been imprisoned for being drunk and disorderly, non-payment of debt or simply to wait the judgement of a magistrate following a dispute with a neighbour or tradesman.

There then followed what might be called the Year of Litigation. Elizabethans were extremely litigious (Shakespeare's father John seemed always either to be suing someone or being sued) and in Shakespeare's early comedies such as *The Comedy of Errors* characters rush about the stage calling on the local officer to arrest one or other of them at someone's suit, for non-payment of debt, non-delivery of goods already paid for and such like.

It is virtually impossible to untangle the web of litigation Forman was involved in during 1585: even the most diligent or those with considerable knowledge of Elizabeltan law have difficulty in unravelling his scrawled stream of consciousness, which is peppered with dates.[7] The root cause of it all was the still formidable Mistress Commin and her long-standing antagonism towards him from the days of his apprenticeship; in spite of this he had remained on friendly terms with Matthew Commin and the rest of the family, so much so that he often entrusted his old master with his financial affairs.

Much Elizabethan litigation had to do with money, for there were no banks in which cash could be stowed for safe-keeping. Usury, professional money-lending with interest, was illegal under ecclesiastical law and even outside the Church was considered unchristian, the province of evil, hard-hearted and rapacious Jews (as in *The Merchant of Venice*). Friends and business acquaintances would often provide loans and also keep cash safe for one another if necessary. This being the case, it is hardly surprising that disputes which were later hard to untangle were often the result.

The trouble started after Forman was called in to treat what he described as 'a wound' on the leg of a Mistress Samways, a relation of Mistress Commin. 'Wounds in the leg' were commonplace not only in Forman's casebooks but also in all the other medical literature of the time and were most likely, in the days before antiseptics, ulcers that were slow to heal. Certainly Mistress Samways had not found anyone able to clear up her problem until Forman treated her, but when he applied for payment for his services neither Mistress Samways nor Mistress Commin would pay his fees. He had been away a fair amount on a wide-ranging tour which had taken in the Mendips, Wells and Glastonbury, during which time he had delegated Robin Grey to dress Mistress Samways's leg on the understanding that he would carry out his instructions and use the prescribed salves. As a result Mistress Commin reasoned that she did not have to pay Forman anything since her relative's leg had been cured not by him but by Grey, 'who had some skill in surgery'.

So far so good, if unfair. But matters became more complicated. Forman had lent money to Mistress Samways's sister, Jane Cole, whom he hints that he fancied, and who also did his accounts for him. In addition to which, because of his long-standing relationship with Matthew Commin, he would sometimes 'make over' to him debts owed to him by other people and Commin would give him the amount of money involved and then collect the sum from the debtor. Also, presumably because of his peripatetic lifestyle, he had taken to leaving his 'books of art and surgery' with the Commins for safe-keeping while he was away.

After the two women refused to pay, there followed a flurry of writs on both sides and on 29 April Forman went to court to claim his fee for curing Mistress Samways. From then on matters went from bad to worse. On 6 May, following an argument, he had a fight in the street with 'the Bishop's man' whom he claimed had hit him without provocation, an attack he blamed (without giving a reason why) on the unfortunate Jane Cole. This resulted in their 'falling out mightily'.

Thoroughly enraged, he then called in an officer and had 'goodwife Commin' arrested on his suit, as well as someone called John Matthews. Chaos followed. Over the next few weeks Forman was put in gaol for odd days at the suits of a whole variety of people who had now become embroiled in the affair, while he, in his turn, continued to have his detractors treated likewise. The mound of writs rose higher and higher while tempers grew shorter, and one Sunday when our hero was coming away from morning service at the cathedral he was set on by a group of men led by Mistress Samways's husband who accused him of 'bewitching' his wife, was soundly beaten up and warned to leave town at once before worse befell him.

When he showed no signs of going, Mistress Commin went to the mayor to 'swear the peace against Simon'. This again was commonplace: one party to a dispute could get an order restraining the other against breaching the peace. It crops up regularly in the records in London, particularly with regard to rival actors and dramatists, who resorted to shouting insults and even violence in a public place. Needless to say, this greatly upset Forman, who considered that he had never breached the peace and that it was he who had been attacked by the parties to the dispute, not the other way around, for he 'hath never brake it nor intendeth to do so in his life'. So, undeterred, he had Mistress Commin arrested yet again on the grounds that she had money of his that she would not repay, whereupon back she went before the mayor to defend herself. This time she did real damage for she reminded him that Forman did not have a licence to practise medicine from either the bishop or any other proper authority and that he had been convicted previously for practising.

As to the treatment of Mistress Samways's leg, which had started the whole farrago, she informed the mayor that it was not worth the twenty marks Forman had charged, following this up with a comment to the effect that 'his life and conversation appear to be such as requireth reformation in this defendant's opinion'. After this he spent another short spell in prison for practising without a licence. Looking back later on months of legal battles he wrote, 'This year was a year of much vexation, trouble, travail, enmity and strife. I was much overborne and had diverse suits at law.' It seems that the stress of the situation took its toll for several times he mentions that during all the excitement of litigation he 'swooned', on one occasion being 'senseless for eight hours'.

However, the one event which might have been thought to take precedence over all the litigious nonsense – the inevitable outcome of months of unprotected love-making – is given only one line in the diary: 'On the 27th day of March A.Y. was delivered at ten minutes past seven a.m. of Joshua.' Anne Young had given him a son.

4

'Wonderful Troublesome Years . . .'

Throughout the mid and late 1580s the country was bracing itself for a possible Spanish invasion. A series of plots to overthrow the queen and put Mary Stuart on the throne increased the climate of fear and uncertainty, in which the authorities saw spies under every bed and an assassin behind every door. But, much as now, for the ordinary person struggling to make a living and get on with their life, such high matters took second place to their own immediate concerns. In Simon's case money problems loomed large, for he was quite unable to manage his finances sensibly and extravagance was always followed by insolvency. Time and again he had to resort to his long-suffering family for assistance, especially his brothers Robert and William, although from the way they always rallied round they must have had some faith in his determination to succeed in his chosen profession.

On the positive side, finally he was making influential acquaintances. One of these was Sir John Davenant who, with a 'Lord Anderson', brought Forman and John Piers, the Bishop of Salisbury, together on the vexed question of licensing, after which, wrote Forman, 'the Bishop and I were made friends'.[1] These were no mean allies. Lord Anderson was the Lord Chief Justice on circuit and Sir John was an influential landowner and close relative of John Aubrey, who described him in *Brief Lines* as 'a most beautiful, good and even-tempered person, of a mild and peaceable nature'. The intervention of two such powerful men ended the bishop's attempts to prevent Forman from practising medicine. This should have been cause for celebration, but summing up the year of 1586 Forman moaned: 'I consumed more than I got and brought myself to beggar's state.'

His reputation was spreading further afield and increasingly he was called away from Salisbury for consultations. One wealthy family, the Farwells of Poole in Dorset, requested his advice about their daughter Eleanor, who was suffering from an unspecified disease. Presumably they were satisfied with him for six months later they called him back on another matter, but shortly after his return in January 1587 he was arrested and imprisoned once more by Giles Estcourt for practising without a licence, in spite of his new friendship with the bishop. Estcourt was joined in his suit by his friend, Thomas Eyre, the mayor of Salisbury, with whom Forman had crossed swords during his legal wrangles with Mistress Commin. In a letter to the Privy Council explaining his continuing actions against Forman, Estcourt went so far as to write that this time Forman 'had been taken at morning prayer with a book in his hand wherein are contained divers bad and foul prayers and devices'.

Possibly Forman had passed the time during a boring sermon studying a medical book or astrological text rather than the Book of Common Prayer. Once more his medical and other books were impounded, and three parchment rolls were taken from his chest. Forman gave a deposition to the effect that he owned all of them, but that some of the marginal notes on the parchment rolls were not in his hand.[2] This time, however, the Privy Council found in his favour and he had 'the Council's letters for my discharge . . . and was discharged from all bonds at the Assizes contrary to the aspect of all men'. In spite of this Estcourt succeeded in having him bound over until the next assize.[3] Forman had to find people prepared to stand surety for his good behaviour, which at first he was unable to do, but he was finally saved when two unnamed men stepped forward and offered to stand bail for him, thus saving him from being returned to gaol. To his great relief all the books which had been seized were returned to him, after which he no longer kept them in his own house or lodgings, but left them with Sir John Penruddock for safe-keeping, although he was to complain later that some had been mislaid.

Estcourt's overt persecution was now starting to rebound on him. It caused a great deal of criticism and there is little doubt that Forman would have found considerable local support at the next assize. But by the time it came around Estcourt was no longer present to see the outcome, for soon after having Forman bound over again, he was himself arrested in London and taken to the Fleet Prison on a charge of 'falsehood done in fellowship'. This suggests a fraud of some kind either on his own part or in collusion with others, but the matter never came to court for in April 1587 he died suddenly, a few days after his son-in-law. In his will he left a fine mourning ring to his friend the mayor, Thomas Eyre.

Just before Christmas 1587 Forman was consulted by a member of one of the most powerful families in the land. George Carey, then governor of the Isle of Wight, was the son of Henry Carey, Lord Hunsdon, the Lord Chamberlain. Henry Carey was the queen's cousin and possibly, so it was rumoured, her half-brother, since his mother Mary Boleyn had been mistress to Henry VIII before her sister Anne and had been married off to William Carey in great haste. He had been one of the queen's foremost counsellors since her accession and she trusted him absolutely, later putting him charge of all land forces at the time of the Spanish Armada. Simon does not tell us what was wrong with George Carey that required his presence on the Isle or Wight, or who recommended him to its governor, but the outcome must have been satisfactory because Carey figures in Forman's casebooks for years. Carey also consulted Forman as an astrologer when he wanted advice on the outcome of the various ventures in which he was involved.

Forman was now having problems in his personal life. In cryptic diary notes he alludes to his deteriorating relationship with Anne Young, including the puzzling entry: 'The 1st January [1587] A.Y. and I were like to have been betrayed.' How? In what way? Since by now Joshua was nearly two, his birth could hardly have been concealed. Even more mysterious is an entry in November: 'the constable came for A.Y. and there followed much sorrow after it'. Was she also arrested in some petty suit of supposed debt or other controversy, or was this something more serious? While bearing a bastard child was not a criminal or civil offence and did not carry quite the stigma it did throughout the nineteenth and much of the twentieth centuries, it met with little sympathy, especially if the girl was from a respectable family.

Great pressure was put on the father to regularise the situation and refusal or inability to do so could be punished by his sitting in the stocks with a notice around his neck to the effect that 'John Smith [or whoever] hath got Alice Brown with child' or by parading through church for three weeks, dressed in a white sheet and with a placard bearing the words 'fornicator' or 'adulterer'. The same penalty was also exacted from women who admitted to adultery though, not surprisingly, while men could often pass it off fairly lightly, a woman's reputation could be ruined for life. However, a dim view was taken of either a single man who did not marry the mother of his child or a married man who could not. In both cases they could be taken before a magistrate and ordered to maintain the child until it was seven years old.

There is one possible answer, not only to the mystery of the cryptic notes but also as to why Simon and Anne never married, despite her having had his child. Until the end of her life Simon always referred to her as 'A.Y.' even though she had long changed her name, having married a man called Ralph Walworth. But although the dates of the marriages of women far less important to him than Anne Young litter the casebooks, he never noted when her marriage took place. The assumption hitherto seems to have been that it happened some time after he finally moved to London. But suppose Anne had married Walworth and ceased to be A.Y. much earlier and that she was already married when she and Simon took up with each other again? Or that when she found she was pregnant, realising that her lover was not prepared to marry her, she hastily accepted an offer of marriage from another suitor to give her child a name and so avoid shaming her family, Ralph Walworth believing the child to be his? For although Forman never denied paternity, indeed seemed to revel in it, Joshua was always known in Salisbury as 'Joshua Walworth'.

Either of these possibilities would explain his fear of their 'betrayal' two years after Joshua's birth. Certainly throughout that summer there was trouble between them, resulting in a major quarrel in the August which estranged them for weeks. It might also explain why Anne had been taken away by a constable if information had been laid against her for adultery and it makes sense of Forman's round-up of the events of the year: 'My special friends and I were set at variance and put asunder; it was the beginning of much sorrow and strife.' It might also explain the guilty dreams concerning Walworth that he experienced for years, in one of which he met up with Walworth 'at the door of the Queen's Cofferer', whereupon 'he drew his dagger on me and I had a bush hanged on my back to fling at him and also drew my dagger'.[4]

41

The year of the Armada came and went without any reference to how near the country had come to a Spanish invasion or to the giving of thanks for the preservation of the queen and the safety of the realm. Apart from the unexplained problems with Anne Young, there was much for which he could be thankful. He was finally rid of Estcourt and no longer in fear of the courts, he was earning reasonably well and he had acquired a number of substantial patrons. Yet, at the very time that he had a real chance to consolidate his position and build on what he had already achieved, he was once again recklessly and dangerously dabbling in the occult. It is hard to understand why he should take such a risk just as everything was beginning to look up for him.

Many Elizabethans did believe that it was possible to conjure up the spirits of the dead and the Church agreed, thundering against any attempts to do so. Even the more sceptical could appear ambivalent. When Owen Glendower appears in Shakespeare's *Henry IV, Part I*, he is made to look a ridiculous figure, boasting of magical powers including necromancy. After a lengthy speech asserting that the earth shook at his birth and the heavens were full of fiery shapes, he tells Hotspur, 'I can call spirits from the vasty deep', to which Hotspur makes the joking reply 'Why, so can I or so can any man; but will they come when you do call for them?' This always gets a good laugh and presumably did at the time it was written, yet Shakespeare later used the conjuring up of spirits to deadly effect in *Macbeth*, while the most frightening claim Prospero makes in *The Tempest* is:

> graves at my command
> Have wak'd their sleepers, op'd, and let them forth
> By my so potent art.

Prospero, of course, is a fictional character who uses magic to bring about a desired end and the real Owen Glendower was a clever, well-educated soldier and a very real threat to the English Crown, whereas those actually claiming to practise necromancy were disreputable characters with deeply unpleasant reputations. The most notorious necromancer in the 1580s was Edward Kelley, who, in spite of having had his ears cut off in Lancaster for digging up corpses for sinister purposes, and being branded on the thumb for coining (counterfeiting money), was a sufficiently plausible and charismatic figure to fool at least two prominent people of his day, Ferdinand, Lord Strange, the superstitious Lancashire peer who may or may not later have been murdered, and the great Dr Dee himself. Dee's attraction to Kelley amazed all who knew him and arose out of Kelley's claim to be a seer or 'scrier' who could interpret messages from spirits by peering into a crystal globe or even mirror glass. So convinced was Dee that Kelley had supernatural powers that he took him off with him on a tour of Europe. Shortly after the two had left, a warrant was issued for Kelley's arrest on a charge of murder, though whether he was guilty of the crime remains unknown since he never returned to England. It was said that he had offended a German prince and had, variously, been executed, strangled secretly in a dungeon, or had broken his neck trying to escape.

In the autumn of 1587 Forman came under the influence of another supposed 'scrier', a John Goodridge, whom he described oddly as 'a gelded man', who held some kind of a seance at which he 'saw' for Forman. What he saw, Forman did not say, but whatever it was greatly impressed him and in May 1588, after further consultations, he invited Goodridge to stay with him for a month, after which he claimed, 'I began to practise necromancy and call angels and spirits.' He could not possibly have advertised this for had he done so he would have called down on himself not only the wrath of the Church but of the civil authorities as well. As was often the case with Forman's more doubtful acquaintances, the two men then fell out and Goodrich was followed later by a man called 'Stephen', who also 'saw' for him in September.[5]

1589 did not start well. While Forman might have been able to ignore the stirring events of Armada year, its aftermath was about to catch up with him. 'On the 27th January being Monday, between ten and eleven a.m., I was pressed as a soldier to serve in the Portugal voyage.' This was Sir Francis Drake's failed attempt to repay the Spaniards for their attempted invasion. Once again the press-gangs were active, looking for soldiers and sailors to serve on ships, for although the English navy had been victorious, disease had raced through the fleet on its return and hundreds of seamen and soldiers had died. This time Forman was to escape from impressment with far more difficulty than on the previous occasion for, in spite of his protests, he was 'restrained', forcibly removed from his house, patients and friends, and taken away to Southampton. For the next fortnight he tried everything to avoid a fate which appeared to be inevitable and on 10 February he was sent to gaol for his intransigence. Since he was let out two days later instead of being taken aboard by force – it was not unusual for the unwilling to be knocked out to make their shipment easier – he must have either bought himself off again, prevailed on someone else to do so, or been released on the orders of some person of influence. One possibility is the intervention of George Carey, nearby on the Isle of Wight.

He returned to Salisbury bruised by the experience to be faced with a more private and personal problem and one he shared with a good many fellow Elizabethans. 'The *gonorrhea passio* came on me,' he records, referring to the 'gonorrhea pain' and using the medical term for it rather than the usual 'clap'. It is possible, though unlikely, that he contracted it from Anne Young and suggests a more casual intimacy. At this time he did not record the names of the women involved in his brief liaisons, as he would later, or where the intimacies took place. Nor does he reveal how he set about trying to cure himself. The only supposed prophylactic against the disease was to wash the genitals in vinegar and white wine coupled with what is described as 'hard pissing' and in the best-run brothels a whore would offer a client a chamber pot to use for the purpose.[6] Contemporary remedies for the clap included dosing with sarsaparilla mixed with the West Indian drug, *guiacum*, or washing the member in water distilled with 'saponaria' or soapwort, a concoction also used for soothing bruises and helping cut fingers to heal. However, if the disease had taken a firmer hold then the treatment was deeply unpleasant: suffice it to say it involved the insertion of a thin lead pipe.

He summed up 1589 as 'a wonderful troublesome year for me. I went from place to place. I was glad to forsake all and changed my lodging often. I got little; spent and consumed all until Michaelmas. Then it began to mend with me. I practised again necromancy, magic and physic.' Somewhat gnomically he added, 'My enemies prevailed against me and I was like to have run into many mischiefs.' He does not elaborate on whether this was in his personal or professional life or both.

Whichever it was, on 18 August he decided to try his luck again in London, this time with far more knowledge of the city and its hazards and with a great deal more experience of life. When he first arrived he took a succession of cheap lodgings, sometimes for as little as a night or a couple of weeks, joining the host of hopeful young men lured to the capital by the promise of success and riches, who lived and often shared rooms either just inside the City proper or in the growing sprawl of lanes and streets on its outskirts. At this time Marlowe was living just off Hog Lane, while Shakespeare, who arrived in London around the same time as Simon Forman, had a room in a street in Bishopsgate ward. (We know that because he left it without paying the equivalent of his council tax and thus appears in the Register of Defaulters.)[7]

Forman lodged first with a Mistress Gott, then took a chamber 'at James Ash's in the Barbican', where once again he succumbed to a dose of the clap 'which took me again in my yard'. (Throughout his diary and in his medical notes he always uses the old word 'yard' for penis.) Towards the end of the year he went back to Salisbury for a few weeks before returning to rent a room in new lodgings with a Mistress Clover in Cow Lane. As an example of his restless nature, after making this arrangement with his new landlady he rode off to Oxford the same day on some pressing purpose which he did not explain.

By January 1590 he was getting by in London with the help of money borrowed from his brothers and had become casually involved with a woman called Bess Vaughan, who, he recorded gloomily, gave him nothing but trouble: later on in the year she slandered him repeatedly, finally involving him in 'a great brawl during which I was like to have been killed'. Forman was a great self-dramatist and the phrase 'like to have been killed' crops up fairly regularly. While sometimes it can be put down to dramatic licence, it was not just paranoia: he had a talent for making enemies.

He was now thirty-seven, still unmarried, and therefore considered a rapidly ageing bachelor. Acutely aware of his status, he started actively looking for a wife and between Easter and Whitsuntide 'I was offered a wife many times and had the sight and choice of four or five maids and widows'; but none suited him. He clearly remained emotionally involved with Anne to some extent, and throughout this time continued to cast their horoscopes to see what the future held for them, although by then she was definitely married to Ralph Walworth.

His activities are also recorded in a very different source. In June that year Forman's name appeared in a Star Chamber case concerning an incident which took place in the Bull Inn in Lambeth Marsh when he was called in to help an acquaintance, Henry Milton, with a legal matter.[8]

45

Milton had asked for his assistance in dealing with a document for a general release of debts, since he himself could not read. The release was to be signed by a widow, Mistress Sweyland, regarding debts for which she had been pursuing a man called John Bawd, which he denied he owed. It is not clear why Milton was involved: the most likely explanation is that he was a friend of Bawd's.

Milton considered Forman to have 'a persuasive tongue', so he asked him to help him encourage Mistress Sweyland to sign the release, which Forman agreed to do. Milton's wife was then asked to bring the old lady along to the Bull Inn, where, in an upper room, Forman and Milton 'welcomed her and desired her to sit down by the fire and drink with them'.

This she did and they passed a pleasant time together, during which Forman explained to her that 'she were best regard her own quietness, for it would be greatly to her discredit, when it should appear before the Lords of the Council, that she should sue Bawd when he never owed her anything'. He then read her the words of the general release and explained it again. She agreed, signed it and promised him a reward for his pains. However, within days she was regretting her action and accusing him and Milton of living by 'shifting [procuring abortions] and lewd practices, cozening and deceiving the Queen's Majesty's good subjects'. Fortunately a gentleman in the next room, who had been observing the proceedings through a hole in the wall made for the purpose, did not consider that anything underhand had taken place. This happened in June and on 26 July 'Simon Forman' was called before the Star Chamber in person to explain what had happened.[9] Presumably he satisfied them since that is all he records in his diary of so daunting an event.

He continued to dabble in necromancy and during 1591 wrote a 'book' on the subject.[10] There are a number of these 'books' among the manuscripts in the Bodleian, but none of them are books as we understand the term today for they are only of the length of a moderate pamphlet or, at most, a short academic paper. In this one he describes how he has learned to call up the spirits, but stops short at saying that he was successful. Five years later he was still having to ask John Goodridge to do it for him and there is a graphic description of how on one occasion the 'spirit' appeared, claiming that he had been sent to the netherworld for killing his father, 'but we could not bring him to human form: he was seen like a great black dog and troubled the folk much in the house and afeared them'. There are echoes here of the later play by Dekker, Rowley and Ford, *The Witch of Edmonton*, in which a supposed witch raises a demon in the shape of a black dog. Goodridge's black dog 'cast out such fire and brimstone that it stank mightily'. However, Simon adds truthfully, 'I saw him not. I saw the fire then saw a kind of shape, but not perfectly. [It was] Salathiel.'

In the same treatise on necromancy he lists the 'secret' names of various angels and demons. Christopher Marlowe in *Dr Faustus* makes dramatic use of the superstitious belief that those with knowledge of their secret names could raise spirits by the proper exercise of magic: it is how Faustus calls up Lucifer's henchman, Mephistopheles. *The Faust Book*, on which the play was based, was published in Germany in 1587 and may have been a useful source for both Marlowe and Forman. Bound in the same folio as Forman's 'book' on necromancy is a discourse on the heavens based on the work of the mathematician Jerome Cardan, as well as notes on how to cast to discover the identity of a thief. (Unfortunately, as the author admits, this did not always work.)

In many respects Forman was extremely credulous. He really did believe in the raising of spirits, in the power of charms to ward off evil, the making and use of 'sigils' (small metal amulets engraved with planetary signs, which were attached to silk or taffeta ribbons and worn round the neck), rings and stones engraved similarly, and in a whole variety of love potions and love tokens. Yet interspersed with his writings on such matters are his own interpretations of the Bible in the form of pages of doggerel verse and lengthy prayers for his salvation. He is a strange mixture, for alongside the raising of spirits and conventional supplications to the Almighty, he was also clearly fascinated by the new sciences, the questions being raised as to the real age of the world, the reassessment of the cosmos, the urgent need to discover a method of measuring longitude now it was certain the world was round, and the flora and fauna of the New World.

The year ended for him with some kind of necromantic seance with music, followed by a visit to friends in Sussex. He was still finding it hard to make ends meet in London and once again had recourse to his brother William for a loan. But from now on, in spite of some setbacks, he would make steady progress towards the status and position he craved: that of Dr Simon Forman of London, gentleman, physician and astrologer.

5

Medical Matters

During the next two years Forman really started to establish himself and become widely known within the City of London, finally feeling secure enough to have the rest of his precious books and chests of possessions sent up from Wiltshire. He was soon very busy, with little time for the jaunts into the country he so much enjoyed. He also began to make valuable and influential friends, including the famous globemaker Emery Molyneux to whom, he boasted, he taught 'the longitude'. Although the discovery of how to calculate longitude was to take well over a century, the increasingly urgent need to find a method of doing so was already exercising minds all over Europe as a result of the huge expansion in merchant venturing and the opening up of the New World.

Convinced that he had found a solution, Forman wrote *The Grounds of Longitude*, his only printed 'book'.[1] It begins in grandiose style:

To all true students of Geography and Cosmography for the discoverie of Straunge Places and Ylandes [*sic*] or Countries, to all students of astronomie and to all those that are desirous to augment their skill and knowledge by the help of Longitude and to all others, well lovers of Art and favourers of Learning, Simon Forman, student in Astronomy and Phisique, sendeth greetings in the year of our Lord everlasting 1591. Imprinted at London by Thomas Dawson 1591.

The printer's sign is of storks or herons set against vine leaves and the dedication alone is set in four different typefaces. He then adds: 'With an admonition to all those that are incredulous and believe not the Truth of the same.'

The book starts off well enough, noting that man has 'learned by the use of various instruments such as the astrolabe to take the height of the Sunn, the height, longitude and latitude of the stars, to know the height of countries and the latitude of places, islands and cities from the equinoctiall that thereby they may better know the place they be and how and where to direct their voyage and their ship and thereby may also attain more speedily and safely to the haven they long for'.

What is needed now, he declared, 'is certainty in Longitude which many men have shot at with cross-staff and instruments, but no instrument [has] yet to measure it'. All of which is obvious enough. 'Ptolemy' had been wrong when he wrote that all navigation could be undertaken by using the positions of the sun and moon, 'since mariners and travellers cannot have [these] at all times to help themselves, after they are beaten and driven by foul weather or with some uncouth storm and raging of the sea unexpected or hath got lost in some strange land'.

Unfortunately, after these brave words the book is a disappointment. Forman lists at length what God has given to mankind, from the ability to count and measure to setting the sun, moon, stars and planets in their courses. He notes that the world turns once every twenty-four hours, the sun, moon and stars passing from east to west, that earth and water are on the face of one round body, that there are two poles, 'Arctick and Antarticke and an Equinoctuall in the middle', that latitude is taken from pole to pole and is the opposite of longitude and so on and so forth, all of which must have been known to most of his readers.

If the reader has stayed with him so far he must by now be eager for the meat, but it never comes. Forman made it clear that he believed the solution to lie in astrology, not astronomical knowledge or the exact calculation of time. All that follows is a succession of vague and intriguing hints that 'the Author' has the ability to chart the position of the 'fixed stars' without error, using 'that method known only to him', and that he will shortly publish tables 'showing how it is done, using astronomy and natural and artificial magic'.

The idea for writing such a book, he claimed, was put into his head by

Emery Molyneux and 'Robert Parker, merchant of London who asked him to take sore pains therein. And by the grace and help of God, I have brought it to pass, which any man that is desirous of the knowledge thereof may learn the truth at the Author's hand if they repair unto him or else they repair to Master Robert Parker in Pudding Lane.' The 'book', in fact, is little more than an advertisement to encourage those interested to visit Simon and learn from him in person. If, as promised, he ever did publish more on the subject then no record of it remains. He ends: 'Finis per me Simon Forman'.

On 17 March 1590 he made a major decision, taking a lease on chambers in the Stone House in the ward of Billingsgate. The Stone House had been what is strangely called a 're-vestry' to St Botolph's Church on Thames Street but the building had been secularised and converted into chambers and tenements. It was a sensible move, Billingsgate was an excellent choice as a place to set up in medical practice. On a large inlet east of London Bridge, it was a port in its own right and had been so since the days of Edward the Confessor when it was used mainly to import goods from France. A fine new Custom House had been built on the riverside between the harbour and the Tower of London, replacing the medieval building where Chaucer had been employed for a time. Now merchant ships put in to Billingsgate from all parts of the known world, although the bulk of the trade was still from France and the Low Countries.

The Stone House was in an ideal situation, for only a few minutes' walk away to the north was bustling East Cheap with its craftsmen, artisans and merchants. A tally of the Crafts of London, dated 1600, lists sixty. Almost every craft and trade is there, including mercers, fishmongers, goldsmiths, jewellers, printers, stationers, waxchandlers, cordwainers, carpenters, coach-builders, paviours and scriveners, to name but a few.[2] Given this amount of commercial activity, as well as a nearby port and its ancillary businesses such as chandlery and sail- and rope-making, Forman speedily increased his busy practice and from now on his casebooks show a steady stream of clients requiring astrological castings and medical consultations. At last, after so many moves, he had a substantial base in which to settle down; he was to remain at the Stone House for years.

However, he was still complaining of being hard up and having to borrow money from his brothers, in part to purchase the ingredients for his medicines. But once safely established in his new lodgings he went out immediately and bought a new horse, 'a red mare', redeemed his eagle stone ring from a John Kempton to whom he had pawned or pledged it, 'bought me much new apparel' (increasingly he loved fine and fashionable clothes) and 'went a-wooing Anne Noke', a lady of whom we hear nothing more.

Thanks to the folios interleaved in the King's College manuscript we know what cures, remedies and supposed prophylactics he prescribed to his patients, both those he had copied out of Boorde's *Breviary of Health* and others which he discovered for himself. He dated only a handful of his notes and it is clear from the different shades of ink and the handwriting that he added to them over a considerable period of time. They are quite distinct from the astrological writings and forecasts in the casebooks and give a general picture of what a patient seeking advice on a medical matter might expect when they visited the Stone House. Much of the material concerns elixirs, salves and poultices, but it also mentions other types of treatment as well as his methods of diagnosis.

It has been suggested that Forman disapproved of bloodletting, never recommended applying leeches, and that he scorned diagnosis from the examination of a patient's urine.[3] No doubt this was a fair conclusion on the basis of the Oxford manuscripts alone, but the Cambridge papers tell a rather different story. He had actually embarked on bloodletting with one of his first patients, John Waller, back in 1579 and it is clear from his drawings, including one particular astrological figure, that he felt it had its uses. Also, on the drawing of the naked man to which he appended the relevant planetary signs to the parts of the body, he drew attention to the main veins for bloodletting, including one in the sole of the foot from which 'can be let blood for all diseases of the body and especially those of the heart but few know of it for it is not in their books'. It was on the page opposite this that he gave his views on the process of ageing, which bring home dramatically how short life expectancy was for those living at the end of the sixteenth century.[4]

He then made various points on bloodletting and its uses. The correct time to draw blood should be on the 'natural day' for it, 'as declared in the almanac', but if a patient is very ill then his blood must be let at once, although even then it is preferable for the moon to be in the right phase. Children under the age of fourteen should only have their blood let in exceptional circumstances, but a rider informs us that 'I Simon forman the Coter [quoter or author] of this booke have let children blood of 5. yers or lesse'. He also used leeches sometimes for head pains, recommending the application of horse leeches to the forehead. If they did not get to work at once then the forehead 'should be anointed with wine and then the leeches would do what was wanted of them by and by'. But compared to many physicians of his day, he is cautious as to the efficacy of the routine bloodletting so often recommended as a cure-all.

He also copied out several pages from Boorde on diagnosis by the use of urine. According to Boorde it should be as fresh as possible, delivered quickly either on horseback or swiftly on foot, for 'if it is not fresh the best physician can be deceived for urine is a strumpet and an harlot and will lie'. We do not know how much store Forman himself set on examining a patient's urine, but what the public at large thought of such divination is proved by the popular and derisory epithet 'piss prophet' applied to those physicians who relied on it.[5]

Thankfully some of the diseases Forman and other physicians of the day were regularly called upon to treat have virtually disappeared, at least in the West. Immunisation and sophisticated medical practices have played a great part in this, but equally important have been the provision of clean water, the use of antiseptics and the recognition of the need for good hygiene. Regarding water alone, a London maid or housewife might throw her night slops out of the window into the kennel in the middle of the street (which ran down to the Thames or one of its tributaries), then take the same pail down to the river bank or a flight of water steps, fill it up with water and take it home for household purposes, including cooking. It was a fortunate household that had its own well.

Elizabethans rarely bathed, indeed it was considered extremely risky, a point made strongly in *The Booke of Sovereigne Medicines* written by John de Feckenham, once bishop of Westminster, at about this time. You should not, he writes, bathe for at least two days after a journey and not then if it 'be not a fair clear day'. In general, rather than taking an open (public) bath you should bathe in your chamber in the morning, an hour or so after dawn, after thoroughly digesting your food and having had a good night's sleep. Before even thinking of getting into the water you should also walk for an hour or half an hour in your chamber or elsewhere.

You should always go into a bath with an empty stomach and 'so remain as long as you are in it except great necessity require the same'. Once in, you can 'tarry there as long as you can abide it', but an hour and a half at most and certainly not until you feel faint or your strength fails you. If this does happen then it is recommended that you drink 'some ale warmed with a toste or any other supping or green ginger or, if need be, *aqua vite*'. It is hardly surprising that even the rich balked at such a performance.

So what remedies did Simon Forman recommend to his patients? Lack of hygiene and antiseptics resulted in Elizabethans being prone to skin infections and abscesses, 'carbuncles, kibes, boils, cankers, bubuckles and whelks'.[6] To ripen an imposthume or swelling and rid it of venomous matter he prescribed a mixture of 'mallows, hollyhocks, rose leaves and sheep's suet, boiled all in beer together then thickened with crumbs of brown bread' and applied as a poultice. This was also useful for suppuration or gathering of the breast, which should first be cleansed with white wine mixed with what appears to be 'burned lead'. Another prescription for 'an anthrax' (a carbuncle) was a mixture of honey, beaten egg, salt and treacle or linseed, boiled in milk with red rose leaves, dry or green salad oil, and thickened again using either flour or breadcrumbs.

A thick potage of meat and parsley or broth from an old hen cooked in wine and saffron 'til she falls asunder' was the prescription for strengthening the heart, either that or 'warm women's milk', especially in the morning. For quinsy or tonsillitis one should apply a plaster of honey and grease mixed with the nest of a swallow or magpie (making sure to use all its constituent parts in the poultice) or, for an ordinary sore throat, a gruel of oatmeal sieved through a cloth and mixed with ground almonds and a little sugar, to be eaten with bread and honey. For cleansing the blood there was nothing to beat barley water made from ripe barley and clear running water 'that hath its course towards the east'.

For severe pain he used pills of opium, henbane and 'white poppi' and for sleeplessness a drink made from lettuce boiled in water was particularly effective for restless or fretful small children, while adults might also try a syrup of violets in warm water 'a good drink for one that sleeps poorly at night'. Those stricken with cramp, 'tinckling in the toes or flesh', should take 'of vinegar half a pint, of oats a handful, of black sope half a pound and boil all together well in a pipekine', then apply often.

Young girls or women suffering from anaemia, 'the greensickness', were offered a pleasant, but expensive, 'elixir' of rosemary, hyssop, bugloss, borage, fumitory and winter savory simmered in white wine then brought to the boil, strained and mixed with cloves, powdered cinnamon, nutmeg, raisins (with the stones picked out), figs, saffron and that great luxury, white sugar, the whole mixture then being reheated and stirred well until it thickened. For those afflicted with agues, fevers or other common ailments, the remedy was a syrup of wild chicory, lettuce, pomegranate juice and water-lily flowers.

Men must have consulted him on the subject of impotence, for there are two entries, one under 'when one would gladly be provok'd but cannot do it' and another headed 'virga virilis, a man's yard'. The prescription for the latter is civet taken in a poached egg. For infertility the newly discovered potato roots, boiled and eaten with pepper and honey 'doth encrease the sperm mightily and provokes venery'. He does not, however, appear to recommend the Elizabethan equivalent of Viagra. This was *eringo*, sea holly, which for many years was cultivated in the area around Colchester and widely used both here and on the Continent. Sea holly has exceptionally long straight roots and these were boiled, cut up in pieces and candied.[7]

Other more homely remedies include 'a hote cow tord clapt on' for a bad knee; for baldness 'a lye of ashes burned of dog's dung', or if that was not available the ashes of 'littel grene frogs' (little green frogs simmered in water could also be used as an anaesthetic when pulling teeth); chewing the flowers of cinquefoil for sweet breath and the application of the 'lices' that breathe under wood or stones 'having many feet', pierced with a bodkin and applied to a tooth, for toothache; while an effective way of stopping a man's nosebleed was to 'lay his cod and stones [scrotum and testicles] in vinegar'. There is even the odd beauty hint: for instance, to make hair 'yellow as gould', one should wash it in a mixture of mashed rhubarb and lye and dry it in the sun if possible or, failing that, by the fire. Repeat frequently, 'for the oftener they do it the fairer they become'. Lye, made by mixing wood or vegetable ash with water then straining it, was commonly used in the laundry.

Forman was very interested in hernias, which he notes were often caused by too much lifting of heavy loads, and recommends manipulation and a truss made from white fustian stuffed with carded wool or cotton as a practical and helpful measure, with a surgery only as a last resort. A sufferer who opts for surgery must choose 'an expert work man' and not trust to 'common cutters' and 'runners about'. A description of what one might expect from such common cutters, including removing part of the peritoneum 'without tyeing or cautrising' would almost certainly make the victim prefer to die with the condition rather than attempt such a cure.

There are also occasional sad case histories. 'I know of a child of eight years who had a dropsy in his belly. It became hard and sometimes made a noise and a croaking.' For some months he was treated by an 'outland man' (a foreign or strange doctor) and 'sometimes he seemed well and played with other children . . . and sometimes he played not and sometimes was very ill. He was very leane and eat littel and slepte littel and', most poignantly, 'in the falle of the lefe he died'. Simon goes on to add that he was at the 'cutting of him up'. His belly was full of red water yet 'he had littel bloode in his bodie and his milt [spleen] was shronke up to the armpit allmoste and was lyttle and square & covered with a velme [film]'.

That Simon Forman was present at 'the cutting of him up' raises the question of dissection, which in general was against the law unless it was carried out on convicted felons. The Barber-Surgeons of London's charter of 1540 gave them the right to take the bodies of hanged criminals for their dissections because 'being anatomised' was considered to be part of the punishment. Such dissections for the purpose of anatomy teaching were common by the 1590s. The College of Physicians, however, was not granted the right to carry out autopsies on ordinary patients until the mid-seventeenth century.

The position was somewhat different abroad. In the interests of furthering medical knowledge a fifteenth-century Italian physician, Antonio Benivieni, was allowed to perform autopsies over a number of years in cases where the patient had died from unknown causes and he had been given permission to do so by the person's family.[8] His descriptions of the procedures he used are very similar to the account given by Simon of the post mortem on the little boy. The suggestion in this case is that Simon had been allowed to attend a rare anatomy demonstration at the Barber-Surgeons' Hall in Cripplegate, the parents of the child having given their permission to discover what had killed their son.

So far as precautionary measures against disease are concerned, then Forman, echoing Boorde, recommends that men should avoid new ale and beer, red wine, hot bread, oysters, mussels and whelks (which were considered to have aphrodisiac qualities and 'provoke venery'), eels, riot, late drinking, walking or riding in wet shoes or boots and too much standing, sitting, studying and playing of cards of dice. This, if followed, would have virtually destroyed the Elizabethan male lifestyle ... On a number of occasions he gives advice he certainly never followed himself, to the effect that both men and women should 'avoid venerous acts'.

He carefully copied out the words of Boorde on the art of medicine: 'that it is to preserve a man's natural complexion or to restore it to a natural course when necessary ... for medicine is for the whole man'. In a tiny note written inside a rectangle at the top of a page he added that 'hit is most worthy to be set off and had in memory'. It has been suggested that he leaned towards the philosophy of Galen rather than Paracelsus (though not sufficiently to satisfy the College of Physicians), but this note on respecting nature and treating the whole man owes more to the philosophy of Paracelsus.

Forman was something of a hypochondriac, for he often cast horoscopes and his writings are peppered with entries about his bad back, headaches, stomach pains, falls, cuts, knocks and head colds. But in the summer of what had up until then been by far his most successful year he became seriously ill for the first time in his life, close even to death.

One of the greatest scourges of the age was bubonic plague. It was endemic, but there were always years when it flared up into a major epidemic, killing thousands. This happened in both 1592 and 1593; 10,675 people died in London alone in 1593. We know from the diaries of the theatrical entrepreneur Philip Henslowe that for much of that time the authorities closed all the theatres to prevent the disease from spreading and that in order to keep going the various theatre companies had to leave London and go out on tour. The officials who bore the brunt of the responsibility for seeing that Plague Orders were carried out were the lord mayor and aldermen. They had to ensure that the beadles checked there was a lantern or candles over every man's door at night so that all could see if the household had succumbed to the plague, while two church-wardens and the clerk of each parish were held responsible for ensuring proper burial and for searching out infected households and seeing they were shut up.[9] The local constables had the thankless task of marking infected houses with a cross, keeping a tally of deaths and arresting vagrants in case they spread the disease. Penalties for laxity on anyone's part were severe: one constable was sent to Newgate for not marking a house with a cross, as were two churchwardens for concealing deaths in the Angel Inn in Bishopsgate Street.

At the beginning of an epidemic corpses were taken straight to graves in the local cemetery without a burial service or any other solemnity, but later, when the disease had really taken a hold, the victims were disposed of as quickly as possible. Thomas Dekker, playwright and journalist, describes seeing the dead 'tumbled into their everlasting lodgings (ten in one heap, twenty in another), gallant and beggar together, scholar and carter in one bed'.

People were no nearer knowing the cause of 'King Pest', as it was commonly called, than they had been when the Black Death swept through Europe two hundred years earlier. Some still believed it was God's punishment for public wickedness and some speculated that it was caused by planetary conjunctions. Others considered it was due to 'corrupt and superfluous humours' and that each victim should be treated according to his 'humour'. The sanguine had their blood let, but the choice of treatment for the choleric depended on how much they could afford to pay: the poor were purged with an infusion of rhubarb, the wealthy with an 'electuary of roses'. Since the activity of the plague bacillus is affected by atmospheric conditions, then the theory of 'corrupt humours' and 'corrupt air' was, in part, correct.[10]

Possible prophylactics included chewing garlic, angelica or gentian root, sucking lemons, sniffing an orange stuck with cloves, drinking wormwood steeped in vinegar and burning a mixture of rosemary, juniper and bay in a chafing dish. A more inconvenient measure was to keep two or three sheep in one's living room so that they might take the infection. Quacks, of course, did a roaring trade in amulets, 'dragon water' and specifics such as powdered unicorn's horn and 'sack, salad oil and gunpowder' to make one sweat. One quack, Simon Kellaway, published his own *Defensative Against the Plague*, allegedly full of advice on how to avoid becoming infected. Those who could not afford to buy the whole book were able to purchase its most practical hint on a small piece of paper. After paying for it, they opened it up to discover Kellaway's great preventative was 'Fuge Loci', flee the place!

On 11 June 1592, Simon Forman rode down to Ipswich on business. He stayed in the town for over a week, returning to London on the 20th. Whether he contracted the plague in Ipswich or immediately on his return to London he does not say and quite possibly did not know, but next day he began to feel ill and the first swelling or bubo appeared in his groin. By 6 July it was very serious and he took to his bed with 'the plague in both my groins and some time after that I had the red tokens on my feet as broad as halfpence'.

However, while all around him were dying and the death carts could scarcely cope with the nightly tally of corpses, he managed to survive. He put this down in part to his being fortunate to have contracted the 'red' rather than the 'black' plague, which he deemed to be almost always fatal. According to his notes, he treated himself by drinking 'strong waters' he had distilled earlier, lancing the buboes as soon as they appeared and cleaning up the consequent wound and letting his own blood once only when the disease first took hold, a regimen he was to use to good effect on victims of the 'red' plague the following year.[11] But while he thanked providence for sparing him, the illness was so severe that 'it was twenty-two weeks before I was well again'. It was hardly surprising therefore that, when he finally recovered he was once again forced to borrow money, this time from both his sister, Joan, and a friend, Hugo.

During his long convalescence London slowly came back to life. The theatres and bear pits opened again and the Court returned to Whitehall, while those who had fled to the country returned to their city houses, some to discover that they had been lived in during their absence or even rifled. Among those whom the plague had carried off was the poet, Thomas Watson, a friend of Marlowe and Thomas Nashe. Later Nashe mourned for him, and all the dead of those two terrible plague years, with haunting beauty in 'Summer's Last Will and Testament'.

> Beauty is but a flower
> Which wrinkles will devour;
> Brightness falls from the air,
> Queens have died young and fair;
> Dust hath closed Helen's eye;
> I am sick, I must die –
>   Lord have mercy upon us!

6

The Terrors of the Night

'She had wit at will but was somewhat proud and wavering, given to lust and to diversity of loves and men; and would many times overshoot herself, was an enemy to herself and stood much on her own conceit. And did, in lewd banqueting, gifts and apparel, consume her husband's wealth, to satisfy her own lust and pleasure and on idle company. And was always in love with one or another. She loved one Cox, a gentleman, on whom she spent much. After that she loved Dean Wood, a Welshman who cozened her of much; she consumed her husband for love of that man. She did much overrule her husband.'

Forman then turned to the lady's body and behaviour: 'She was of long visage, wide mouth, reddish hair, of good and comely stature; but would never garter her hose and would go much slipshod. She had four boys, a maid and a shift [a miscarriage]. She loved dancing, singing and good cheer. She kept company with base fellows such as she was herself of, of lewd conversation – and yet would seem as holy as a horse. She was never without one bawd or cunning woman or other, to keep her company, to her great shame, to paint her, etc.'[1]

So who was she? The mistress of a smart brothel? The willing and promiscuous hostess of an East Cheap tavern? She was, surprisingly, the wife of Dean Blague, a respectable Bachelor of Divinity of Oxford University and a Doctor of Divinity of Cambridge. A careful and academic young man, he had been given preferment by no less a person than Lord

Burleigh and acquired a clutch of livings in various places including Ewelme in Oxfordshire. In 1591 he became dean of Rochester, though for most of the time he lived in London. The red-haired lady who never gartered her hose was his second wife, Alice, married off to him at the age of fifteen when he was over thirty by her family, who were deeply impressed by Blague's religious standing and status. His first wife had died young. Both he and Alice were firm believers in astrology, continually worried about health problems and over the years consulted Forman regularly.

Alice Blague first visited him in 1593, whether for a medical problem or an astrological casting he does not tell us, writing only that on '11th June I did halek Alice Blague and on the 15th June'.[2] That seems to have been the extent of that side of their relationship, for she does not appear again in his 'halek notes', although she was to involve him for years in her affairs with other men.

Forman was still trying to find a suitable wife. The previous year he had taken a strong fancy to a young woman he met in the street, whom he 'liked well and, by enquiry, understanding whose daughter she was and where she dwelt, [I] intended to make some errand to her father's house to come acquainted as well with her friends, intending to espouse the wench if I could obtain her good will, her being free of others'.[3] He was serious enough to cast to know how he would fare. (Castings for his own use are almost always under the heading 'a certain gentleman wishes to know ...'.) The result informed him that he would have 'good entertainment' and so he went round to the girl's house, where he found her at home with a girlfriend.

Simon sent out for a quart of wine and everything seemed to be going well, the young lady encouraging his interest so much that when another suitor turned up he was sent about his business, much to Simon's satisfaction. After some time the girl's mother returned and invited him to stay for a meal (with gammon and cheese) together with another guest and the girl's father, who came home shortly afterwards. At six in the evening Simon went back home, having found the opportunity to kiss the girl twice, with high hopes of taking it further. But unfortunately he could not leave it there and at once cast to see how he would fare if he married her. The astrological forecast was that she would 'prove a whore and bear outward in her behaviour a fair show, but she will play the whore privily'.

This was sufficient to ensure he never saw her again. He then went a-wooing a Mistress Lodwick, of whom we hear no more.

He was soon caught up in far more serious matters. With the return of the plague, almost all the physicians of any standing fled to the country to save themselves and Forman was almost overwhelmed by pleas for help. He remained in London to bring relief to plague victims, and though he must have considered it highly unlikely that he would contract it again, this did him nothing but good with the local citizens. 'I began to be known and came to credit,' he wrote, then ventured into doggerel to make his point:

> And in the time of Pestilent Plague,
> When Doctors all did fly,
> And got them into places far
> From out the City.
> The Lord appointed me to stay
> To cure the sick and sore,
> But not the rich and mighty ones
> But the distressed poor.

After the worst of the epidemic had abated he wrote a pamphlet on the subject, into which he put everything he considered relevant and had learned from his experiences of treating himself and others. It is called 'A *Discourse of the Plague* written by Simon Forman, practising physician and astrologer 1593 and Notes for other Men to read and Himself to Remember'.[4]

He starts by considering its cause and hedges his bets by going along with both of the most popular theories of the day. 'The nature of the Plague,' he writes, in part one, 'is two-fold, affected by the motion of the Planets.' There is the black plague, caused by the positioning of Saturn, and the red, caused by that of Mars. He then describes how the swellings, the buboes, appear either under the armpit or in the groin or both. It is possible to cure the red plague, from which he had suffered himself, either by lancing the buboes or, if the swellings 'broke of themselves', by 'careful dressing of these sores for they are dangerous and very infective'. Modest bloodletting might help, as it had done in his case, and possibly a purge. On the other hand, the outlook for those suffering from the black plague was almost always fatal though 'if red spots [appear] on one with the black plague he may escape', but one must be careful not to confuse such red spots with flea bites.

Tudor physicians were correct in differentiating two kinds of plague, although modern medicine recognises a third type, which is rarer. In Forman's day the most common was bubonic plague, with its classic symptoms of purple pustules followed by red lumps (from which it was possible to recover), and after that the pneumonic plague, which affects the lungs and has a higher fatality rate. The third variation is septicaemic plague, which presents with a rash and and almost always ends in death. But most of the cases in 1592–3 were bubonic.

Part two of Forman's plague treatise dwells at length on the second supposed cause of the disease under such headings as 'The Plagues of God' and the 'Plagues Sent by Devils', the latter apparently with God's agreement. Plague, Forman pontificates, is most often a punishment for wickedness, women being particularly at fault for drawing it on a population. He cites Potiphar's wife and Jezebel in the Old Testament as examples, Jezebel, who, having been 'lascivious and adulterous ... with her painted face and whoredom, enticeth men to come in to her to fulfil the lusts of the flesh, provoking the Lord to wrath and indignation'.

The plague left him far better off and with a greatly enhanced reputation. He moved downstairs into superior ground-floor accommodation in the Stone House, had a splendid gown made trimmed 'with velvet fur' to advertise his status, redeemed a ring from pawn (possibly the same one as last time) and bought another for forty shillings. He had acquired, he wrote, more knowledge of both astrology and medicine 'and my credit increased and I got much'.

But the epidemic was not the only event that made 1593 a dark and uneasy year; there was to be much else besides, for the plague's return brought with it the popular human need to find scapegoats for the visitation. During the early part of the year the spread of the disease was blamed increasingly on the wave of immigrants who had come to London to escape religious persecution on the Continent. A rash of threatening posters and handbills appeared in public places, of which one gives the flavour:

> You strangers that now inhabit this land,
> Note this same writing, do it understand,
> Conceive it well for safeguard of your lives,
> Your goods, your children and your dearest wives.

To their credit the Privy Council acted quickly and an Order in Council was made prohibiting the further publication of such 'libels' under pain of severe punishment. The order also obliged officers of the law to search the lodgings of anyone suspected of promoting such material and to arrest them if they had any cause, however slight, to believe the offence had been committed. If, when questioned, the accused refused to confess willingly, then they could be tortured. The order ends with the chilling words: 'We pray you use your utmost travail and endeavour in this task.' It is easy to understand, how innocent citizens might become apprehensive that their houses could be searched at any time and their private papers examined on the pretext that they had published anti-immigrant material.

The order was of special concern to those dabbling in forbidden knowledge. They were aware that they might be brought before the authorities to answer for all kinds of other material discovered in their possession if they were subjected to a search, and Forman ended his general round-up of the year with a note to the effect that he was taking care, for 'if I did intend to do anything whatsoever, if I did tell anybody of it I was prevented and did not do it or could have no power to proceed with it'.

He had cause for caution. Devil-raising and necromancy were in the air in 1593, arousing concern in high places, and *Dr Faustus* was playing at the Rose Theatre to packed houses in the periods when the playhouses were allowed to open. It was so successful that the Lord Admiral's Men also took the production out on tour, giving rise to the famous anecdote that when they performed it in Exeter the players found a real demon had joined the cast and were so terrified that they spent the night on their knees in Exeter cathedral praying to God for forgiveness.

The authority for the making of the order regarding immigrants had come from Sir Robert Cecil, son of Lord Burleigh. Sir Francis Walsingham, Elizabeth's spymaster, had held the post of Lord Privy Seal and Secretary to the Privy Council up until his death, but Cecil had to be content with the title of 'Acting Secretary' while the queen procrastinated about ratifying his appointment. However, this did not prevent him from assuming all the powers of the position while he waited for her to make up her mind, even secretly entering into negotiations with King James in Edinburgh to ensure he was well placed when she died. He was clever, ruthlessly ambitious, calculating and ferociously anti-Catholic. He was also slightly hunchbacked and there was gossip at the time that this was the reason why Elizabeth kept him waiting so long, her penchant being for straight, handsome young men.

While Cecil might be able to claim some credit for the order on anti-immigrant publications since he had great sympathy for all those fleeing from Catholic persecution, there is little doubt that he found it useful to have an excuse to investigate other activities which were of concern to him under its cover. Certainly by 1593 he was looking askance at the activities of a loose club or gathering of scientists, mathematicians, astrologers, astronomers and writers, who met under the joint aegis of Sir Walter Ralegh and Henry Percy, Earl of Northumberland, nicknamed 'the Wizard Earl'. It was known as the School of the Night.

It is hardly surprising that this circle, which investigated many subjects proscribed by the university curricula of the day, soon became the object of rumour and speculation. It is not certain how many people were involved for no comprehensive list exists, but it was known to include Thomas Hariot, the great mathematician and astronomer, Robert Hues, the geographer, Walter Warner, a mathematician and alchemist, Christopher Marlowe, who was a close friend of Hariot, Emery Molyneux, the globemaker and friend to whom Simon Forman had 'taught' longitude and who was the patron of his book on the subject, and the poets George Chapman and Matthew Roydon, as well as Sir George Carey, who had consulted Forman since 1587.

Others who were interested in such subjects as navigation, algebra, alchemy, chemistry, geography, medicine, literature and poetry were also invited, sometimes to Ralegh's Tower Room in his fine house overlooking the Thames, sometimes to the residence of the Wizard Earl with its laboratory, crucibles, furnaces and 'speculative glasses'. There were short stays in the country at Sir Walter's country estate, the Old Castle, Sherborne, a gift from the queen when he was at the height of her favour. Forman was friendly with Molyneux and Carey and interested in the subjects discussed, including longitude. He lived in the right place and knew the right people and it is probable that he attended some gatherings, since it was not necessary to be wealthy, well-born or university-educated to take part in the school's discussions: the passport was an enquiring mind. As the gatherings took place discreetly, it is not surprising that he made no specific mention of them, although he he did refer to meetings of an unnamed and unexplained 'circle'.

During the spring of 1593 Christopher Marlowe was put under surveillance and the kinds of topic discussed were listed for the authorities by Cecil's informer, Richard Baines, and later published in his notorious 'Note'.[5] What was learned from Baines and from the dramatist, Thomas Kyd, under torture, was that Marlowe regularly attended meetings with his friend Thomas Hariot, at which shocking and forbidden matters were allegedly discussed (though it hardly needed the services of a spy or the use of the rack to gain this knowledge, since Marlowe, especially in his cups, was notorious for going out of his way to be offensive and outrageous).

They covered a wide range of topics: the real age of the earth, the truth or not of early Old Testament stories, the size and scope of the universe (Hariot had a splendid telescope), and the new sciences and mathematics, which were spreading across the Continent. But Marlowe, according to Baines and Kyd, went much further, informing all who would listen that the 'woman of Samaria and her sisters were whores and Christ knew them dishonestly' and 'that St John the Evangelist was bedfellow to Christ and leaned always in his bosom [and] that he used him as the sinners of Sodom'. Add to that the rumour that both Hariot and Marlowe were atheists who sought to convert others, and Marlowe's notorious remark that all who loved not tobacco and boys were fools, and it is hardly surprising that the authorities began to think it was time they found out exactly what was going on.

Marlowe's pronouncements were doubtless exaggerated, but he certainly said enough to frighten his friend, drinking companion and fellow Cambridge University wit Robert Greene, who, when he was dying, warned him of the perils of atheism, ending with the chilling prophesy 'for little knowest thou how, in the end, thou might be visited'.[6] It also prompted another friend, Thomas Nashe, to tell everyone that he himself had 'never been an atheist like Marlowe'.

On 20 May Marlowe, now the most popular poet and dramatist of his day, was arrested on charges of blasphemy and treason and, astonishingly, allowed out on bail so long as he reported each day to the office of the Star

65

Chamber. Ten days later he was dead, supposedly killed in a fight in a Deptford tavern owned by one Eleanor Bull, over who should pay 'the reckoning' (the bill). We now know that Marlowe had been one of Walsingham's spies, that he spent his last day in the company of three others and that there was no tavern in Deptford owned by an Eleanor Bull, but that a lady of that name, who happened to be related to Sir Robert Cecil, had a house in the town.

Rumours of what might lie behind Marlowe's death added to the general climate of fear. Shortly afterwards Cecil announced that he would be setting up a formal inquisition to look into the School of the Night, its membership and Ralegh's involvement with it. Ralegh would always arouse strong feelings; he was described on the one hand as 'the best hated man of the world in Court, City or country' and on the other as 'this beautiful daemon'. Whatever the real reasons were for setting up the inquisition, members of the School felt themselves to be under attack.

As if this was not enough, a month later Thomas Nashe published a pamphlet called *The Terrors of the Night*, the content of which was to influence attitudes towards Simon Forman for the next four hundred years. Nashe was capable of writing beautiful poetry and also wrote plays in partnership with, among others, Robert Greene and Ben Jonson, but he earned his living mostly from the publication of witty, polemical and sometimes scandalous pamphlets under titles such as *Pierce Penniless* and *A Cup of News*. He was perennially hard up, always trying to find himself a patron, and he applied at different times to both the Earl of Southampton and the Earl of Oxford, but his was a difficult, prickly personality and he never succeeded in acquiring sustained patronage.

The Terrors of the Night ranges over such topics as superstition, the raising of spirits and the meaning of dreams and nightmares, 'for as touching the terrors of the night, they are as many as our sins', and 'the Night is the Devil's Black Book'. Nashe, while unconventional in many respects, did not hold with involvement in the occult and had no time for those who claimed expertise in it. However, his most blistering invective is reserved for the impostors and charlatans who set themselves up as physicians and astrologers:

Shall I impart to you a rare secrecy how these great and famous conjurers and cunning men ascend by degrees to tell secrets as they do? First and foremost they are men which have a little sprinkling of grammar and learning in their youth, or at least I will allow them to have been surgeons' or apothecaries' 'prentices. These I say, having run through their thrift at the elbows, and notoriously among harlots and makeshifts and spent the annuity of halfpenny ale left to them, fall a-beating their brains how to botch up an easy and gainful trade and set a new nap in an old occupation.

Hereupon presently they rake some dunghill for a few dirty boxes and plasters and of toasted cheese and candle-ends temper up a few ointments or syrups; which, having done, fare North or into some such simple country they get them and set up. Scarce one month have they stayed there, vaunting and prating and speaking fustian instead of Greek, then all the shires round do ring with their fame; and then they begin to get them a library of some three or four old rusty manuscript books, which neither they themselves nor any else can read and furnish their shops with a thousand *quid pro quos* that would choke any horse; beside some waste trinkets in their chambers hung up, which may make the world half in jealousy that they can conjur.

The supposed physician talks 'doubtfully', hinting that he knows far more than he says and so, having had some small success in fooling people in the country, finally draws nearer and nearer to London until he settles, first in the outskirts then in the City, 'where he sets out his stall like a cobbler or stocking mender'. Many poor people come to believe in him and bring him their urine to divine and soon he is famous throughout the taverns and ordinaries. Later he 'trudgeth off' to dine with a nobleman, where he dismisses all the learning of Galen and so gains even greater acclaim. If such as he are of any sect then they are in reality 'metal bearing Paracelsians', alleging they can cure any number of diseases by the 'great cures' they have in hand. The reputation of such a so-called physician is enhanced the more by claiming either that the illness he has cured was one of 'unrecoverable extremity' or, if there is no hope, then he gives 'peremptory sentence of death'.

Naturally such a charlatan also dabbles in alchemy and pretends to be an augurer, so has people running to him for forecasts, 'where he, like a crafty Jack, as if he had a spirit at his elbow', tells them what they want to know without recourse to any familiar, having learned it out of their own mouths. At the end of the day it is left to the hangman to call a halt to the villainy of such people and so 'knit up their knaveries'.

The Terrors of the Night was widely circulated and proved so popular that it was reprinted several times. Was Nashe casting his net wide or did he intend it to refer to Forman? Certainly the quack doctor follows a similar course; he emerges from some country place, goes north, ends up in London, lacks any kind of professional qualifications, owns only two or three books and claims to summon up spirits. But since Forman was only just getting himself properly established in London at the time it was written, it is by no means certain that Nashe was aiming at him. It is possible that he was harking back to Edward Kelley, who claimed great and fantastic powers and was a convicted felon. Although it was now some years since he had left the country and by this time he was almost certainly dead, he had been notorious throughout London in the 1580s, when Forman was still unknown and living in Salisbury. However, there is no doubt that *The Terrors of the Night* has contributed to his bad reputation.

Against this troubled background Forman fell passionately in love. The affair did not stop him taking other women to bed whenever the opportunity arose, or from searching for a suitable wife, but no other woman was ever to affect him so deeply. For four years he wrote continually and eerily about the affair in his diary and in pages of notes interleaved with his astrological castings, expressing his feelings of love, sexual frustration and jealousy. He became obsessed.

It was a relationship doomed from the start. He first met Avisa Allen in November 1593 when she came to consult him on a health matter. She was thirty-two years old, a neighbour who also lived in Thames Street not far from the Stone House. She was married to William Allen who, since references are sometimes made to 'one of his ships', must have had merchant-venturing interests as well as business in the City which took him away from home regularly. The Allens were obviously comfortably off for they had a substantial house and servants, while Avisa was able to employ a personal maid.

The liaison was dangerous in more ways than one, for not only did Avisa have a husband but she was also a Catholic recusant. For years recusants had been left alone so long as they remained loyal to the Crown and paid a small fine if they did not attend church, but by the 1590s, after the events of the previous few years, the climate had changed completely and for Catholics, however loyal, these were now dangerous times. Catholic priests were forbidden entry to the country and any who came were hunted down without mercy. If caught, they were tortured before being hanged, drawn and quartered at Tyburn, while the most severe penalties were imposed on those who had harboured them. Nor could a blind eye be turned any longer to Catholics who did not attend church regularly on Sunday. However much they might protest their patriotism, non-attendance was punished by increasingly draconian fines.

Forman's note of her Catholicism and recusancy is corroborated in the Recusant Roll for 1594, where she is listed as 'Avisa Allen of London, spinster, alias Avisa Allen, wife of William Allen of the parish of St. Botolph in the ward of Billingsgate, London'.[7] At that time she was liable for a fine of £100 levied on her in the previous April for failing to attend church, although there is no record of any further proceedings being taken against her. Possibly this was because William Allen did not share her faith, for he does not appear in any of the relevant Recusant Rolls and, as he was a substantial and respected citizen and presumably paid her fine, she was left alone, at least for the next three years. But she must always have been aware of the shadow hanging over her.

Forman has left us no physical description of her, whether she was dark or fair, plain or pretty, but the sexual attraction between them was almost instantaneous. They had another interest in common, for Avisa 'distilled', that is she was sufficiently skilled to make up medicines and elixirs herself. He mentions this several times and the way in which he does so suggests that this was more than the mere concoction of domestic remedies for run-of-the-mill household sickness, arguing a much more advanced knowledge of the craft.[8]

His detailed notes tell us a good deal about Avisa's household and the way it was run, but he never referred to children or nurses, which suggests that until his arrival on the scene the marriage had been childless. Nor are there medical notes of her having given birth to sons, 'maids', or suffering 'shifts', as was the case with many other female patients. As to her husband, William Allen might well have been a good bit older than Avisa, for over the years he consulted Forman almost continually on a variety of medical matters.

It did not take long for the relationship between Simon and Avisa to become a physical one. On 29 November 1593 Simon writes: 'at 3 p.m. Avisa Allen and I first *osculavimus* [kissed].' Bed followed soon afterwards. 'She rose and came to me; *et halek Avisa Allen primus* [and I made love to Avisa Allen for the first time] the 15th December, Saturday p.m. at 5 p.m.' For the next four years we follow the ups and downs of this love affair, while his casebooks show frantic castings to see if they might ever come together as man and wife; the only event he considers worthy of note in his restrospective survey of 1593, apart from minor grumbles about his troubles, is that he 'cured Avis Allen'. Only rarely does he use her name. She is most often referred to as 'A.A.' or by two triangles. He was now firmly embarked on a dangerous love affair with a married Catholic.

Hauntingly, among those early castings, when he was asking the stars what the future had in store for them, one entry stands out. On 2 July 1595 he wrote: 'A.A. that now lives obscure for religion's sake – when thirty-six years be come and gone – [will] be constrained to live more obscure and be in peril of imprisonment and forced by law to go to church. And then she shall die and be buried without Christian burial in the thirty-seventh year of her age.'9 This was prophetic.

7

'Many Brabbles and Brawls'

For the next three years Forman lived a double life, the professional one with its medical practice, astrological castings and mounting trouble with the College of Physicians, the other the secretive and emotional roller-coaster of his relationship with Avisa. From start to finish the latter was a story of stormy rows, jealousy, apparent endings, reconciliations, love-making, even violence. We know from the poetry and drama of that era that Elizabethans showed their emotions far more overtly than we do today, coupled with which they were ever aware of the fragility of life; they lived, in Marlowe's words, on 'the slicing edge' of death. Death might take them at any time, by disease for which there was no cure, by accident, in childbirth, or in a casual quarrel on the street which could lead to a drawn knife or sword.

There is, however, less mention of spirit-raising and meetings of inner circles at this time, possibly because in March 1594 Sir Robert Cecil finally set up his Inquisition into the activities of the School of the Night. It was held at Cerne Abbas, close to Ralegh's country home, the reason given being that there had been complaints about the supposedly scandalous goings on at Sherborne Old Castle whenever the members of the School met there for a few days. Its main object was to examine the accusations made against Ralegh and his 'damnable crew'. The statements of some of the witnesses who gave evidence bear a remarkable resemblance to what was alleged of Marlowe in Baines's note: that Hariot denied the resurrection; that Thomas Allen, Lieutenant of Portsmouth Castle and a devout Catholic, had been seen to tear pages out of the Bible to dry tobacco on and had made lewd jokes about Moses and concubines; that Ralegh himself had instigated a blasphemous discussion on the nature of the soul and had invited Dr Dee along to perform experiments in alchemy and occultism.[1]

Cecil had set up the Inquisition when Ralegh was out of favour with the queen after his hasty marriage to Elizabeth Throckmorton, but by the time it started taking evidence Ralegh's star was once more in the ascendant. After weeks of evidence from the School's more prominent members, from complainants, those with axes to grind and various informers (one of whom had infiltrated the School), the Inquisition came to a sudden halt and there is no record of its conclusions. However, it had its effect. If the members of the School continued to meet then they did so in secret; in a letter to Johann Kepler, Hariot deplored the times in which they were living when it had become impossible for a serious man to express his views freely.[2] Coincidentally or not, Forman's notebooks at this time contain an increasing number of 'religious' writings including a leaden rewrite of the first chapters of Genesis.[3]

However, he now had much else to occupy him, His casebooks record a steady increase in the number of those consulting him both as patients or for astrological predictions, until by the end of the century his advice was being sought by over a thousand people a year.[4] Women came to him with queries about pregnancy and childbearing. 'A certain young woman great with child and married posed the question to know when she would be delivered and how long she would labour.' He had told her she would be delivered on 4 May 1592 and a note added later, which we may believe or not, confirms this was the case – that she was delivered of a son at seven minutes to ten and that the labour was not 'hard'. Another, a Joan Horton, had a pregnancy which lasted 'thirty-eight weeks and six days. He [the child] was begotten at night at about the fourth hour. He was born black and a breech child.' A note adds: 'the father died when he was two or three years old'.[5]

Some arrived desperate to know if they would ever become pregnant, others fearful that they might be because they were unmarried or their husbands had been from home at the crucial time or because they had too many children already. As well as making predictions, Forman prescribed draughts or salves for them when he thought it necessary, but there is no reason to believe that he ever procured abortions; in any event desperate women would have been far more likely to resort to the local wise woman or midwife, who would be known to offer such a service, than to approach a male physician. Abortion was a last resort: for both parties it might mean death, for the woman from blood loss or septicaemia, for the practitioner, if discovered, by hanging.

Men wanted astrological castings to see if a proposed bride was likely to be fertile, if their betrothed or their wives were faithful to them, if a child was theirs. They wanted to know if their servants were honest, if they were likely to be left a legacy or acquire wealth, if their latest venture would succeed. They came for potions to make them more virile or to cure impotency, the clap, or the French pox (syphilis). Seafarers wanted to know if their voyages would be successful; their wives, when they were away at sea, if they would be safe from shipwreck. City merchants asked for assistance in tracking down thieves and getting the better of their competitors; over-indulgers tottered in for hangover cures. As a result Simon sat down and wrote several brief pamphlets or papers on subjects such as 'The Importance of Knowing the Hour of Conception of Men and Women', 'How to Discover if a Man be like to be Drowned, Hanged, Poisoned or Suffer Any Other Accidente', 'How to Know the Terme of Lyfe in the Nativity of a Man' and 'Whether a Wife or Other Women be Honest or Noe'.[6]

1594 began and ended with Forman falling downstairs. He gave no explanation as to why he should have done so, perhaps he had simply drunk too much wine, but it was at this crucial point in his career, when money was coming in steadily and the numbers consulting grew by the week, that the College of Physicians finally moved against him, an action which was to lead to years of confrontations, fines and further imprisonment.

It was necessary for the College to show publicly how jealously it guarded its prerogative to examine, license, set standards and police medical practice, and Forman had received a number of warnings: to be recognised as a properly licensed physician the practitioner must be a university-qualified doctor of medicine, and since he had no such qualifications he must cease practising forthwith. This stipulation was extremely useful, for it had the added attraction that it excluded virtually any other category of practitioners, especially 'women and Jews', while the need for recognised practitioners to be able both to read and write Latin eliminated many others, whatever their practical skills. Those trained within their own family or by apprenticeship to a 'doctor', therefore, could easily be dismissed as ignorant or incompetent; only 'book knowledge' counted.

Those who fell foul of the College and refused to heed their warnings were hauled before a special committee of censors sitting in the College hall in Knightrider Street. Volumes of such hearings now in the archives of the Royal College of Physicians show that the censors' apparently harsh treatment of Simon Forman was not unique. Most often a formal hearing before the censors ended with a homily, the imposition of a fine and the culprit agreeing to an injunction that he would cease to practise, but if the culprit still refused to learn his lesson the College had powers of imprisonment, the recalcitrant being sent to the Counter Gaol in Wood Street to teach them a lesson.

The most effective way of forcing the College to withdraw its proscription was to have a powerful patron, as one particular case shows which was a rarity in that it involves a woman. Alice Leevers was described as an 'unskilled and demented wife who has long practised medicine as she herself admits'.[7] But in spite of many warnings and having previously been brought before the censors, Goodwife Leevers refused to be bound over not to practise further and on 15 March 1586 was gaoled for her disobedience. A letter then arrived from Henry Carey, Lord Hunsdon, the Lord Chamberlain to the queen, enquiring why this had been done.

Surely it was obvious, the president of the College wrote back, after thanking him in flowery terms for his letter in 'favour of Alice Leevers asking that she might be admitted to the practice of physick and surgery'. This was not possible, since 'the said Alice, *being only a woman* [my italics] is therefore utterly ignorant in that profession – therefore our society must admonish, punish and correct all such offenders'. She has, he asserts, continued to practise whatever the College might say 'and is meddlesome in what she does not understand'. Lord Hunsdon remained unconvinced, repeating his demand, and a final letter to him from the President, 'who in truth your Lord may, and shall during our life command whatever', reluctantly agrees to 'remit all offences committed by her and . . . touching such part of surgery as are of less danger to the party effected and wherein by track of time she has a little loose skill, she [may] use her outward medicine and devices without interruption'. He ends by humbly beseeching his 'honour to continue your honourable favour towards our poor society which is wholly devoted to your good lord in all services that we shall be able to perform. We most humbly take our leave this sixth of April 1586.'

There are others. A peremptory letter from Sir Francis Walsingham, in his capacity as Secretary of State to the Privy Council, in September of the same year[8] demands to know why the College has confined one Nott, 'a practisioner in physicke' to the Counter Gaol in Wood Street and demands that he be released forthwith from his 'suffering and utter undoing' at his (Walsingham's) request 'without putting him to further trouble'. A letter back, explaining that the man had been 'insolent' and refused to give a bond not to practise medicine, received short shrift and Nott was promptly released. There is even a letter from Queen Elizabeth herself,[9] intervening on behalf of a John Bannister, much praised by her late 'coosins, the Earles of Warwick and Leycester for excellence in the arts of Physicke and Chirurgery . . . given under our signet the 28th day of July 1593'. The college did not even attempt to argue this one.

Simon had already been called before the 'Barber Surgeons' (the College of Physicians had no jurisdiction over surgeons or apothecaries), the outcome of which he does not detail, when he was 'warned again by the Physicians' on 14 February that he must cease practising immediately. This he ignored and on 8 March he was called before the President and five censors to explain himself.[10] The first hearing was brief:

Simon Forman of Wiltshire appeared: he confessed that he had practised medicine in England for these sixteen years and here in London for only two years. He claims to have cured a Master Anize, a Master Nicholas and Master Allen [presumably Avisa's husband] all in Thames Street and all suffering from a fever to whom he gave an electuary [medicine] of syrup of roses with wormwood water and twenty others he had cured in the same way. When asked what authors he had followed and what medical books he had read, he replied that he had read through one [by] Cox and another called Wainfleete.

He boasted that he had made no other help in diagnosing diseases than his *Epherimides* [almanacs] and that by heavenly signs, aspects and constellations of the planets he could instantly recognise any one disease. When he was examined on the principal of astronomy as well as in the fundamentals of medicine, his answers were so inadequate and absurd that it caused great mirth and sport amongst the Auditors. He was forbidden to practise and for his wicked and illegal practice he was fined five pounds to be paid within sixteen days. This he readily and faithfully promised to do.

The misunderstanding over the the 'Cockis or Cockys' book was obviously the crux of the matter. One possibility as to how it arose is that the censors simply did not know of the correct book, or that if they did, none of them had read it because it was only available in manuscript form and had never been printed.[11] Yet, had they done so, they would have found nothing that would have seemed unlearned or ignorant. But there was a yawning cultural gap between the academic physician with access to whole libraries of printed works and the self-taught empiric with his medieval manuscript, even if the two parties shared the same belief in the basic tenets of Galenic medicine. It is also difficult to imagine that Forman, who made such copious notes on his medical treatment of patients in the margins of that very book, would have 'boasted' that he needed no more to diagnose and treat illness than his almanacs.

As to his supposedly 'inadequate' answers to the censors' questions on astrology, which caused those listening to fall about laughing, he was not condemned for casting horoscopes since they all practised astrology themselves, but for his supposed methods. Medical historian, Michael Macdonald, comparing Forman's astrological methodology with that of other practitioners of the period, puts much of their prejudice down to the fact that there was no definitive source book on the subject, each practitioner being certain his own method was best. He describes Forman's 'book' as remarkable, giving high praise both to him and his friend and colleague Richard Napier for their meticulous record keeping, notes on patient interviews and the way in which they both recorded the treatment they prescribed and its outcome. Both were more systematic in observation and record keeping than the regular physicians whose papers have survived.[12] Be that as it may, at the end of the hearing Forman agreed to pay his fine, although he had every intention of carrying on exactly as before. For a short time he was to be left alone.

Soon, however, he was in trouble of a different sort, for there are a number of entries in his diary which, taken together, suggest that he had fathered a second illegitimate child: 'The 11th March. Alice Barker prorit [is pregnant] and on the 12th day she sent for me.' This is followed by, 'the 21st day I was before the Bench of Aldermen for Alice Barker'. (It was on the next day that he went to Knightrider Street and paid his fine of £5 to the College of Physicians.) The next entry informs us that 'on the 20th April Anne was christened'. That the infant 'Anne' was his daughter is also suggested by a further entry the following year when he carefully recorded, 'I have put Anne to a new nurse, to Clemens the tailor's wife of Great Bookham in Surrey.' Why else should he go to so much trouble for some unknown child? Presumably Alice Barker had had him brought before the Bench to ensure he recognised the child as his and agreed to maintain her according to the law.

That this supposition could well be correct is borne out by the fact that on the very day of baby Anne's christening he had a monumental row with Avisa, one so bad that they were estranged for the next eight months. It began with 'a variance between Kate Nicholl and me and Nurse Dandley' during which unspecified things were said and it ended in Avisa refusing ever to see him again. Usually he gives a reason for their quarrels, but not on this occasion.

Unable to persuade her to change her mind, he turned for comfort elsewhere, this time to a Mistress Bradedge, who 'thought I would have married her but I intended it not and she disliked me much until St. John's tide [24 June]', but continued to ask the stars what future there might be, if any, for him and Avisa, 'whether she would continue the friendship and be faithful' and, more significantly, if she would become a widow and marry him.[13] On 9 December he fell downstairs 'again', but this was a red-letter day for at last 'the friendship between Avisa Allen and I was renewed'.

'I got much and spent much,' he wrote in his final round-up of the year, 'and had many brabbles and brawls.' He could not resist a further note on his own health. 'This summer, in July or thereabouts, I had the wet gout in my feet; it broke under the toe next the great toe in my left foot. I cured myself with the dregs of my strong water, through God's help.' Gout was another affliction which interested him.

The 'brabbles and brawls', however, were to carry on well into the next year and throughout 1595 he was to record his thoughts and actions on an almost daily basis, from his preoccupation with his own health to the problems and irritations besetting medical practitioners of the time, one of which was payment or rather lack of it. He gives the example of the 'Greenwich man' who called him out on a home visit early in January, promising him twenty shillings for doing so, only to have the patient then refuse to pay for his treatment 'and thus was I cozened'. Not only did the Greenwich man not pay him, he compounded his action by passing on the 'bad sore throat which afflicted him', leaving Simon suffering from it for the best part of a month.

There are also the first signs of trouble from William Allen, who called round to tell Forman that he 'misliked certain speeches I had made'. Frustratingly, he does not explain what they were, only that Avisa visited him later the next morning to make the peace between them and sent the cuckolded William back to invite Forman to supper that evening. Whatever suspicions William might harbour, he was continually either sending for Forman or calling on him, sometimes because he was ill, on other occasions for an astrological casting, but also with complaints which are recorded only in illegible cryptic or cypher notes. As Forman and the Allens were such close neighbours, it stretches the imagination to breaking point to believe that the lovers were able to keep their liaison secret for nearly four years. It is difficult to decide what William Allen's attitude towards them really was, whether he turned a blind eye, took no action for fear of losing his wife, or allowed himself to be persuaded that his suspicions were unfounded. Whichever it was, he must have had a hard time.

Meanwhile, however passionately involved Forman was with Allen's wife, making love to her whenever the opportunity arose, it never prevented him from enthusiastically accepting other offers. 'On the 4th of February I and a gentleman were like to fall out for standing at the garden by a gentlewoman,' (whom he later 'haleked') and on that same day, a Tuesday, he was visited by Ellen Flower, 'a seaman's wife from Ratcliffe' to the east of the City, a woman who was to become a regular visitor when her husband was away at sea to have, among other things, her horoscope cast. She came to see Simon accompanied by her cousin and as a result the following morning he received an unexpected visit when 'an old quent merchant came unto me that was a confederate of Mistress Flower', a term which hardly requires great expertise in Middle English in order to understand what Ellen Flower had in mind.

The day after the visit of the quent merchant (or pimp) and following a busy morning, during which he had been consulted by a 'divers number of gentlewomen', he had another unexpected and rather more respectable visitor. This was Hugh Fort, an old friend from his Salisbury days, bringing news of his former mistress, 'A.Y.', who was asking after him. As if this were not sufficient for one day, almost without a pause he went out on a house call to a Mistress Johnson, possibly the wife of the Henry Johnson who had taken him off to Holland some years earlier. Mistress Johnson was staying at the Red Cross Inn in Watling Street and was worried about her child. Simon reassured her so successfully that she allowed him to 'oscula illam in domu sua', kiss her right there in the house.

He returned some time later to find to find a note from Avisa inviting him to supper. He did not go, 'whereupon she took great grief and was sick', sending for him again five days later to make it up. Hugh Fort returned to Salisbury shortly afterwards bearing messages from Forman to Mistress Anne Walworth, née Young, while William Allen sent him 'a discourteous note', criticising him for 'lifting up the cup'. It has been suggested that this phrase might have magical significance, but a more prosaic meaning could be that Forman had drunk too much when he last visited them or even that it was a veiled reference to Allen's suspicions that he was involved in an adulterous affair with Avisa.[14]

The month ended with his listing in his casebooks the enormous variety of subjects on which he had been asked to make castings, to which he added that in spite of suffering from some minor ailment he had 'haleked one, Joan Wilde, at a quarter past eight on the morning of Tuesday the 25 February'. Unless this was an early-morning call, the lady presumably had stayed the night. She seemed to enjoy the experience, for a couple of weeks later she called round at the Stone House again, this time in the afternoon 'at 4 p.m.' and they spent the rest of the afternoon in bed.

Almost daily pages of scrawl chart the disturbed progress of the affair with Avisa. How the two of them were invited aboard 'my Lord Cumberland's ship', the Scourge of Malice, but the excursion was spoiled by yet another quarrel, and how within two days they were 'frayed' yet again, after she had told him how one John Davies had spoken against him to her husband. They quickly made it up, but in May she discovered Joan Wilde's apron 'left at my house' and 'was sick about it', though he managed to allay her suspicions and 'we were friends again'. It was well that she never read what he wrote about the lady since it would have confirmed her worst fears.

On 19 May she informed him that she did not want him to make love to her any more, and that no matter how hard he might try to persuade her she would never go to bed with him again or even visit him unless she had need of him in his professional capacity. Her resolute stand lasted a whole week until they met secretly in 'a garden' where she once more gave in. 'Deo gratias!' he records. There were a number of small gardens in the city to which householders living nearby held keys, as is the case with the private gardens of squares in London to this day. 'The garden' plays a continuing role in the affair as a place of assignation, which suggests it must have been one of these: even if the Allens had a garden of their own, the lovers could hardly have taken the risk of meeting secretly in it with a household full of servants only yards away, let alone the danger that William might arrive back unexpectedly at any time.

On 7 June, coming back to the Stone House from the garden with Avisa, they found Joan Wilde standing at his gate waiting for him 'whereupon Avisa was sore angry'. The next time he he called to see her he was told she was out, visiting the Fleet Prison. Possibly she had gone to see fellow recusants imprisoned for non-payment of fines since this was where they were usually confined. When he tried again he was told this time that she was away visiting friends in Walham Green. Over the Whitsun holiday he wrote to her a number of times without a reply until, on 12 June 'at 11 p.m.' (he is very precise about these matters) Avisa came to see him, joined shortly afterwards by her husband. But the next day, at exactly '52 minutes past 2 p.m. A.A. sent me her first letter saying she would come no more to me'. The day after that, walking downstairs while at the same time reading 'John Ward's articles', he heard a cat mew thrice, 'but I could not see her [the cat], which prophesied ill'. An hour later he had another letter from Avisa repeating the message of the first, which sent him rushing round to her house, this time to find her in her stillroom busily involved in distilling elixirs and strong waters.

Their joint fascination with the art swiftly brought a rapprochement. Later in the afternoon she came round to the Stone House 'and at 30 minutes past four *halekekeros harescum tauro*. And at that instant time we renewed our friendship, and made a new league of friendship for ever to endure: God grant it may and never break again.' This was obviously specially significant for a few days later he rode down to Wiltshire 'to Salisbury to see my friends, where I had not been in seven years before', and on 30 June 'there was a final conclusion and end of all our friendship between A.Y. and I'. He even returned to her the tokens of affection she had given him over the years and 'I received back my rings and jewels again from her'.

In his professional life he was continuing to acquire prestigious clients, one of whom was Lady Margaret Hawkins, the wife of the great seafarer and hero of the battle against the Armada, Sir John Hawkins. She came to him on the eve of the fateful venture to the West Indies from which neither her husband nor Sir Francis Drake was to return. Whether she called to ask Forman to cast to see if the venture would be successful and her husband return safely or to consult him on a medical matter is not recorded, though she could be among the casebook notes of anonymous castings or consultations, headed simply 'a certain lady asked . . .'.

Through Sir George Carey Forman had made the acquaintance of a number of seafaring men, one of the most prominent of whom was Sir William, later to be Vice-Admiral, Monson. He and his family were regular visitors to the Stone House. Monson had been sent to Oxford, but left of his own accord and ran away to sea. His career after that sounds like the synopsis of an old Hollywood film. By the time he was eighteen he was captain of a privateer and then volunteered for the queen's pinnace, *Charles*, in the fight against the Armada. After this he served in the of Earl of Cumberland's ship, *Garland*, before being put in charge of a Dutch vessel which was captured by the Spaniards, who condemned him first to the galleys and then imprisoned him in Lisbon Castle. In 1593 his father died and he was left sufficient wealth to buy his freedom, after which he continued as a privateer. During the next few years he had several narrow escapes, one of which was particularly daring and left him with a lifelong leg injury. He then went back to Oxford and finally took his MA before being drawn once again into authorised piracy.

Monson had first asked Forman to cast for him as far back as Armada year, when he had wanted to know how he would fare on a venture he was undertaking on behalf of George Carey. Forman was doubtful as to its wisdom and later noted: 'He came home about the 26th May 1588 and brought nothing but sped very evil; but met with such a rich ship as I told him he would. But took her not and through his own negligence, let her pass by him 'til it was too late and she got under a castle on the coast of Spain.'[15] But at least he had come safe home as Forman had also foretold. After that Monson consulted him almost every time he went to sea, although he did not always take his advice. In May 1595 he asked Forman three times if it would be lucky for him to go to sea in a ship called the *Alcidor*, owned by a Master Watts, but in the end he decided to throw in his lot again with the Earl of Cumberland, sailing on the very ship, the *Scourge of Malice*, which Forman had recently visited with Avisa.

Forman warned Monson that if he sailed on her he would have no luck, but he went anyway. There followed nothing but trouble; the earl turned back not long out of Plymouth and put another captain in charge. Off the 'South Cape', where the ship's mainmast broke, they were becalmed; the food went rotten because it had been insufficiently salted and they had to limp ignominiously back to Plymouth, 'and so', concluded Forman, 'he was glad to be home'. Monson then married a comfortably off widow (without, so far as can be seen, asking Forman's advice).

Possibly because of all this maritime interest, Forman wrote a number of notes on various calculations: 'To Know How One Shall Speed on a Voyage at Sea upon a Question', 'Whether a Man is Like to be Drowned at Sea', 'Whether to Sende a Letter, to Know What Would Become of it and Whether it will be Well Regarded or not', 'Whether Goods are in the House or Not and Whether an Absent One be in Prison'.

All year he was also dodging the Widow Sweyland, who was still trying to sue him, once hiding out at the Allens' house for three hours to avoid being served with a writ. Back home, he spent some time perfecting the recipe for a syrup of violets and, like so many others before and after him, began serious work 'on the philosopher's stone and . . . made my furnace and all for it'. As we know from many accounts of the time, the search for the philosopher's stone was the obsession of sixteenth-century alchemists, for it was believed that if such a 'stone' could be created, it would have the power to transmute base metal into gold, a theory used hilariously in Ben Jonson's great comedy, *The Alchemist*.

During the summer he passed several weeks in the country visiting friends and family, returning again to London at the end of July. His holiday had obviously done nothing for his temper, for he quarrelled with almost everyone on his return and admits that he offended many of his friends, although he was careful not to further antagonise William Allen, who was ill again and had sent for him, asking him when he came to 'draw up the reckoning' of his recent treatment so that he could pay him for his advice.

He and Avisa were still putting themselves through emotional hoops and by 15 September were again at odds. A week later, in an attempt to bring about yet another reconciliation, he gave a supper party at the Stone House for the Allens and William's brother John, landlord of the Ship Inn in Thames Street, and his wife Bridget. The evening turned out to be a disaster, for Avisa was convinced he had taken a fancy to Bridget and was consequently consumed with jealousy, bustling round in the morning to tell him, yet again, that she had finished with him. A day later, on 26 September, he returned the visit to beg her to forgive him, but 'she would not be friends with me and we again departed in ire'. That afternoon 'at 55 minutes past 3 p.m.' he bought a pair of expensive new black stockings (they cost twelve shillings) and returned home to find he had a visitor, whom he describes as 'Master Roche, the Queen's physician', who 'wished to be acquainted with me'. The College of Physicians' list of queen's physicians suggests that the official post was then held by a Dr Roger Marbeck (a view supported by the *Dictionary of National Biography*), but it is possible that Roche was one of a number of medical practitioners who also attended on the queen.

That night Forman slept uneasily, dreaming a muddled dream in which his new black stockings turned into three black rats which perched on the end of his bed, but also that he had finally succeeded in making a powder for his philosopher's stone. He awoke the next morning to a message from Avisa to say that she had forgiven him. We know this to be true for she came back to his bed and Simon records that on 27 September 1595 at exactly 5.30 p.m. she conceived a child.

8

Disturbed Dreams

Throughout the summer and autumn of 1595 Forman was again in trouble with the College of Physicians. On 2 June at eight o'clock in the evening he was knocked up by a constable, accompanied by officers, who came with a warrant for him. Three days later he appeared in court at the magistrates' sessions and was ordered to cease practising 'forthwith'. Although he ignored this, his behaviour suggests that this constant pressure was having an effect on him, for throughout September and October he was in a quarrelsome mood, falling out with neighbours, offending acquaintances, dismissing and then re-employing his man-servant. He even quarrelled with Avisa in the early months of what was to be a sickly pregnancy.

Then on 7 November the college demanded he appear before them in Knightrider Street immediately, this time before a larger committee of eight censors. The session was a briefer version of the one he had attended previously and covered virtually the same ground, involving the trouble-some 'Cox'. The record states:

> Simon Forman appeared: he was examined but found to be completely ignorant. Moreover he confessed he had never read any writer in medicine except one, a certain Cox, an English writer and very obscure man and absolutely unknown and certainly of no merit. He was forced to confess he practised medicine only by astrology; and

when he was questioned in that, he was discovered to be ignorant even of the fundamentals. He was therefore committed to prison with the fine of £10 to be paid for the use of the College.[1]

He spent the next eighteen days in the Counter Gaol in Wood Street, where there were four classes of accommodation: the Master's Side, the Knight's Ward, the Twopenny Ward and the appropriately named 'Hole'. Once inside everything operated on bribery (known as 'garnish'), the amount increasing the longer a prisoner remained inside. Prisoners housed on the Master's Side had their own cell with straw on the floor, a pallet and, perhaps, a straw mattress on which to sleep, a couple of dirty blankets and some candle ends, and, so long as they were prepared to pay through the nose, they could have food, drink and writing materials brought in and receive visitors. Conditions were similar in the Knight's Ward, but there were several prisoners to each cell and as most of the accommodation was right beside the prison jakes it was even less salubrious. The Twopenny Ward was worse again (and below ground), while the Hole was notorious throughout London – a vast and appalling underground dungeon, in which the prisoners, even if they had any money, were not allowed to send out for food, drink or blankets and were entirely dependent on charity. Needless to say many ended their punishment there, dying of cold, semi-starvation and disease. Epidemics of 'gaol fever' were rife throughout all prisons.

Forman did not say in which part of the goal he was confined, but it was most likely to have been the Master's Side since he was in a position to pay for the privilege. He wrote that while inside he was much slandered by a villain with the name of Tutsham and felt it added to his disgrace; but he had no intention of remaining in the Counter and at once sent a petition to the Lord Privy Seal – none other than Sir Robert Cecil – pleading for his freedom.

Whatever he put in the petition proved effective as Cecil promptly ordered his release. The College President and no less than seventeen infuriated censors 'who were all present in the College that day' met to discuss the matter again on 22 December and recorded that Simon Forman, who a short time before 'had been put in prison on account of his illegal practice and remarkable audacity', had been freed from prison on the authority of the Keeper of the Great Seal of England. The meeting resolved therefore that four of the censors and a chairman should be sent to Sir Robert to inform him why 'the impostor, Forman' had been committed to prison and to demand that he be sent back again. What transpired at the meeting between Sir Robert Cecil and the censors, or indeed whether it even took place, is not recorded, but in any event the college failed in its attempt to have Forman returned to gaol.

The censors had no intention of giving up. In September 1596 they hauled him in again, threatening instant imprisonment if he disobeyed. First he was accused of giving 'compound water to a Master Sotherton, who was suffering from a burning fever', and later died, and then questioned on what grounds and for what reason he practised medicine 'and how he thought he could safely give medicines to the sick. He [Forman] said he understood the nature of diseases and could prescribe by astrology.' He was finally questioned by Dr Smith, 'the Queen's physician', on the rudiments of the subject and was found to be 'a mere impostor and ignorant in all that science which confirmed the opinion of all present. He was forthwith committed again to prison.'[2]

Within days he was out, but on 15 September the College had him re-arrested and taken before the Lord Mayor, who committed him to the Counter. After a week he was released on bail but, determined not to be beaten, on the 30th the college brought him up before the magistrates yet again and this time he remained in the Counter for a fortnight, the College refusing any requests from whatever source that he should be released until he agreed to be bound over not to practise. He cast to know if he should agree to these terms and the answer was that he should not do so but fight on for the right to continue in his profession. However, to play for time while he worked out future tactics, he agreed to be bound on the sum of £40 'not to practice after Mayday next'.[3] It was a shrewd move, for by that time he felt secure enough to meet any future challenge head on.

His domestic life was equally fraught. The lovers bickered continually and the situation was made more tense when William showed obvious displeasure after coming home one afternoon to find Forman sitting alone with Avisa. Was the child she was carrying Forman's? It seems likely and from his exact recording of its supposed time of conception Forman obviously thought so. But if she was still sleeping with William as well, there was at least a possibility that it was her husband's. There is no evidence to suggest that William did not believe this to be the case or that he was anything but delighted at the prospect of having a child.

If Avisa had succeeded in convincing William that he was the father, then she was taking foolish chances. Two days after Christmas Forman recorded that 'Avis Allen and I were friends again perfectly and *halekekeros harescum tauro*', while a few days later he even risked taking her to bed in her own house. After this it is hardly surprising that he reminded himself that 'suspicion [is] like to grow'.

There is no doubting the depth of their feelings for each other, but any joy they felt was transitory for they were never at peace. The smallest thing sent one or other of them into a passion of jealousy and suspicion, emotions exacerbated by their situation and Avisa's pregnancy. Forman resented everything she did which did not include him, refusing to believe her when she told him she had other calls on her time such as her busy household, seeing to her husband's needs and keeping up with her friends and acquaintances. But having taken her to task for neglecting him and accusing her of being unfaithful, it never crossed his mind that he should modify his own behaviour and on '29th January, Thursday, at twenty past two [I] haleked Julian in Seething Lane.' Three untranslatable lines in cipher written at the same time record how Avisa's pregnancy was progressing.

The early new year had brought its usual crop of illnesses and he was rarely at home for long, being called out continually to attend on sick people. He was also brought before the magistrates by a Dr Stamp for continuing to practise without a licence, though whether this was official and on behalf of the College of Physicians or a more personal battle is unclear since he was now on good terms with some of his colleagues, discussing a suitable medicine for Mistress Elizabeth Watts with a Dr Moseley, being asked for a second opinion by a Dr Fulke and talking over general problems with a Dr Jones 'in the garden'. With increased wealth came more new clothes and he proudly describes putting on 'my fine velvet jerkin and new furred gown' of a morning before going off to visit his patients in the City.

Avisa was now having trouble with her pregnancy. One day she collapsed in a fainting fit from which it was difficult to arouse her and which worried William so much that he immediately sent for Forman. He was told of it on his way back from visiting a patient by a woman he

describes somewhat mysteriously as 'the garden Katherine' and went to see
Avisa at once to prescribe an elixir. However, his anxiety did not prevent
his sleeping with other women: first Margaret App, then Julian Clark a
week later and on 28 February he 'haleked' Anne Nurse at three p.m.,
'Ankers' at six p.m. and 'Judith' overnight, all within twelve hours.
Possibly it was so much indulgence, coupled with his busy days, that made
him sleep so heavily that one Friday, blundering out of bed to answer a call
of nature, 'I cut the ring finger of my hand almost off, having left my sword
hanging by my bed.'

When Avisa was six months pregnant and feeling increasingly unwell,
the relationship took a dramatic turn for the worse. Feeling as wretched as
she did, it was scarcely surprising that she no longer wanted him to make
love to her, but although he had taken up again with Joan Wilde (she who
had left her apron at his house) Forman refused to take no for an answer.
Avisa was obviously finding the whole business of coping with her
pregnancy, a suspicious husband and an importunate lover too much. By
the end of the month she was so beside herself that when he remonstrated
with her for refusing him sex and grabbed hold of her, she slapped him
hard across the mouth. For a week he left her alone, then called at the
house to see if she had changed her mind. This time she went for his eyes,
scratching his face so badly that it bled.

After this he did not see her again for some weeks, using the time in
another vain attempt to 'create' the elusive philosopher's stone. An
undated verse[4] very likely written at about the same time gives advice on
how to choose a wife or friend, under the title 'This Is a Circle of my
Spirit':

> So thou shouldst know if thou be wise,
> Thy friend from foe for to discern,
> And how to save thyself from harm,
> And whom to trust for happy mate
> Ye then will be in quiet estate.
> And who shall be thy friend or foe
> Among the rest and others more,
> And whom to admit thy counsel to
> If thou hast matters great to do,
> And if thou art like to wed a wife

How thou shalt shun both rage and strife
And all by letters of their name
Shall know the truth of all this same.

Left to himself, he began casting to see if a certain Appellina Fairfax would make him a suitable wife. Appellina was a young and handsome widow, daughter of one Master Southwick, and he continued his pursuit for some weeks, eventually casting again to seek an answer to the question 'will she make me a good wife'. The answer was favourable so he sent his servant to Appellina with a letter pressing his suit, but she did not deign to reply.

He continually cast to see if he should 'visit the Allens or no' and was finally spared from having to make a decision when at the beginning of June William Allen sent for him. He was experiencing a severe pain, which Forman diagnosed as an abscess on his liver and 'a melancholy' in his blood.[5] Avisa's sister-in-law, Bridget, also asked his advice, complaining that she was suffering from 'pains in the head and stomach'. He sent her away with a purge, noting this was due to her having over-indulged in 'sturgeon and Rhenish wine' the previous day. He does not say if Avisa consulted him on her own account, although by this time the birth of her child was imminent.

A series of notes in the casebooks and a single line in the diary recount the sad outcome of Avisa's pregnancy. On 26 June 1596 she gave birth to a son, but from the beginning it was clear that something was badly wrong with the baby. There was no question of Simon being present when the child was born for it was unheard of for a male doctor to undertake a delivery at that time. A woman turned to the local wise woman or unqualified midwife to deliver her child. Many were extremely skilled, but in this instance the woman was either careless or there were complications with which she was unable to cope.

Forman was called in almost immediately after the child's birth, attending Avisa on a daily basis until on 8 July, already desperately anxious, she asked him outright to cast to see what the future held, if any, for her sickly son. The casting is headed 'whether a child should live or die', and notes that it is for 'Allen'. Inserted above this and in a different ink is the name 'Alexander', presumably added when the baby was hurriedly baptised. Beside the question is a figure for 'a casting for a child ten days old, Alexander, will he live or die, asked by AA after a dream'.[6] No answer to the question is given, but underneath he has written: 'He died on the 9th July at six o'clock in the morning.' It is also noted that the length of the pregnancy 'lacked two days of forty weeks by my reckoning' and that the reason for the baby's death was that during the delivery the 'the nurse [midwife] had overput the mould of the head by striking it too hard'. The diary entry records simply: 'On 26th June Avis Allen was delivered of a manchild named Alexander which died shortly after.'

Following this domestic tragedy, Forman had unlimited entry to the Allens' house, almost immediately advising Bridget Allen as to whether or not she was pregnant and whether it was safe for her to ride into the country on horseback, some of the notes being in cipher. But his behaviour towards Avisa appears inexplicable even by the standards of the day, for in spite of what she had been through, he was soon pressing her to resume their physical relationship well before what Shakespeare calls 'the childbirth privilege', a month's lying in, was over. By 16 July he had persuaded her to do so and although they quarrelled the following week, three days later he again cajoled her into bed, although 'she was sick'.

His bald account of the resumption of their love-making, apparently without problems other than their usual quarrels, is belied by one of the longest notes of a casting in any of the casebook folios.[7] One day, the morning after they had made love, Avisa went to see Forman complaining of pains in the head, kidneys, heart and womb, but there was more to it than a simple medical consultation. Her state of mind suggests that she was suffering from postnatal depression. Any woman in such circumstances would be distraught, but in Avisa's case her feelings must have been intensified by the situation in which she found herself. She was involved in an adulterous liaison which had resulted in a son unlikely to have been her husband's, a sin for which her religion might well convince her that she had been 'punished' by his almost immediate death.

Nor, because of the interdict on Catholic priests, could she seek help and solace in the confessional, unburden herself of her guilt and be given penance. According to Simon, during the consultation she became hysterical, eventually 'threatening to take her own life voluntarily', a mortal sin for a Catholic, and even for a Protestant an offence so grave that suicides were denied Christian burial. In view of her mood his casting which, among much other irrelevant material, promises her life and health 'if she will be ruled under the influence of Venus', is staggeringly insensitive. He was less concerned about Avisa's health and feelings than about her maid, Kate, who was often present when he visited her, because he thought her deceitful, 'for she dissembled much and spoke much ill of me behind my back'. He also cast yet again to see if he and Avisa would ever marry, but received no answer.

As if his troubles with the censors and his fraught relationship with Avisa were not enough, he was now involved in another bout of litigation, this time with a man called Peter Sefton and again to do with money. Sefton had taken Holy Orders and Forman described him as 'a preacher', which suggests he was of the Puritan tendency. He had no benefice or parish to begin with but later, when he had become a deacon, he 'trafficked in the sale of benefices' to others. Sefton and his wife also lived in the Stone House, which made this falling out highly inconvenient.

The immediate trouble started with an argument between Forman, Sefton and Sefton's friend, Atkins, in which Mistress Sefton also joined, addressing 'lewd speeches' to him. Forman then claimed Sefton owed him money. Sefton rejected the claim, and filed a bill of covenants against him, which was refuted. Next Forman countered the charge by bringing a suit against Sefton in the Court of Common Pleas for the debts he alleged he was owed. There was then a short pause in the proceedings, but later in the year the legal battle flared up again, to the point where a fight broke out in Forman's chambers between his friend, Jarvis, and Sefton's associate, Atkins. The two men drew daggers on each other and Jarvis stabbed Atkins. Sefton had a warrant issued against Simon by no less a person than the queen's own attorney, Sir Edward Coke, causing him to hide out in a friend's house until things had quietened down, after which he dreamed he was in a copse or orchard, closely confined within a fence and that many people stood outside shooting arrows at him. An acquaintance, John Davies, came and looked on, but did nothing while Peter Sefton 'in a white waistcoat' looked as if he were to be hanged.

Forman had been haunted by disturbing dreams throughout 1596, in counterpoint to what was happening in his life. However insensitive he might sound about the emotional upheavals of the previous few months, he too must have felt guilt, especially if he believed the dead child to have been his, for he shared all the popular beliefs in the power and prophetic nature of dreams which we see very clearly in drama, particularly Shakespeare's plays.

In both *Richard III* and *Julius Caesar* the ghosts of the dead visit the guilty before battle, while Prospero tells us at the end of *The Tempest*, 'We are such stuff as dreams are made on, and our little life is rounded with a sleep.' 'O God! I could be bounded in a nutshell and count myself a king of infinite space, were if not that I have bad dreams', says Hamlet, who later, in the great soliloquy, fears that there will be no peace even in death:

> To die, to sleep;
> To sleep: perchance to dream: ay, there's the rub:
> For in that sleep of death what dreams may come
> When we have shuffled off this mortal coil,
> Must give us pause.

Many of Forman's dreams were of women in his life. In August, at the height of the emotional turmoil with Avisa, he dreamed of Jane Cole, to whom he had taken a fancy so many years ago in Salisbury then later fallen out with, and that she was now looking ill-favoured and out of fashion and talked as if 'she were mine enemy'. A letter from Avisa 'containing vile words without cause', provoked a dream in which he was feeling her belly, for she had become very fat. She told him she had lost all her pigeons and asked how she might call them back again and he told her to do it with peas and salt cake, then '[I] took a fair white pigeon and tied her by the leg; her mate came and wanted to tread her'. The pigeon was willing 'but they would not because we were looking on'. He thought this a hopeful dream, as he did another, in which he and Avisa and one of her friends were in the garden and both 'strove for me'. Emboldened by the dreams he went to her once again and made love to her, but had to leave immediately afterwards when his man came to tell him that his wealthy patron, Sir William Monson, urgently required his services.

In the autumn William Allen was ill again and Avisa sent Kate to ask Forman to cast to see if he would survive, the answer being that he 'will not die yet'. Pragmatically, he also cast again to see if he should continue to pursue Appellina Fairfax and whether to marry her if she agreed. He cast a horoscope for himself in Latin, the translated outcome of which is that he would be loved by many women and honoured by great persons.[8]

When he was not treating the sick, he busied himself again with engraving sigils and making other charms and tokens.

Avisa was still far from well, suffering with 'pain and faintness at heart and in her womb'. She thought she might be pregnant again and brought her water to be tested. This time she must have been having sexual relations with William, for she wanted to know whether, if she was, the child was his or her lover's. He told her she might have conceived and asked her what William would think about it if she had, but did not record his view on the possible paternity. She also told him that her maid, Kate, feared that she too was having a child and was in much distress.

What becomes clear from the casebooks and medical notes is how the threat of pregnancy hung like a millstone around the necks of sexually active women, when every act of intercourse was akin to playing Russian roulette. Kate's lover was fourteen years younger than herself (she was thirty-six) and she wanted to know if he would stand by her or run away. In the event, Avisa did not rely on the response from the stars but, along with Kate's friends and family, ensured that the young man did his duty and married her, 'even though', Simon recorded, 'he bears a mind to some other poor wench' who was also pregnant by him.

Within a month Avisa was ill again. She knew now that she could not be pregnant for she was suffering from a flux of blood and water from her womb, but of more immediate concern to her was the lump that she had found on her neck 'as big as half an egg', which she asked Simon to examine. It must have sent a shiver through him. It needed no astrological casting to diagnose what was wrong, for he recognised immediately that she was suffering from the early stages of scrofula, tuberculosis of the glands of the neck, the disease popularly known as 'the King's Evil.'

Forman had made a particular study of scrofula, dating back to his very earliest ventures in medicine. He claimed to have 'cured' two men, the first by holding his mouth open with a key and giving him a medicinal drink. The second was more complicated, being the young man who had twenty-four holes from ear to ear and 'a very great hole in his throat'.[9] The disease also presented with lumps and abscesses and when he saw the symptomatic swelling on Avisa's neck Forman must have realised that, short of a miracle, all he could do was alleviate the symptoms. To this end he used the conventional methods of the day, bloodletting, vinegar gargles, cleansing the wound with hot oil and plasters of turpentine, and dressing it with red wax. 'I dressed the throat first,' he records on 28 November,[10] 'but did no good but did draw down the humour more. It now swells more and pimples very much more.' Some lines in cipher follow.

At about this time he was offered the chance of a voyage on a ship, the *Centaur*, belonging to an Alderman Watts, who had been to consult him on the advice of Sir William Monson. The alderman had privateering interests and the voyage offered an interesting interlude, but, though sorely tempted, Forman turned the invitation down very possibly because of the state of Avisa's health. He did, however, go for a short holiday with friends to Sandwich in Kent, but was unable to shake off his fears; he dreamed that she was very ill and that Kate and William Allen were wrapping her in a white sheet and then laying her beside him in his bed, 'but she was exceeding cold like one dead'. In his dream he asked them if they could not heat cloths and put them on her to warm her, but Kate replied 'let her lie, for she will be hot enough anon', so he clutched her to him to warm her. He returned home to find that she had been ill during his absence and, eerily, she told him that at one time she had felt so cold she supposed she had been poisoned.[11]

In spite of his very real anxiety for her, they quarrelled after he accused her of having taken a fancy to his servant, William, while he had been away and 'she confessed that she bore him a good mind . . . and [he] was somewhat bold with her. She fancied him much . . . and I had great suspicion that he had lain with her and she with him. But she denies it absolutely.' She also asked him to cast to see if they should continue with their own relationship. The result of the casting sounds almost Delphic:

It is better to continue than to leave off, for fear of a further inconvenience that may follow. They two shall be more together or die; or else the woman cleave only to her husband. She is unfortunate to herself, forward and overthwart and hurteth herself – works against her own quiet and will not be ruled by good counsel. She hath a marvellous distempered body that is soon well and soon ill and she is loathe to take physic and anything that will do her good, follows the counsel of those that will do her hurt.[12]

She was now suffering almost continual pain in her throat, and when he visited her a couple of days later while Allen was out, he found her in bed.

She asked him if he thought she might be carrying a dead foetus, then, significantly, if her ills were caused by her adultery and if her behaviour was driving her husband into the arms of another woman.

Forman's bad dreams began to affect him: for nearly a week he never left his house until, hearing that Allen was away from home, he went to see Avisa, begging to make love, but she refused 'for fear'. After this he dreamed that he was back behind the stall in Salisbury marketplace as in the days of his apprenticeship. He was wearing a white apron, very white sleeves and was all in white but with a *black doublet* under all and many pretty maids came to buy from him including a big wench who was very free. He was only too well aware aware of the significance of being in white without but black within. Two days later he dreamed he sent a message to Avisa by his man (the one with whom he had accused her of infidelity) and was told that she and Kate had taken a wherry over to Southwark to avoid him, so he pursued her only to find that she had deceived him. 'I lost her and sought after her, but could not find her for she was in black and hidden.' When he finally discovered her she was in bed with his manservant and when he awoke 'I was sorely vexed'.

Shortly afterwards Avisa called him in again, telling him that this time she was sure she was pregnant. It is difficult to know if it was true or a symptom of her illness, though there are suggestions over the coming months that she might have been. Once more he propositioned her and again she refused him. This time he dreamed he was back in Quidhampton and that he and a friend, Dick Howes, were by the river looking for trout. While he was there he filled a bucket for a neighbour and left it under the bridge. He then found a book in a wall beside the pond which contained a picture of Our Lord, illuminated in colours which shone out over the black, dark water. Then two children appeared, one of whom was given to divination. That same night Avisa dreamed she was in prison and heard someone say he was sorry to have brought Master Forman there, but he had been compelled to do so. He spent all the following day with Avisa from early in the morning until late at night (presumably Allen was out of town) and in spite everything 'haleked twice in the morning and again at 6 p.m.'

A few days later, thoroughly alarmed at Avisa's state of health, the Allens consulted Simon together and he prepared a special potion for her. She had now convinced herself and William that she was pregnant and

Simon told them that if she was then she should feel the child quicken within the next two or three weeks. That night he dreamed he was riding pillion to Quidhampton and on to Old Sarum, behind an old friend, Thomas Cumber. On their way they saw a woman winnowing corn in a farm close by, although all the meadows were under water. A young girl who was with her called out to them, asking if they would take her to Sarum and tried to reach them, but she was unable to cross over the flood. They left her staring after them until they vanished from her sight.

Within days it was Christmas and the Allens gave a great feast. But Forman experienced little joy at that season of good will, fearing that Avisa was unlikely to see another.

9

Death and a Dark Lady

At the beginning of January 1595 Forman had had a most strange and erotic dream, which reveals something not only about his own state of mind but also about the effect on men of the Elizabethan age of the Virgin Queen as icon. In it he found himself walking beside her 'through lanes and closes', talking and reasoning with her. She was all 'unready', dressed only in a white shift and white petticoat over which she had thrown a coat. They came upon a group of people laughing and talking from whom emerged a tall man with a reddish beard, who Simon recognised as a weaver, who spoke to the queen in a familiar manner then kissed her. Simon rescued her from the importunate fellow by hustling her along a dirty lane, where her shift and petticoat trailed in the mud and became soiled, telling her that she would do him a favour if she let him wait on her and she agreed that he should. So he raised her clothing, telling her, ' "I mean to wait *upon* you and not under you, that I might make this belly a little bigger to carry up this smock and coat out of the dirt." And so we talked merrily; then she began to lean upon me, when we were past the dirt, and to be very familiar with me, and methought she began to love me. When we were alone out of sight, methought she would have kissed me.'[1]

Dreams played a major part in his life during the early part of 1595 and several directly affected his actions. For a few brief weeks in January he and Avisa resumed their love-making, but instead of dreaming of Avisa he began once again to dream of his old love, Anne, in spite of having supposedly broken off with her for good, so much so that he sent a letter to her begging her to let him know how she was. She wrote back to him straight away, encouraging him again to cast their horoscopes to see if she was likely to be widowed and if, in spite of everything that had happened during the years between, they might still marry; he was no longer under any illusion that William Allen might conveniently die and so leave Avisa free since everything now pointed to her predeceasing him.

On the day that he received the letter from Anne, Avisa came round to the Stone House, bringing him 'a little hot pie' (she had been entertaining people for dinner) and that afternoon they made love, possibly for the last time since it is never mentioned again. That night he dreamed that he was passing over a mixen (dunghill) which shook under him. As he was doing so 'a fellow thrust at me with a dungfork and I fell into the water'. Someone else held him up so that he would not drown, but he emerged stinking and dirty.

Next he dreamed that William and Avisa both sent letters by a 'blackamoor to a certain man and the man was like to rob him but Allen had written certain matters against the blackamoor in his letter who, when he discovered this, attacked Allen with a knife', at which point Simon came to his rescue and in the nick of time saved his life. The next morning William Allen arrived at the Stone House to ask Simon to cast a figure for him on a weighty matter. He had stood surety for a merchant friend for the enormous sum of £30,000 and he wanted to know if he would suffer by having done so. Simon was convinced that his dream had been sent to him as a warning for Allen and told that he would most certainly come to grief 'unless he discharge himself of it', which Allen duly did.[2]

One other 'action' dream that month was of a somewhat different nature. He dreamed that he was in a place 'where many boys and maids were like to die and I too'. Suddenly he realised he was able to fly and so 'flew to a plum tree and saw green plums but ate many red plums'. Realising his new-found ability, he flew back to the place where the young people were held prisoner and assured them that if they tried they would find they too could fly. When their enemy appeared, he made them hold hands and rise in the air. Some could not fly as high as others, but he encouraged them along and they managed to perch on the roof of a house until they were sufficiently rested to fly over fields, hedges and water until they reached a place of safety on a bleak hillside and there rested again.[3]

This, he decided, was a hopeful omen for any business he might have in hand and so the next morning, without more ado, he had Peter Sefton arrested on a suit against the money he claimed the cleric still owed him and the matter was brought before the queen's attorney. It was finally settled by Sefton giving Forman a silver bowl to the value of the money owed. The the two men agreed to a rapprochement after the queen's attorney intervened and asked Forman to 'stay the matter'. Sefton then apologised, asking Forman to forgive him 'and so end the matter'.

The truce lasted barely a month. Within no time they were wrangling again because Sefton had refused to pay Forman's legal costs. Furious at Forman's continued demands that he do so, Sefton began spreading tales about him, slanders which he repeated when they were brought to arbitration in an attempt to settle the matter once and for all. Sefton told the arbitrators that Forman had a dire reputation going back to his youth in Wiltshire, where he 'had stood in a white sheet in Sarum', the inference being that he had undergone penance in church for fornication or adultery. Also that he had once actually seen him 'occupy a wench on a stool' in a public place, 'for the which I could have killed him with good will', wrote Simon.[4] The litigation against Sefton continued and Forman even conferred with Avisa as to whether or not he should bring him before a magistrate and have him bound over to keep the peace.

She remained convinced that she was carrying a child. Her elaborate calculations pointed to its being born late in the summer, but as time went on she asked him if it was possible that it had died in the womb, as although she had all the symptoms of pregnancy she could still feel no quickening. If this was indeed the case then there was nothing Simon could do about it unless the foetus spontaneously aborted. In April, before going out with a woman friend to visit one of the Allens' ships which was bound for Ireland, she consulted him on the general state of her health. He recorded that 'she is an enemy to herself and has taken evil drink or medicine'.

On the same day he proudly notes that the barber had been to trim his beard and hair and that he washed himself almost all over, 'arms, breast and legs', a major event evidently considered worthy of record. Possibly as a result of the shock of the experience, that night he dreamed he had died and was washed and laid out in a coffin on two tables and that he heard people say he was dead and that they should bury him.

He was becoming increasingly desperate to find a wife, preferably one who could bring him a dowry as well as being considered a suitable match for a successful physician. However passionately he felt about Avisa, he had never stopped looking for a respectable young girl or a comfortably situated widow but his efforts always came to nothing, and it is at this time that, buried away in a marginal note, he ponders on whether this has anything to do with his appearance.[5] Yet it is clear that, in spite of his red hair and 'speckled face', he had a way with women. Had he deliberately written of his sexual conquests for publication, then one might well take his 'halek' notes with a pinch of salt, but they appear only in his most private papers and while he wrote 'books' and 'notes' on how to do a whole range of things, there is nothing entitled 'how to succeed as a seducer' or 'how best to persuade a woman into bed'. Nor, any longer, did he suffer from lack of means or status. Thinking of his failure to marry, one can only wonder if some of the mud thrown at him had stuck.

However, determined to keep all options open, he called again on Appellina Fairfax but received as little encouragement this time as he had before. After she had rejected him yet again, he recommended casting figures in the vain hope that Anne might yet be a widow. The following night he dreamed of a child falling into a ditch, of a field full of people put to the sword and that he was among a great many young maids and he laid his head in one of their laps as an archduke passed by. After which he knocked at Anne's door and she came down to him dressed only in her nightdress, calling for her mother to 'stay till this strange man be gone out of the house. Her house was decorated with green boughs for it was holiday and fair time.' Disturbed by the dream, he wrote to her urgently and this time she asked him to come down to Salisbury to see her. He rode down almost straight away, though what passed between them he does not record; nor does he say anything of Joshua, who was now twelve years old.

During this time, when he was fearful for Avisa's life, turning again to his old love and pursuing prospective wives, he was visited by two young women, both of whom, although they came from very different backgrounds, had minds of their own and had used their sexual attraction to improve their lot. They were Emilia Lanier, née Bassano, and Frances Pranell, née Howard, daughter of Viscount Howard of Bindon (not to be confused with her wealthier and more powerful relative and namesake, Frances Howard, who became Countess of Essex). Both, in their different

Engraving of Dr Simon Forman, by Godfrey. The only known portrait of him. 'This summer I had my own picture drawn', he noted in his diary in 1600, 'and bought my purple velvet gown, my velvet cap, velvet coat and breeches and a taffeta cloak...'

One of the fantasy genealogies Simon Forman invented for himself. (Bodleian Library)

The Licence to Practise Medicine issued by Cambridge University in June 1601, 'after long exercise and experience'. (Bodleian Library)

Astrologaster or the figure caster', woodcut by John Melton. The astrologer wears the furred gown of a 'doctor'.

Woodcut of a young woman consulting an astrologer or fortune teller to have her horoscope cast.

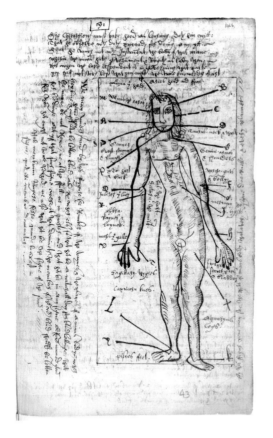

Drawing by Simon Forman of the parts of the body governed by the planets and signs of the zodiac. (Mss.16. King's College, Cambridge)

A doodle on a page of the Cockys manuscript. (Mss.16. King's College, Cambridge)

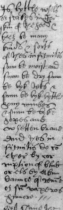

Caricature of *Thomas Nashe in Irons*, from *The Trimming of Thomas Nashe*, 1596. Author unknown.

Thomas Hariot,
Mathematician
(Trinity College, Oxford)

A section of Vischer's *View of London*, 1616, showing London Bridge as seen from the Bankside.

The Signs of the Zodiac and the Four Humours. Engraving from Thurneysser's *Quinta Essentia,* 1574.

Sir George Carey, later Lord Hunsden. Carey, who succeeded his father as Lord Chamberlain, was an early patron and client of Forman and allegedly a member of The School of the Night.

(*Clockwise*) Sir Thomas Overbury by
Sylvester Harding; engraving of the Earl
and Countess of Somerset at the time of
their trial, in 1616; miniature of Robert
Carr, after the manner of Hilliard; woodcut of Anne Turner on her way to the
gallows at Tyburn.

Engraving of Frances, née Howard, Countess of Somerset, by Simon Van der Pass.

ways, made sufficient impression on him for him to record far more about them than is usual in the case notes, where generally all he tells us of a woman patient is her age, her husband's – or in rare cases her own – employment, an extremely brief medical history, the reason for the consultation and its outcome.

A. L. Rowse's identification of Emilia Lanier as the Dark Lady of Shakespeare's Sonnets has always been controversial. Suffice it to say that she is a substantially better candidate than Mary Fitton, one of the queen's ladies, who for a long time was thought to be the most likely contender. It is unclear where this latter notion first arose, but one look at Mary Fitton's portrait, which hangs in a gallery in Arbury Hall in Warwickshire, would have suggested it was unlikely, for it shows a fair-skinned, grey-eyed, red-head wearing a gown on which caterpillars, spiders and other strange creatures crawl, possibly an oblique way of relating something of her colourful history.

Emilia's family, the Bassanos, came to England from their home in Venice towards the end of Henry VIII's reign, and were such skilled musicians that the king immediately employed them at Court. Emilia was the daughter of Baptista Bassano and his common-law English wife, Margaret, who had settled in St Botolph's ward in Bishopsgate. Baptista died when Emilia was six, her mother when she was sixteen, by which time her elder sister had made a respectable marriage. Baptista had left Emilia a hundred pounds in trust, which she would receive at the age of twenty-one, but that was still five years away.

There were few opportunities in late sixteenth-century England open to poor but intelligent young women with ambitions well above their station. Emilia had no desire to go into service, take up some menial occupation, or marry the first penniless man who asked her. She therefore thought long and hard about her two most marketable assets: her skill as a musician and her undoubted attractions for the opposite sex. She determined to find herself a rich keeper and with that in mind sought a position in the household of the Countess of Kent, where her lively disposition and musical ability so charmed the countess that she made Emilia her lady's maid and took her with her when she next went to Court. There Emilia soon attracted the attention of the queen, who was so impressed by her performance at the virginals (and the queen herself was no mean performer on the instrument) that she regularly had Emilia play for her.

Not surprisingly, Emilia began to attract a great deal of male interest, most of which she kept at arm's length, until finally she came to the notice of the Lord Chamberlain himself, Henry Carey, Lord Hunsdon. Although he was old enough to be her grandfather, he made her his official mistress, setting her up in a rich apartment and showering her with beautiful dresses and jewels, with the proviso, however, that should he get her with child then she would agree to be suitably married off. It is this relationship which possibly links Emilia to Shakespeare, who was by now a member of the company of the Lord Chamberlain's Men and so regularly played for him and at Court. Given her privileged position, Emilia would have known all the actors in his lordship's company, including the man destined to become England's greatest dramatist. Nor, according to gossip at the time, did her liaison with the Lord Chamberlain prevent her from seeking solace elsewhere. Shakespeare's patron, the Earl of Southampton, reputedly became one of her lovers.

Emilia visited Forman for the first time on 17 May 1597, after which he wrote that 'she hath had hard fortune in youth. Her father died when she was young; the wealth of her father failed before he died and he began to be miserable in his estate. She was paramour to my old Lord Hunsdon that was Lord Chamberlain and was maintained by him in great pride; then, being with child, she was for colour married to a minstrel.' So her elderly lover had remained potent. The docile husband was Alfonso Lanier, another Court musician, and from what she told Simon and anyone else who would listen she did not reckon much to the bargain that had been made for her.

The second young woman, on the other hand, most certainly did not come from the wrong side of the tracks. Frances Pranell had been born into one of the great families of England but her father, Lord Howard of Binden, was from a cadet branch of the family. Her mother had been his third wife and Frances was orphaned as a small child with only a modest dowry, the rest of the inheritance having gone to the children of the first two marriages. She was nineteen and already married to Henry Pranell, a vintner, when she first consulted Forman. Pranell was a great deal below her in status, but he was smitten by her beauty and he had one tremendous advantage: his father, Alderman Pranell, had left him exceedingly rich. She told Forman that she was born at Lytchett in Dorset on 27 July 1578 at 9.30 p.m., was frank about her reasons for marrying Pranell and became one of his most regular clients through three marriages, each one a pragmatic step up the ladder of wealth and influence.

Frances's first visit, also in May, was for a horoscope casting, not for herself but on behalf of her sister-in-law, Catherine Howard (born a Neville) who was married to the admiral, Lord Thomas Howard. Catherine wanted to know if her husband was likely to die soon and, if so, if she might then hope to attract the attention of Henry Wriothesley, the much-sought-after, epicene, Earl of Southampton. Simon rightly predicted 'no' on both counts and Catherine settled down to amassing riches instead, going on to build the great house of Audley End. She is another of those reputed, along with Mary, Countess of Pembroke, and Lady Audrey Walsingham (wife of Marlowe's patron, Sir Thomas) to have been a mistress of Sir Robert Cecil. If that was indeed the case then this apparently cold and unattractive man might well have had hidden depths, but there have always been women sexually attracted by power.

In the same month, Forman was consulted by William Evers, who would also feature in the casebooks for years. William's brother was Ralph Evers, Warden of the Middle March, on the English side of the border of England and Scotland. Forman had other clients, the Careys, who also played a part in peacekeeping in the area, two members of the family in succession being wardens of the West March. At this late stage in the queen's reign, the Marches and the 'Debatable Lands' beyond were of strategic importance to both London and Edinburgh. Both governments therefore agreed to appoint three wardens each to liaise with each other in an attempt to keep the peace. The task of controlling the inhabitants of the Marches was not an easy one. 'The Borderers', as they called themselves, felt they owed little or no allegiance to either crown and while they regularly crossed the border to raid and pillage each other, they were equally capable of ganging up together to fight off any external threat. The reivers, their roving bands of looters, gave us the word 'blackmail', for they would descend on an unfortunate village or farmstead, their mail painted black to enable them to merge into the night, and demand protection money for not stealing their cattle or razing the buildings to the ground. From time to time border feuds erupted even on the streets of London and the anarchic situation provided ideal cover for spies, who passed each way largely unhindered.

William Evers was twenty-seven when he first came for a consultation, complaining that he was suffering from poisoned air and bad medicines.

'He hath a slimy flux,' recorded Simon, 'matter in bowles and reins', who sent round to him the next day three shillings' worth of strong water. During this visit Evers told Forman, who loved to hear of marvels, of the Boy with the Golden Tooth in Prague 'who was a wonderful prophet though only eleven or twelve years old'. In June Evers returned again, this time for a casting as to how he would fare on the forthcoming Island Voyage to the Azores under the command of Robert Devereux, Earl of Essex. Forman told him that his state would alter three times during the period of the voyage, from worse to better, then from better to worse, but that he would afterwards be 'dignified' by Essex; to which he later added a note to say that Evers had indeed been knighted, thus proving him right.

The following day Emilia Lanier returned on a similar mission, for her husband, Alfonso, had volunteered for the same venture and she wanted to know if he would be successful in a suit for preferment which he was pressing. This time Forman added a few more details about her, that she was 'brought up' by the Countess of Kent and had been married for four years, 'but the old Lord Chamberlain had kept her long. She is high-minded, she hath something in her mind she would have done for her. She hath £40 a year and was wealthy to him that married her, in money and jewels. She can hardly keep a secret. She was very brave in youth. She hath had many false conceptions. She hath a son, his name is Henry.' She appears in the relevant folio under the often used anonymous 'a certain lady', but Forman later wrote her name, 'Emilia Lanier', beneath it in a different ink.[6]

By the beginning of June Avisa was clearly dying, whether from tuberculosis or septicaemia caused by a dead foetus, or a combination of both, it is impossible to tell. On 6 June she sent urgently for Forman and on the 10th William came round himself and brought him to her as the situation was now desperate. The next morning, as a last resort, Forman bled her and then gave her his 'strong' medicine, but there was nothing more he could do for her but stand helplessly by. Less than forty-eight hours later she was dead. The single diary entry for that year reads:

1597   Avis Allen died 13th June[7]

There is no way of knowing if this really was the only entry he made in his diary that year or if he destroyed everything else in it, considering that the event so overshadowed everything else it was the only one worth recording. What is uncanny is the truth of the prophetic casting he had recorded two years earlier. For Avisa *did* die in the thirty-seventh year of her age, she had been forced by law 'to go to church', had lived in threat of imprisonment for her Catholicism, and certainly seems to have been buried 'outside Christian [or at least Church of England] burial', for there is no record of her burial in any of the relevant London parish registers.

But life went on. This does not mean that Forman recovered from his bereavement overnight, without even mourning Avisa's passing, or that he was never as fond of her as he pretended, it was simply that early death was a fact of sixteenth-century life. Perhaps in those last months, knowing her illness to be terminal, he had begun withdrawing from her emotionally, but since there are no records of their relationship during that period we cannot know.

Three days after Avisa's death, Emilia Lanier came to the Stone House desiring further information about her husband's future. By now he had sailed off with the Earl of Essex to the Azores and rumours were circulating that the venture, designed to intercept a plate or treasure fleet en route to Spain from South America, had been a fiasco due to Essex's miscalculations and that his ships had missed the Spanish fleet altogether.

Following Avisa's death, Forman redoubled his attempts to find a wife and actually got as far as a contract or understanding with an Anne Waller of Ashby in the Forest of West Bere, one of two daughters of a wealthy landowner. It seems a most odd arrangement, for on payment of a silver groat from him she bound herself in the sum of £500 not to marry anyone without his consent; if she did so, the money was forfeit. She did not marry him, but he does not say if she paid up. He also continued making advances to widows, in one instance persuading a female friend to take a letter from him to the lady concerned. She was a Mistress Boothby in Leicester Street, but she apparently had not even heard of him and asked the bearer of the letter to tell her all she knew of 'Dr Forman'. He had asked his friend not to say anything unless the lady agreed to see him for herself; the friend kept his confidence, but the widow lost interest and sent back that she was not ready to marry until her troubles were over.

He had never been faithful to Avisa during her life and felt no compunction about bedding women within weeks of her death. He 'haleked' Elizabeth Hipwell for the first time in his study at the Stone House when she came for a consultation. The lady was, in the Cornish phrase, rough as rats. Her husband, he noted, was a lewd fellow 'who spends all he gets, keeps bad company, is a thief and is like to have been hanged for robbing'. He was a 'faint-hearted fellow with a yellowish beard and a brown head'. A note in Latin is not very clear but seems to suggest that Hipwell's preference was for anal intercourse with his wife and sodomy with boys,[8] while Elizabeth regularly 'haleked' with two men in Finchley. The Hipwells, being thoroughly disreputable, were not at all the kind of people a well-known physician would wish to be seen consorting with, but Elizabeth continued to console him for some time.

Frances Pranell returned in August, this time requesting him to test her urine and to see whether or not she had conceived. 'She hath taken some grief or discontent and a cold,' he wrote. 'A rheumatic body, weak in the reins and a heat in the *renus tenorea*.' A month later she was back again, still worrying that she might be pregnant as, 'she hath not had her courses, *sed non est gravida* but she is not with child'. (There may have been some medical reason for her inability to conceive since she was to remain childless in spite of having three husbands.)

Forman was increasingly being consulted by theatre people or their families. One of these was Philip Henslowe, merchant, entrepreneur and owner of the Rose Theatre. He also had ambitions to become the queen's Bearward (a keeper and preparer of bears for bear-baiting). His first visit was to enquire if Forman could discover the whereabouts of some stolen goods, to which the reply was that they were nearby, 'buried in the earth of a neighbour's house'. Six months later he came again, this time on a medical matter, for he had pain in the kidneys, side and head, and water in the stomach. Henslowe must have felt very concerned about the state of his health as he considered himself to be something of a specialist on medical matters. His own advice, along with 'receipts' for medicines and remedies (some of which make pretty gruesome reading) are set out in notes in his own diaries.[9] A few will suffice to give the general idea:

Take ants and stamp on them then strain them through a cloth, then take swines' grease and some knot grass then stamp on the same and take juice and mix it with the strainings of them [the ants] and put it in the ear as drops and it will help and hold deafness, if God permit.

To help clear eyes that be blind take fennel and vervain and beat it with pimpernell known as eyebright and mix the whole with sage and celandine of each half a pound. After boiling in a pan, they should be mixed with powdered peppercorns and white wine and . . . with the urine of a boy.

Forman's own prescription for Henslowe's affliction was that he should purge himself, and the owner of the Rose must have been sufficiently satisfied to recommend Forman's services to others, since he was later consulted by a female Henslowe relative who, at the age of forty, was suffering from the effects of a miscarriage.

Among other theatrical families who consulted him was that of the Cowleys, who lived in Shoreditch. Richard Cowley was an actor in Burbage's company and his name appears in cast lists for the two parts of Shakespeare's *Henry IV* and for *Much Ado About Nothing*, in which he played the part of Verges. Forman took a fancy to Mistress Cowley and at six o'clock in the evening on 20 August, after debating most of the day whether or not to do so, he decided to pay her a clandestine call, but to his disappointment he found her husband 'had but newly come in', presumably from the theatre after that afternoon's performance. He cursed himself for not going round in the afternoon when he could have been sure her husband was fully occupied.

Emilia Lanier consulted him again, this time demanding he look into what the future held for her, particularly whether she was ever likely to be a lady of title and, if so, how she should best set about it. Forman recounts: 'A certain gentlewoman – Emilia Lanier – whose husband was gone to sea with the Earl of Essex was desirous to know if he would be knighted tho' there was little chance that he would, and also whether she should be a lady or no. She hath been much favoured of her Majesty and of many noblemen and has great gifts and been much made of – a nobleman that is dead hath loved her well and kept her. But her husband hath dealt hardly with her, hath spent and consumed her goods. She is now very needy, in debt and it seems for lucre's sake will be a good fellow, for necessity doth compel. She hath a wart or mole in the pit of the throat or near it.'[10] A later note records that 'he [Lanier] was not [knighted] nor worthy of it'.

It is clear they had taken a fancy to each other. Within the week she was back again on some unspecified medical matter and after she had gone he cast to see 'if I should go to Lanier this night or tomorrow, whether she will receive me and whether I shall be welcome et halek'. A note on the same page to the effect that 'the woman hath a mind to the quent but seems she is or will be a harlot' may also refer to Emilia. By 11 September he was fairly lusting after her, heading a question 'A certain man longed to see a certain gentlewoman whom he loved and desired to halek with.' The question was 'whether he should send his servant to find out how he might be received and whether she would bid him come to her or no?' The answer was hopeful, so he duly despatched his man to her to ask if he might call round that night and she sent back word that he would be very welcome.

She gave him an intimate supper and after much fondling and leading him on, invited him to spend the night with her. 'She was familiar and friendly to [me] in all things, but only she would not halek.' She allowed him the utmost licence to feel 'all parts of her body willingly' and kissed him often 'but would not do [it] in any wise'. Whereupon he took 'some displeasure and so departed friends, but not intending to come at her again in haste'. To this he added, 'but yet we were friends again afterward but at that time never obtained my purpose'. Later still he wrote, 'she was a whore and dealt evil with me after'. If this account is true then this, too, fits the pattern of Shakespeare's teasing Dark Lady. Over the next few weeks he kept away from her in spite of her persistent invitations, but finally, after she had sent her maid to the Stone House begging him to come, he returned with the maid. With what success he does not say.

Certainly the 'halek' notes do not diminish, his conquests including maidservants, patients and women of all classes, married and single. On one occasion he remained in an upstairs room with an Isabella Webb (who was sewing) while her husband was teaching below, kissing her and making open advances to her, but on this occasion, not surprisingly in the circumstances, she did not allow it to go and 'so in great kindness [I] left her'.

Towards the end of the year an interest in what was going on outside the immediate confines of his own life begins to creep into his writings and in October we find him casting to know 'what should be done in the Parliament and what would come thereof in the end – quietness or strife?' The troubles at Westminster were about the passing of statutes to relieve the sufferings 'of the poor', a problem exacerbated by the large numbers of soldiers and sailors now discharged from active service who, in order to feed themselves and their families, had been reduced to begging or robbery to survive. In the event, the proceedings passed off peacefully, though those needing alms were forced to return to their birthplace, while begging and robbery were treated with increased severity.

The political situation brought inflation and Forman grumbled that 'currants were now 28s cwt [a hundredweight]; grains 12d a pound; ginger 12d a pound; woollen cloth 23s a yd; Castille soap [was dear]; black soap 23s cwt; hops 40s cwt; peas 8 groat [a farthing] and butter four pence a pound [that in the old currency].'[11]

There is one further link between Simon Forman and Shakespeare, for that November he was consulted by Mistress Mary Mountjoy. Her husband was a Huguenot refugee, a well-known maker of wigs and headdresses. The family lived in Silver Street, which crossed from Cripplegate, near to London Wall, to Wood Street, which in turn ran down to Cheapside and their house and shop are actually marked on Ralph Agas's pictorial map of London.[12] It must have been a lively and somewhat notorious household, for the elders of the French Church in London formally reported that the Mountjoys lived 'a licentious life' and that both Mountjoy and his daughter's husband were 'debauched'. The Mountjoys regularly took in lodgers and for a number of years one of these was William Shakespeare. The received wisdom is that we know nothing at all about Shakespeare, but in fact his long-standing connection with the Mountjoys and his involvement in their affairs are well documented, along with other records of his activities in London.[13] Mistress Mountjoy came to enquire if Forman could discover where she had dropped her purse when hurrying along Silver Street the previous week, since it contained a gold ring, a hoop ring and a French crown. She gave her age as thirty. Ten days later she returned, this time with a medical problem. She was suffering from pains in the head, side and stomach, weakness in the legs and a swimming head, and Simon diagnosed her as being eleven weeks pregnant, 'seven more and it will come from her or stay hardly'.

Forman's practice was now well established in the Stone House, but quite suddenly, and without explanation, he decided he wanted to get away from Billingsgate for a while, so he moved upriver to Westminster, taking a lease on a property known as Lambeth House. To avoid any confusion which might arise from the word 'Lambeth', he wrote 'I took Lambeth House and entered it a month before Christmas, Lambeth House at *Westminster*, nota.' He did not feel certain enough about the move, however, to give up his lease on his apartments in Stone House, which was just as well, for while he was in Lambeth House his study was rifled, with the connivance of that very John Goodridge, 'the gelded man', who claimed to read the future in pools of ink and had purported to raise demons for him years before. The thieves stole a number of his books including some on astrology, Richard Anglicus on the testing of urines, a book of notes on the use of the astrolabe and a Geneva Testament, a gift made to him by Anne years earlier, which he must have kept when he returned her other gifts.[14]

The thieves were not very smart and took the books along to an amateur astrologer, Master Coomy, proposing to sell them to him. Coomy was honest, the books were retrieved and the thieves caught. They turned out to be no common London villains but 'Cambridge men': Thomas Russell, son of a respectable man in Lewes in Sussex; William Grange, 'a Northern man' and sizar of St John's, who graduated from Trinity in the following year; and George Nicholas, another Trinity scholar who had taken his BA in 1592. Books were valuable commodities and one can only assume the thieves, short of cash, saw them as way to make some quick money. Simon notes that neither of the last two came to any good, for 'Nicholas, whose mother dwells in Westminster is gone beyond [the] sea and become a seminary priest'.

There is a footnote to the death of Avisa. In the autumn of that year, as the leaves were turning, Simon paid a visit to friends in Worcestershire, who took him to Stourbridge Fair. While he was wandering around among the crowds he saw a girl whose appearance rooted him to the spot. She turned out to be an acquaintance of his hosts, a Mistress Withypoll, and the reason for his being so struck was that she was 'much like Avis Allen, for whose sake I now have a good affection for her'.

10

Friends and Acquaintances

By February 1598 anything from five to ten people were consulting Forman every weekday and the money was rolling in. Each case was given due consideration on medical or astrological grounds, remedies being prescribed for alleviation of the former and figures drawn for casting for the latter. He says himself that this was the year in which he first made plenty from both, and spent it too, on good living, fine clothes, a chased fencing sword and other extravagances for 'I now had good credit'.[1]

Among those of high and low degree seeking him out, one name stands out. Richard Napier was to become Forman's closest friend as well as colleague. At first the relationship was that of pupil to teacher, but soon Napier was practising on his own account and as time went by they were to influence each other more and more, both using similar meticulous recording methods. They were the most popular astrological physicians of their age and the best documented.[2]

The Napier family originally came from Scotland, but by the end of the 1590s had been settled in England for a considerable while. One of its members, Robert Napier, became a substantial merchant with a property in Bishopsgate, which is possibly how Richard Napier and Forman first became acquainted. Richard Napier (later Sir Richard) was a pious and scholarly man who had taken a degree in theology at Wadham College, Oxford. By the time the two men met he was the rector of Great Linford in Buckinghamshire, a post he would hold for the rest of his life. In spite of

111

being in Holy Orders, he was fascinated by astrology and firmly believed in astrological medicine as a tool, a view which the Forman casebooks prove was shared by other clerics, but rarely, as in Napier's case, to the point of studying it and setting themselves up in a successful practice.

He had first contacted Forman in 1597 while visiting London and asked him for a casting to see if he could find some stolen property. A few weeks later he consulted Forman again, this time about the state of his health. Simon noted that he was thirty-seven years old and had 'heat in the back and reins and is troubled with gravel'. 'Gravel' or 'gravel in the reins' features frequently in Elizabethan medical practice, probably due to the state of much of the unboiled water, particularly in the towns and cities: it was not always possible to quench one's thirst with ale or cider. 'His humour is melancholic, full of red choler,' he wrote. The remedy was a purge and Simon sent one round to him.

The two men took to each other immediately, drawn together by their mutual enthusiasms, and before long they were visiting one another regularly. Just as people setting out on long cross-country car journeys today make a list of road numbers and towns, on the first occasion Forman ventured to ride into Buckinghamshire he made a note of the best route to Great Linford. His journey would take him through 'Barnet, St. Albans, Dunstable, Hockley-in-the Hole, Stony Stratford and so to Linford', taking 'the great Roman road, the Watling Street' almost all the way. He was soon to know the road well, though sometimes they met elsewhere, most usually in Cambridge.

Between visits, they wrote to each other regularly.[3] Possibly to differentiate him from his father, who was also called Richard, Napier was known to family and friends as 'Sandy' and this was how Forman addressed him. Not all his letters are dated, but one, written on 19 September 1599 to 'Brother Sandy', records that the book on which Forman has been working is now half done. 'Therefore I pray forget not your promise for the answering of all invectives against our profession. I do wish you had *Bruceldoro*, my gelding, to keep this winter. If so, send word by the carrier next week. If you come to London on him you shall be welcome. This winter I mean to study hard. I thank you for my cheeses.' Bruceldoro is the name of a horse in Ariosto's story, *Orlando Furioso*. Robert Greene made a play out of it, which Forman would almost certainly have seen since he was a keen theatregoer. Typically Greene, as always short of cash, managed to sell his script to three separate theatre companies for the sum of twenty nobles, assuring each one that it had been written only for them, a ploy which was only discovered when the various companies began preparing to put it on to the stage.

An undated and joking letter from Forman to Napier begins, 'Scholar, I received your letter by carrier and withal a pasty of some turkey, as I suppose, fast closed in boards like a wooden dagger on a leaden sheath. A worse I saw not these seven years. I gave the fellow two shillings for his pains: for the messenger was worthy of his hire.' It continues, 'and I also know that your goodwill was better, or else my deserts and goodwill have been in vain; for I have done that for thee, scholar, that I have done for no man the like. Men say a man should not look a gift horse in the mouth. No more did I this, but I looked in his belly and there I thought to have found gold ... alack, alack, poor jennet [horse] metaphorised! Other demands also I find in your letter, namely to know in which side of a man or woman the disease lieth. I have oftentimes told you this question before.'

He then sets out various astrological figures and answers questions his friend had put about the buying and selling of land and other matters, ending 'my business is such now that I have much ado to have time to write this letter. And so with a thousand commendations I commit you to Christ Jesus and the Holy Trinity, my schoolmaster and teacher, to whom be bliss. And to yourself, thank for ever.' In return, whether or not this was strictly allowable, Napier conferred on Simon the powers of blessing and cursing according to the laws of the Church.

Over the years Forman purchased medicines, drugs and herbs on Napier's behalf, since such items were hard to obtain in rural Buckinghamshire, and Napier reciprocated with good country food. Another letter, probably written a few years later, informs Sandy that 'I have brought and sent you such parcels of drugs as are specified in the note herein enclosed. But we have no hypocon water, nor can get none. Endive water is to be had but we know not how to send it for spilling. In the meantime make your infusions with white wine; for every dram of rhubarb put half a pint of white wine or Rhenish wine.' Also enclosed was 'only half a pound' of an indecipherable drug or herb which had been requested 'because it is somewhat old'.

Napier had wanted to know what signs Simon used to discover whether or not a maid was still a virgin, bearing in mind that a physical examination was out of the question, except in very rare cases when it was undertaken by a midwife. The first point made is the obvious one. 'I answer you this, when the velme [film] or string of her virginity is broken. If you will know otherwise then it must be upon a question and by sight of the party', and, of course, astrological castings. Asked for advice on menstrual irregularity, Forman told him 'that when you will open a vein to bring down the course of a woman, do it in the middle of the foot under the ankle, and sometimes the vein lieth above the ankle on the inside of the foot; that upon the ankle on the outside of the foot is to stop the course. You will find it in the little written book I gave you. Your brother paid me twenty shillings for the drugs but they came to 26s. 9d. My boy delivered the things to Warren the carrier, packed in a candle basket.'[4]

The Condwells were on a very different footing to Sandy Napier. Either they were genuinely unfortunate and often ill or they were both hypochondriacs, since they consulted Forman continually, first coming to him in 1598. They lived in the City in Old Jewry, a street which led up from Poultry to Moorgate. John Condwell suffered from stone and the ubiquitous 'gravel', Anne Condwell had 'the languishing sickness'. The prognosis from the first casting for her was grim, 'her time draws on to die, she cannot live long', but happily this proved to be wrong, for not only was she still consulting Forman years later, but she soon began to feature in the 'halek' notes, the relationship continuing both before and after Forman's marriage. Over the months and years Simon diagnosed catarrh in her stomach, trouble in the reins (the Elizabethans seem to have been obsessed with their kidneys), jaundice and that she was 'sick of a melancholy'. This, along with her bouts of the 'languishing sickness', suggests that she was seeking something other than a purge or herbal remedy for her condition.

Anne Condwell was always asking Forman if he thought she was pregnant, as did another regular client, Frances Pranell. Almost as often, Frances wanted to know when, if ever, she would be relieved of her husband. She had decided, since her sister-in-law had given up her pursuit, that the Earl of Southampton might be a suitable candidate just as soon as Pranell accommodated her by dying, so how long would she have to wait? Should she encourage the earl's advances? A few months later she repeated the questions, but by that time she had, all unbeknown, missed the boat. Forman had consoled her by telling her that Southampton would eventually leave his old love and marry her. Southampton had made Elizabeth Vernon, one of the queen's maids of honour, pregnant and however much he wished to avoid marrying her, the two families, appalled at the looming scandal, insisted that he did the right thing. He resisted for as long as he could, for Forman noted that the young woman was twenty-nine years and two months old when the wedding took place and that the child was born less than two months later. The news made Frances unwell, suffering 'grief and cold' and she sent a specimen of her urine to Simon to see, yet again, if she was with child.

1598 also saw the reappearance in the records of the red-haired and slatternly cleric's wife, Alice Blague. Alice had embarked on an affair with another man of the cloth, Dean Owen Wood, Dean of Armagh since 1590, a position he oversaw from London; later he would succeed Blague at Ewelme. He was wealthy, having married a Mistress Ballard, the rich widow of a Cheapside goldsmith who was much older than himself and had bequeathed him her substantial property both in London and the village of Tottenham. The wealth side of the bargain was most satisfactory, but the age and unattractiveness of the widow were not. Wood therefore looked around for younger blood and, like Forman, tended to take what came to hand. As his wife's maid later told Forman, when consulting him on her own behalf, 'one day Dean Wood did occupy her against the bedside, her mistress being abroad in Tottenham'.

Wood then turned his attention to his colleague's wife, a state of affairs which kept Alice Blague continually on Forman's doorstep asking for advice. First she asked him to cast to see if she might get 'restitution' from Dean Wood for her services, and the next month to know 'if he bear her any love or no'. The answer was 'he hath done and will do again'. In March she wanted to know if it was true that Wood was now involved with an Anne Haybourne and also if Blague would ever become a bishop. Unhappy with what she was told, she repeated the questions the next day, shortly after which Dean Blague also consulted Simon, complaining of a 'stuffed stomach'.

The Blagues had their uses, since they recommended their physician to other clerics, including the celebrated scholar and divine, Hugh Broughton, from Shropshire. He was something of a controversial figure since while holding that the text of Holy Writ was sacrosanct and written by the finger of God, he declared openly that he had doubts about how

115

some of it was interpreted, one of his notions being that Hell was never meant to be a place of torment but merely a sort of waiting room for erring souls, a view which provoked something of a storm. Broughton's most pressing need was to know what his fortune might be in terms of preferment and whether a rival of his, Dr Dodd (who also came from Shropshire and was vicar of Epping), was likely to become the next Bishop of Chester or even of London. Broughton was quite prepared to turn to astrology rather than prayer or the scriptures to discover what the future had in store, constantly wanting to know if he would beat Dodd to a bishopric. Dodd did eventually become Bishop of the Isle of Man, thus winning the race, though the post could hardly be described as a pinnacle of achievement.

Fame and fortune did not stop Forman from trying his hand again at magic. For days together he was busy engraving rings and stones with magic symbols for would-be lovers and, on one occasion, preparing hazel wands for some unspecified purpose. 'Just before moonrise at 7 p.m. and 9 p.m. I did let to be cut eight hazel wands within the day and hour of eight just. Jane did cut them, being a virgin and in that hour they were whited and written on.' He also continued his unsuccessful quest for the philosopher's stone.

He could have made a fortune as a blackmailer, for he was constantly at the receiving end of the confidences of adulterous wives or husbands. In March 1598 Shakespeare's landlady came to him again, asking if her husband was likely to be sick in the near future, shortly after which a Master Wood, who lived in Coleman Street close to the Mountjoys' premises, enquired on behalf of Mistress Mary Mountjoy 'whether the love she bears him will be altered or not'. The answer was that 'they may join, but take heed they trust not out their wares much or they will have loss'. An unexplained marginal note states that at one time Mary Mountjoy had to be 'concealed'. Later in the month, Mountjoy came along himself to find out whether his two French apprentices were honest and likely to serve him well.

A number of Forman's patients also feature in Aubrey's Brief Lives, one of whom, a colourful character, appeared on the scene for the first time that April. Sylvanus Scory, son of the Bishop of Hereford, is described as a very handsome gentleman of an excellent wit.[5] He had been indulged since birth, given the best possible education and then been sent abroad to complete it. Aubrey makes no bones about where his wealth came from. His father loved him so dearly 'that he fleeced the Church of Hereford to leave him a good estate; and he did let such long and so many leases, that, as Mistress Masters told me, they were not out till above these sixty years. To my best remembrance she told me that the estate left him was £1500 per annum, which he reduced to nothing (allowing himself the liberty to enjoy all the pleasures of this World) and left his son so poor, that when he came among gentlemen, they would fancy a crown or ten shillings for him.'

As well as running through his fortune, Scory became a favourite at Court and a Member of Parliament and acted as a go-between for 'Monsieur', brother of the king of France, who was suitor to Queen Elizabeth. 'I have heard Sir John Denham say,' continues Aubrey, 'that he was the most accomplished Gentleman of his time; and [it] is a good testimonial of his worth that Mr Benjamin [Ben] Jonson, who ever scorned an unworthy patron, dedicated to him.' Unfortunately poor Scory had a problem, apart from suffering from 'the melancholy', which Forman does not appear to have been able to help him with: he was impotent. 'He hath a weakness in his genitals *quod non potest coire* [so that he cannot copulate] and grieveth much. It comes through much lechery.'

The famous printers, the Jaggard twins, who gave their age as thirty-two, consulted Forman jointly as William was suffering from jaundice and John with fever. They were followed by another well-known printer, Richard Field, an old schoolfellow of Shakespeare's, who specialised in printing foreign-language books and claimed to have 'swallowed a portugue [a Portuguese gold coin] which lies in the pit of the mouth of his stomach'.

Also during March Forman cast to know whether Sir William Evers, to whom he had been called, 'be slain or not, that is whether he will live or die'. Among the letters of John Chamberlain, a person whose main claim to fame is as a letter writer, is one to a Sir Dudley Carleton which explains the reason for this. Sir William and his brother, the Warden of the Middle March, were walking down a London street accompanied only by a page when they were ambushed by five members of the Widdrington family 'about a country quarrel', a reivers' feud which had spread south from the borders right on to the streets of the capital. The Evers brothers defended themselves manfully, but were both wounded in the subsequent fight with swords and daggers, William so badly that he nearly died.[6]

It is also easy to forget the kinds of problem which brought people to Forman's door in an age which believed in witchcraft and the supernatural. On one occasion worried parents brought him their small child, saying they feared it had either been 'bewitched or was a changeling', while Margery Skelton 'that dwells in the little lane that goes into the fields beyond Holborn bridge, is bewitched and haunted at night with ghost or sprites that she hears often'. And who, most intriguingly of all, was 'the gentlewoman of Deptford that was so behanged with jewels, that left the grasshopper with me'? He does not say the reason for her visit.

To his endless litigation with the Seftons and rows with rival doctors, Forman added problems entirely of his own making. He now needed a sizeable household to see to his needs and keep everything running smoothly, so, as well as employing two manservants, at Easter 1598 he took on two young women, Bess Parker as a housekeeper and Alice as a maid. At midsummer he decided that he no longer wanted to live in Westminster and returned to his old apartments at the Stone House. He had taken a six-year lease on Lambeth House, which he sold on to a James Bainton for £90 since it still had five and a half years to run. However, nothing was ever straightforward where he was concerned and he recorded briefly that he was 'in danger of killing by Bosgrove and Bainton for my House of Lambeth'.

By the end of June he was established back in Billingsgate and on 14 July records how he 'haleked Elizabeth Parker p.m. at ten *et eo tempore fugit matrix virgam virilem*' (thus relieving her of her virginity), after which she told him immediately that she was sure he had made her pregnant. The coupling with Bess must have been a boisterous and energetic affair, for afterwards Forman complained of being taken with 'a pain in my left thigh in the sinews under the buttocks like to a scalp or cramp'. It troubled him throughout the night 'that I could not sleep nor scant stand the next day'. However, four days later he was back for more and 'halek Elizabeth Parker a.m. at one, *bis, et ultimo sanguinata est*', after which he has the nerve to cast to discover whether or not Bess is a 'harlot'. The following night he dreamed she was pregnant. Fortunately she was not – as yet – and the arrangement continued.

Shortly after his return to the Stone House he acquired a neurotic patient, another who would stay with him for years. This was Sir Barrington Molyns or Mullings from Chelsea, one of those popularly known as 'Essex's cheap knights', men he had knighted on behalf of the queen after the failed Islands Voyage. Molyns came with a nasty complaint: 'he is infected with melancholy and salt phlegm and breeds worms in his nose or stinking, sweet and venomous humour'. Forman told him to diet for twenty days to scour the blood and to wash his face with aqua salsa and wormwood mixed with fumitory. Sir Barrington was keen to marry and came asking questions about a Mary Hampden and a Mistress Elizabeth Southwell, sister to Sir Robert Southwell, both of whom he considered would make him a suitable wife. Sir Robert was not too keen on Barrington as a brother-in-law and so the cheap knight wanted to know if he was more likely to obtain the hand of Mary Hampden, although his preference was for the other lady. He pestered Forman continually for answers on the subject for he had gone so far as to obtain a licence to marry Elizabeth Southwell, but she had then refused to go through with it.

His requests for advice did not stop with himself, for he was also concerned for the health of his womenfolk and maids: Bridget, who was twenty-three, had 'the greensickness and hath taken thought and grief, very faint at heart and her mind much troubled while her maid suffered from putrefaction of the womb and corrupted blood'. The records of the ups and downs of Sir Barrington's courtship and health spread through a number of folios. They continued until 1600 when he finally achieved his goal and married Elizabeth, by which time she was thirty. She did, however, give him a son and heir two years later.

At the end of 1597 Forman had received another letter from Anne, requesting his help and advice, an event which prompted the dream in which he and Walworth met in the street and drew their daggers on each other. The next time Anne wrote to him, in 1598, she asked if he would be able to come down and see her soon, so finally he rode down to Salisbury in the autumn, though he admitted to feeling apprehensive as to what his reception might be or even if he would be able to see her at all. Before setting off, ever hopeful, he had cast to see if she might soon be widowed, but the answer was, as usual, that she would not.

In the event nothing was put in the way of his spending time with his old love, arrangements having been made by his brother so that 'he was entertained most friendly'. The journey back to London was fraught with problems and he lists all that went wrong: '1. I lost my rapier, cost 13s. 2. My man's horse tired – much ado to get another, but it was nought.

3. I fainted at supper at Hartley and was very sick. 4. My horse limped and was like to throw me over his head. 5. I was glad to change my own horse for he trotted so hard I could not sit him. 6. I bought a new rapier by the way and my man was like to break it . . . 7. I never slept till I returned.'

Back home he continued to solace himself with Bess Parker, but was annoyed when he discovered she was prodigal with her favours. On 8 November his step-nephew, Stephen Mitchell, came to stay. Stephen was now in the service of a merchant venturer, Alderman Watts, and had made several voyages to the Caribbean and the Mediterranean, distinguishing himself in the West Indies by captaining one of the smaller vessels attached to the merchant fleet. Shortly after Stephen's arrival Forman found 'Elizabeth Parker was on the bed, kissing with him and the boys, I being then abed.' Nothing loath he joined the party 'and stayed with them until almost eleven at night'. The next morning one of the boys, Ted, warned Stephen that from now on his uncle would be watching his every move, but according to Forman 'another lad said that if she were disposed to pleasure any other good fellow, what had I to do with it?' A week or so later he reclaimed his mistress and 'halek E. Parker 9.15 p.m. *et seminavi per multum semen et matrix hausit multum tempusque*'.

At Christmas, however, Bess Parker left his service to go to another household and by this time he was relieved to see her go, unaware that this was not to be the end of the matter. The festive season was a busy one as various members of his family came to stay and he also entertained a number of friends. Then on 30 December 'I heard the piping of the fairies as I was wont before trouble. *Questo*, whether there be any trouble towards me or no? It seemeth there is some trouble or imprisonment towards and it will fall out next week.' He did not go to prison, but there was certainly trouble in store. Almost immediately afterwards Bess Parker sent him 'a token'. 'It seems by this figure', he wrote, 'that she is with child and that her Master hath put her to some other place . . .'[7]

11

Politics, Privateers and Marriage

Forman entered the New Year of 1599 in a grumpy frame of mind. He could see trouble looming ahead over Bess Parker's pregnancy. He also sacked one of his manservants and castigated the other, for 'while I was out of town he played the villain with me in many ways, both with his tongue and also with his hands; and with my distillations was negligent', which sounds even more like something out of *The Alchemist*. The negligence had to do with the pots of strong water on the stills in the corner by his chimney, distilled from fumitory, thyme, angelica, sage, saxifrage, worm-wood, bugle, ginger, senna, caraway seed, liquorice and much else.[1]

Political events were also now forcing themselves on him. The sixteenth century was drawing to its close amid increasing troubles both at home and abroad and he was sufficiently concerned to draw figures and make astrological calculations as to the possible outcome of a variety of events and to take precautions against others. At the end of 1599 he described how, in August, there was a great muster at St James. 'I bought much harness and weapons for war, swords, daggers, muskets, corselets and furniture, staves, halberds, gauntlets, mails, etc.' This staggering amount of hardware suggests he was fitting out a small army, though it is possible he had undertaken to buy it on behalf of his 'hundred' or parish, as was mandatory in times of need. There was good reason for anxiety since Spain's ambition to invade the country had not ended with the defeat of the Armada in 1588. Two further attempts in 1596 and 1597 had both

121

come to nothing due to adverse winds and bad weather, but by the beginning 1599 English intelligencers were sending back reports of ships massing off Corunna.

There were also problems closer to home in Ireland, where considerable resistance was being shown to English rule in the parts of the country now held by the Crown. The government saw Ireland – Catholic, rebellious and resentful – as a back door through which Spain might still achieve its objective. At first it was decided to negotiate with the opposition in the person of the wily Hugh O'Neill, Earl of Tyrone. When these talks broke down Robert Devereux, Earl of Essex, was despatched to Ulster with a great force of men on a mission which was to prove an unmitigated disaster.

The choice of Essex to lead the force was by no means popular. He had already come perilously close to forfeiting everything he had as the queen's great favourite, beginning with his failed venture to capture the Spanish plate fleet off the Azores. He and Ralegh had long been rivals and it was partly to regain favour with the queen after she had taken such offence over his marriage that Ralegh had suggested Essex should join him in the Islands Voyage. Essex had agreed, but refused to take any advice from the experienced Ralegh as to how best to set about it and insisted he be in overall command. The two men returned home, each blaming the other for the ensuing fiasco, to be summoned before Elizabeth, who told them in no uncertain terms that she would never again back such a foolhardy adventure.

Essex's temper was further soured when he discovered the queen had finally ratified the appointment of his long-time enemy, Sir Robert Cecil, as Secretary to the Privy Council and that she planned to send his uncle, Sir William Knollys, to Ireland to negotiate with O'Neill, for he wanted his uncle to help him restore his standing with her. So determined was he to have his way that he was foolish enough to tackle the queen on the subject. She refused to agree to his demand and in full view of the Court he turned his back on her and flounced off, at which appalling piece of lèse-majesté, she ran after him and slapped him on the head. Enraged, he roared at her that he would not have put up with such treatment even from her father, a sentiment which must have amazed bystanders since Henry VIII would undoubtedly have wasted no time and removed his head from his shoulders.

However, over the weeks the queen softened, in part because she was distracted by the illness of her friend and greatest adviser, Lord Burleigh, and also because she genuinely missed Essex's company. At this low point the negotiations with O'Neill broke down finally and it was decided to send an army to Ireland. Essex at once begged the queen to put him in command. For a while she hesitated, but finally agreed against the advice of her ministers and her own misgivings. True to form, Essex immediately surrounded himself with favourites, many of whom were totally unsuited to the posts he gave them, the most blatant case of nepotism being to make his closest friend, the Earl of Southampton, his Master of Horse.

News of the appointment swept through London like wildfire and on 19 March 1599 Forman cast to know whether he would succeed in his attempt to pacify Ireland, recording one of those strange conclusions, like the forecast of Avisa's death, which appear prophetic. The answer to his question was: 'There seems to be in the end of his voyage negligence, treason, hunger, sickness and death. He shall not do much good to bring it to effect. At his return much treachery shall be wrought against him; the end will be evil to himself, for he shall be imprisoned or have great trouble. He shall find many enemies in his return and have great loss of goods and honour, much villainy and treason shall be wrought against him to the hazard of his life, because the moon goeth in Jupiter. Yet he shall escape it with much ado after long time, much infamy and trouble.'[2] Only the last sentence was to prove inaccurate.

Special taxes were levied to pay for the campaign in Ireland. First to knock at Forman's door were 'two who came for forty shillings for the soldiers'. This did not please him, 'but I supposed I ought to pay it'. Shortly afterwards he had to find a further 13s 4d to help equip Essex's army. He calculated that if everyone liable to pay did so at the rate of a fifteenth of their regular 'subsidy' or local tax then the whole 'throughout England would come to £38,000. 6s. 9d and three quarters of a pence', while for Billingsgate the sum would be £39.

Essex set off from London in March in a blaze of arrogant magnificence and Forman was among the thousands who turned out to see him leave from Tower Hill, recording later that 'he took horse at the Tower about one o'clock, up the Crutched Friars and up Cheapside with some hundred horse. At about two o'clock it began to rain and at 3 'til 4 there fell such a hail-shower as was very great. Then it thundered withal and the wind turned to the north; after the shower was past it turned to the south east again. But all the day, before one o'clock, was a very fair day and four or five days before, bright and clear, and very hot like summer.'[3] The storm, he noted, was 'an ominous prodigy'. After the pageant the Lord Chamberlain's men, taking advantage of the public mood, put on a special performance of Shakespeare's *Henry V*.

Towards the end of the previous year, James Burbage, now an elderly man, had taken a decision. For three years he and his sons had been wrangling with Giles Allen, the owner of the land on which Burbage had erected the first custom-built playhouse, the Theatre, over the terms, conditions and cost of a new lease. One had been drawn up back in 1595, but Allen had refused to ratify it, assuming that the Burbages had made so much money that they could afford to pay almost anything he asked. In fact this was not the case, for to build the Theatre Burbage had borrowed the enormous sum of a thousand marks from his wife's father and the repayments, plus interest, were still crippling him.

Eventually Allen told Burbage that he could accept his offer or go elsewhere, assuming that Burbage would have no other option but to give in. He did not know his man. Taking advantage of a clause inserted in the original lease, which stated that if he spent more than £200 on the building he was at liberty to dismantle it and remove it 'overnight', Burbage did just that. The Theatre was taken down and the materials shipped across the Thames. There, early in 1599, a stone's throw from Henslowe's Rose Theatre, he built the biggest and best theatre of its day. It was called the Globe.

Forman wrote in his diary that he left the Stone House again at the beginning of the year, but there is no mention of any other residence until he moved to Lambeth permanently in 1601. Various references strongly suggest that if there was an absence then it was only temporary; possibly another occasion when he was avoiding being served with a writ. Certainly there was no falling off in the number of people consulting him and medical patients and astrology clients, new and old, would need to know where he was to be found.

Two early consultations in 1599 had direct relevance to Essex's imminent expedition to Ulster. Mistress Blague wished to know how Dean Wood's son David, who was going with the earl, would fare and what might happen to him before he returned. Her lover, the dean, was accompanying the troops as far as Wales to see them set sail and Alice Blague paid Forman to make her a magic sigil ring with coral, inscribed with verses of love, presumably designed to keep the erring dean faithful to her while he was away.

Frances Pranell also came again, now thoroughly depressed by the time it was taking her husband to die and with her sights still set on the Earl of Southampton in spite of his marriage. With that hope in mind, she asked if Pranell would return safely from some unspecified venture on which he was about to embark (suggesting he too was planning to go with Essex). The answer was that he would return 'about 23 May or Bartholomew Tide; he will have loss in his goods and want of money to spend. He bears her little good will now, or none.' Wherever Pranell went, he disappears from history and must have died soon afterwards, for by the autumn Frances, now a brisk, desirable and wealthy young widow, was back for advice on whom she should marry next.

Forman had more on his mind than Essex's expedition. In early March he was visited by Bess Parker's brothers, demanding to know once and for all if he had fathered the child she was carrying and, if so, what he proposed to do about their pregnant sister. Forman blustered and tried to make excuses. The story of the bedroom romps with Stephen Mitchell and 'the boys' was retold and embellished, to which he added that 'on 22 August last she had been sent to Mary Fardell that lay in childbed and Nicholas Fardell did occupy [had intercourse] with her before she came away'.

This cut no ice at all with the Parkers, who promptly began legal proceedings for the sixteenth-century equivalent of maintenance. Faced with this, Forman made some notes for his defence: 'remember these that follow Whitfield, how he had her. That the smith used her. William Casson how he had her. Old Westley, how he did use her. Captain Ruddleston at Mr Bragg's. Fardell of Southwark when I sent her to his wife's lying-in. The time she went to Hackney and went not thither but to Lambeth. The time that she went to Fleet Street, when I went to Lambeth in the afternoon and forbade her to go out. The time she stayed so long at the market.'[4]

In the event the matter never came to court, for Forman, deciding discretion was the better part of valour, made a series of payments, including one to a man persuaded to marry Bess two months before the child was born on 9 June. He also paid for the nurse who looked after her in childbed, though still protesting to the end that the dates were right for the child to have been Fardell's. However, Bess had no such doubts, for as soon as her daughter was born she sent to him at once 'to know my mind' and once she was up and about she arrived on his doorstep, bringing the baby with her, to inform him that her daughter had been baptised with the strange name of Fennena.

Forman's growing clientele among the merchant venturers and other seafarers vividly illustrates the sheer magnitude of the expansion of trade at the end of the sixteenth century. It is there to be seen in the pages and pages of astrological castings he made for many of those involved.[5] The two main categories of entrepreneurs who consulted him were the merchant venturers and the privateers. There were degrees of merchant venturing. Some wealthy and powerful traders boasted what almost amounted to a small fleet of ships, while others owned maybe only one small vessel or held a share in one owned by someone else. Anyone holding a share in another's enterprise would be likely to have a man of their own on board, known as a 'factor', to look after their interests and ensure they received their due at the end of the voyage.

Privateering, on the other hand, was licensed piracy. Privateer captains carried letters of authority or licences from the Crown and were 'allowed' to waylay enemy ships for gain, the word 'enemy' often being used somewhat loosely. Back home in England it was not considered in the least disreputable, indeed rather the reverse, and some of the best families in the realm (not least the mighty Cecils), had shares in privateering ventures. Not surprisingly, the lines between merchant venturing and privateering occasionally became blurred.

In 1599 Forman acquired a client who was to consult him continually over many years. He was Nicholas Leate, 'trader to the Levant and ironmonger'. He appears in the casebooks for the first time in January 1599, asking after his ship the *John Francis* which had sailed for the Levant five months previously and had not been heard of since. He wanted to know if she was now in Algiers or had left for Alexandria. Simon's answer was that she was on her way home with a rich cargo, but that there had been sickness on board which had caused a delay. Nothing happened and in February, March and throughout that summer until as late as August,

Leate was still enquiring after her. A note tacked on to the record of the visits informs us that the *John Francis* finally arrived back safely and with her cargo, but without Leate's 'factor', who died on the voyage.[6] In February of the following year he called a further five times to discover the whereabouts of the *Angel*, 'what has become of her that she comes not?' The answer was that she had left Alexandria, had suffered some 'great mishap', but was now sailing homeward once more. There were many more questions about other ships which he either owned or in which he had an interest, such as the *Charity*, the *Hector*, the *George* and the *Lanneret*.

'What news on the Rialto?' the traders and merchants of Venice ask each other at the beginning of Shakespeare's play and it was no idle question when all too often ships disappeared into the blue taking their owners' fortunes with them, never to be heard of again. The Elizabethan audience would have been accustomed to hearing such queries on the quayside at Billingsgate or downriver in Deptford.

Many of Leate's vessels returned unscathed, indeed the *Angel* had already reached the Dover Straits at the time he was asking after her, while the *Charity* docked at Woolwich on May Day 1600. It also transpired later that the little *Lanneret*, which for safety had sailed with the much larger *Hector* as far as the Adriatic, was safely anchored in the Venetian-owned port of Zante. Zante, on the south-west coast of Greece, was the centre of the currant trade, currants and many other kinds of dried fruit being in much demand.

As for the *Hector*, her voyage is worthy of a film script. She was famed in her day and it was claimed that she opened up direct trade with India. She sailed back from Asia via the Cape of Good Hope, after which her captain took her into the Mediterranean as far as Constantinople and from there on to Zante, where he found five other ships from London and two from Bristol. To protect themselves from Barbary pirates, they decided to sail home in convoy and on their way through the Straits of Gibraltar, the *Hector* sank a 'Biscayan' with 500 men aboard (something of an exaggeration, one imagines), and 'spoiled' a Spanish vessel: a prime example of the blurring of the line between venturing and privateering. The *Hector* finally arrived back home in triumph at the head of a fleet of twelve ships, 'coming into port very rich.'

As well as seeing Forman about his ships, Leate also consulted him on various medical matters. In September 1599 his little son John, aged two, was smitten with the smallpox and was prescribed a remedy for the disease along with a rosewater mixture to bathe the sores, while later Mistress Leate came for a cure for her 'lethargy', possibly caused by the anaemia from which so many women suffered.

Seafaring enquiries continued over the years. When Sir Thomas Shirley decided to put to sea, Master Shaw the elder asked Forman whether or not he should help fit out and victual Shirley's vessel in case he made a loss, to which the answer was that he should not do so for the moon was unfavourable. William Bagley of Ratcliffe wanted a forecast on his forthcoming privateering voyage to the West Indies in Sir John Gilbert's *Refusal* and the response was positive. And it was not only those who had big investments in an argosy or argosies who wanted such information. While prizes for the owners of the privateers and the captains could be great, there was no shortage of volunteers from the ranks of ordinary mariners, for if the voyage was successful a seaman could come home with a share in the prize money as well as his wages and keep, a share of forty shillings or more not being uncommon for a single voyage.

When staying with him in London, Stephen Mitchell would often ask Simon how he would fare on his next venture. On one occasion he was offered a berth on the *Neptune*, bound for the Caribbean, to which the answer was that he should go but would gain little. In this instance Forman was proved wrong, for the venture was successful and Stephen came back with money in hand. He also started bringing back for him the new plant – tobacco – which was becoming much sought after for medicinal purposes.

Another time Stephen Mitchell wanted to know if he should sail with a Captain John Beckett of Limehouse to the Indies or in the *Green Dragon* with a Captain Pepperell to the South Cape. On Forman's advice he chose the latter, which must have been a privateer, for 'on 25 July [they] met thirty sail of the Spanish Indian [West Indian] Fleet', the kind of plate fleet Essex and Ralegh had set out to find. They kept with them for a week, during three days of which there was a running fight, but they failed in their attempt to take any of them. Disappointed, they lay off the Cape for a month then sailed into the Straits and took a French ship bound for Marseilles which 'was not a lawful prize and so they were in trouble'.[7]

From time to time, seeing how much money could be made from such voyages, Forman seriously considered either investing in a venture or even going to the Levant or the Caribbean himself in search of a fortune (or to avoid problems at home), but he never did. Usually, and probably comfortingly, the stars never seemed to be sufficiently propitious. But shipboard life fascinated him and he even made a note on what was needed to victual a vessel, presumably gleaned either from Stephen Mitchell or from a client. 'In a ship they go five to a mess and every mess is allowed 7 lb of flesh; flesh three days a week, four days fish. If you victual ship for one month wherein there are forty men, you must have 84 lbs for every five men, that is fourteen stone [10 stone is 140 lb beef]; for five men a month at 16d. a stone; for fifty 840 lbs.' It was also necessary to carry 'pease [sic], oatmeal, cheese, salt pork, stockfish and vinegar'.[8]

The enquiries continued. A 'Goodman Flowers' of Ratcliffe was due to sail in the *Rose Lion*, a powerful, armed merchantman, but the voyage was delayed and he wanted advice as to its outcome. The ship was owned by a syndicate of City merchants who were prepared to go to great lengths to protect their investment. The *Rose Lion*, like Leate's fleet, traded mainly in the Levant, so was exposed to the pirates who infested the Mediterranean from the Straits of Gibraltar to the far reaches of the Barbary coast. Sometimes they ventured out as far as the Western Approaches and were an added threat to the possibility of falling prey to the Spaniards.

Some years after his first visit to Forman, Leate was asking after the *Centurion* and why she was delayed. He had cause for misgivings, for on an earlier voyage, chronicled by Hakluyt, the *Centurion* had been attacked by no less than five Spanish galleys and 'was fired five several times, with wildfire and other provision, which the Spaniards threw in for that purpose'. 'In every one of the galleys there were 200 soldiers who, together with the shot, spoiled, rent and battered the *Centurion* very sore.' Though grappled and boarded, the crew heroically fought the Spaniards off.[9]

Very often it was the worried mothers or wives who came for advice, having heard or seen nothing of their menfolk for months and with no idea where they might now be. Such enquirers were treated with sympathy: not only did Forman cast horoscopes for them, not infrequently he also made enquiries on their behalf on the quays and among those recently returned from voyages. Joan Ede of Ratcliffe was deeply worried about her husband, who had sailed for the Caribbean four years earlier in a vessel which had not been heard of since. Simon learned that he had been captured by the Spaniards and made a prisoner in Seville. The wife of another Ratcliffe seaman wanted to know how her husband would succeed in his voyage in the *Godspeed*, but Simon was unable to give her an astrological answer. He wrote later that 'she [the ship] went to sea a-roving, but the company were taken about Penzance by the Dunkirkers and lost all. They were stripped of all their clothing and came home naked. The master was taken prisoner to Dunkirk.'

Mary Alcock of St Katherine's came to enquire after her husband and his servant, Daniel Fleshman. Both had sailed in the *Little John* for the West Indies. She had heard nothing: had they been taken? Simon cast and told her that her husband seemed to be not well and in prison; this time he was near the mark for they were both in gaol in Havana. The servant returned safely the following year, but her husband was slain in a sea fight on the way home. Mary Alcock continued with the business, trading on her own behalf, and later appears again asking after one of her men, who was rumoured to be in a Dunkirk gaol. This was not all that unusual, for there were a number of women at the end of the sixteenth century trading on their own account in a variety of businesses. Only a small proportion set up independently, but many took over their husband's affairs if they were disabled or had died and ran them very competently.

A young woman, nineteen-year-old Anne Lock, twice wanted to know what had happened to her husband, who had sailed in the privateer, the *Marigold*. After taking a prize, the ship had been driven ashore at Lisbon, but had then come safely home without Anne's husband. Forman discovered that he had been taken prisoner in Portugal and held for seven months. Some two months afterwards he arrived back in London safe and well, either having escaped or been released, after spending some months on a Flemish vessel which had willingly taken him on board but had business 'sailing eastwards' before returning home.

It was not even necessary to travel to exotic places to come to grief: two merchants asked Simon to cast to see what had happened to their ship, the *Diamond*, which had set sail, heavily laden, from Fowey in Cornwall ten days earlier and had still not arrived. The *Diamond* was never seen again, having either been taken by predatory enemies or, more likely, joining the hundreds of wrecks littering the bottom of the English Channel off the Cornish coast.

Outside his busy practice Forman's troubles continued to mount, Bess

Parker's child being only one of them. Yet again he was having trouble with Peter Sefton. Mistress Sefton had seen one of their neighbours, Mistress Bestow, stealing into a warehouse close to the Stone House to visit two Spanish prisoners or detainees. There had been no further quarrels with the Seftons for nearly a year, but in May 1599 Sefton publicly slandered Forman once again, this time with tales which made those for which he had previously been forced to apologise seem nothing. For, Forman recorded, on the evening of 9 May Sefton was heard to say in front of five witnesses that 'I had six, seven, eight, nine whores and had killed two children. That I suffered Sir William Monson twice to occupy Mistress Bestow in my chamber, also that Master Wheatley and myself did carry her to the Spaniards in the warehouse and that they did occupy her also.'[10] Forman at once cast to see if he should take legal proceedings against such a dreadful defamation of character, found the stars were favourable and had Sefton arrested, 'by Rudgley, the sergeant in Gracechurch St for which I paid him 3s'.

Sefton was put in prison and an amount set for the terms of his release. Within an hour Sefton had agreed, delivering up a 'bond' of £200 (an enormous sum) and Forman settled that he should be set free 'on condition that after this he should abuse me no more in word or deed, but keep himself honest and quiet. On this condition I caused the action to be withdrawn and discharged him.' Trouble between them rumbled on for another couple of years, but this was the last time it flared up in such a dramatic way.

Forman must have lent a sympathetic ear to women as they were continually asking his advice on their various relationships. Martha Webb, a friend of Alice Blague's from Canterbury, had become the mistress of Sir Thomas Walsingham, Marlowe's old patron and probable lover. Sir Thomas had by this time made a suitable marriage, but enjoyed some entertainment on the side. Martha had been married at the age of fifteen and Forman described her husband as a 'tall, slender and very honest man'. She was 'very fair, of good stature, plump face, little mouth, kind and loving; desired to go gay and to have many jewels, to fare well and keep good company', which suggests she must have had a great deal of energy, for by this time she had given birth to eight children. She wanted to know if Sir Thomas would be faithful to her. She continued to ask Forman if Sir Thomas loved her for several months, which he notes, adding, 'it seems she loves him better than he loves her. Their love is at its highest. It will come to nothing . . .'

Forman was now forty-six, a confidant and adviser on sexual, emotional and marital affairs to numerous women, yet still without a wife. Wealthy and established, he had started to give serious consideration to acquiring one well above his original social status. He looked fondly, for instance, on Sir William Monson's widowed sister, Anne Lee, and cast to know whether she loved him and might be prepared to marry him, though it is very unlikely that her family would have encouraged such a match. There was also pretty, wealthy Sarah Archdell, a young woman of twenty. He came across her at six o'clock in the evening on 17 April. She lived in Budge Row, 'on the right going to the church, right against the Rose at the standing steps'. Whether the Rose was the playhouse of that name or a tavern he does not say but Sarah had taken his fancy 'when he had gone to see a play at the Curtain theatre' just outside Shoreditch and she had been sitting in front of him in the audience with her uncle and friends.

'After the play we went into the fields together and so I had some parley with her, but nothing of anything touching the matter. She seemed very kind and courteous and I led her by the hand all the way almost.' On 22 April he cast to see if her uncle would allow his suit. 'This day he and I met at the Curtain again and after walked in the fields; but I never moved the matter to him.' That evening, at supper with his friends and clients, the Condwells, he looked out of the window and saw Sarah passing by with her uncle. He immediately left the supper table and overtook them in the field beyond Moorgate, where they stayed until after ten at night. By this time he had made up his mind to propose, but was thwarted by not being left alone with her. After that he spent some time talking to her uncle and waylaying Sarah, but all to no avail.

Then in July, quite suddenly and with hardly any warning, he took the plunge with an eighteen-year-old girl who had been introduced to him by the Blagues when she was on a visit to London from her home in Kent. Here we have the start of what might be called the 'mystery of the two wives', a mystery which has exercised researchers over the years. The index of manuscripts held in the Bodleian Library states categorically that Simon Forman married twice, first an Anne Baker and then a 'Jane –', the maiden name being left blank. Every source but one has since repeated this information.

It does not take much research to show that the idea lacks all common sense. Several notes at this time do show him casting to discover if 'Jane' would make him an honest wife and whether or not he should marry her, along with similar references to an 'Anne' On 5 July 1599 he asked '[is] it best to marry Jane *Baker* [my italics], whether she will prove an honest good wife, and what her friends will do for her?' On the 6th he enquired again 'is it best to keep Jane and marry her or no?' It suggests last-minute doubts and these had been exacerbated by a series of uneasy dreams. However, clearly for all to see, he wrote in his diary: 'I was married to Anne *Baker* of Kent, Sir Edward Munnings' sister's daughter, the 22nd July 1599, Sunday, in the 47th year of my age.' Other notes inform us that her father was John Baker of Canterbury, who had been a proctor in the ecclesiastical court, and that her mother, the sister of Sir Edward, was now Dorothy Munnings, having remarried after her husband's death.

In a further document, we learn that the wedding took place at seven o'clock in the morning at Lambeth parish church and was performed by the curate.[10] There had been a thunderstorm with lightning at three in the morning, after which it rained hard until five o'clock. Witnesses and guests at the ceremony were a Master Best and his wife, Dick Cook, 'friend Condwell' and Simon's man John Braddedge, along with the bride's mother and her man and a Mistress Cure of Southwark. As the bride's father was dead, she was given away by 'one Fratell'. Others attending included Mistress Blague and Mistress Appleward. Simon paid the curate and attendants eight shillings and twopence and then the whole party repaired to the Blagues for a wedding breakfast, after which the bride and groom returned home 'between one and two p.m.'

If we are to believe that Forman married twice, then why did he never remark on the death of his first wife? Nor is there any entry of the burial of an Anne Forman in the parish records before Forman's own death. Strangest of all, we would have to accept that he gave both wives the same nickname, 'Tronco'. Rowse alone recognised the anomaly and suggested that the most likely reason for the historical confusion is that Forman's wife was known by both names, Anne and Jane: there are plenty of precedents for a child being baptised with one name yet called another. Forman's handwriting is also hard to decipher, especially his capital letters, a common Elizabethan idiosyncrasy.[11] In the weeks preceding his marriage, the names 'Anne' and Jane' are easily distinguishable, but in his general writings Forman frequently used great flourishing capital letters to record someone's name and when comparing the way he sometimes writes a capital A, with a great curving cross piece, and a capital J (written in the old style, with a rounded loop which crosses the down stroke), the two look very similar.

So it was that Simon Forman, at the age of forty-six and after so many years of searching, finally took to wife an inexperienced teenage girl. This major decision was finally behind him. On the whole they were to rub along well enough – though from the first he was not faithful.

12

Domesticity and Success

Forman's young bride was a virgin when she came to the marriage bed and he wasted no time in deflowering her that evening. According to him, she entered into the physical side of their marriage with enthusiasm, 'fully and freely'. One wonders if she would agree with his assessment. Although she was seventeen, she was physically immature for her age and it was not until late into the following year that 'my wife's course came down and it was the first time that ever she had them'. Even so, when she began vomiting and complaining of stomach pains the month after their marriage he cast to see if she might be pregnant, correctly diagnosing that she was not.

Marriage had little or no effect on the way he lived his life, least of all on his pursuit of other women. If he had married so young a girl at his age because he was besotted with her – a situation which is hardly unknown – then she might have had a more of a hold over him, but this was clearly not the case. He had decided he could wait no longer for a wife and that as no one better had offered she would do. Nowhere are there any expressions of the affection or passion he felt for either Anne Young or Avisa Allen, indeed much of the time he sounds as if he is thoroughly irritated by her.

His new wife, however, greatly impressed him in one respect: her family and various ramifications of it had their own coat of arms; more than that, with a little ingenuity it was possible to link them with others of far higher status. Simon thought this should certainly be recorded for posterity and just as he had done on his own account years before, he covered pages and pages with exquisitely drawn reproductions of armorial bearings in full colour, touched with gold leaf, even though his claims regarding her relationship to some of the noblest families of the realm are somewhat far-fetched.[1] He approached the subject with the same enthusiasm he had shown when concocting his own fantasy genealogies and since the latter are undated it might be that the second set at least was an attempt to re-invent his own ancestry in order to compete with Anne's.

Perhaps his delving into the past triggered an interest in fairy tales and mythology, for he jotted down notes on characters out of Arthurian mythology, such as King Mark of Cornwall, Tristram and Iseult and Sir Gawain, which suggests he had read Mallory or Chrétien de Troyes. This, in turn, inspired him to write some quite dreadful poems based on the same subjects, the style of which owed nothing whatsoever to the influence of the early medieval poets.

He also wrote a *Book of Giants*[2] in which he recounts, among much else, that Gogmagog 'with whom Corineus wrestled when Brutus first came to this land, was twelve cubits high and of such strength he took an oak in his arms and plucked it up by the root', while in Thanet was found 'the tooth of a man, standing upright in the cleft of a rock, a mighty battleaxe by him. I judged [it] to be an eye-tooth three-and-a-half inches long. John Russell, a chirugeon of Canterbury and step-father to my wife was there when found in 1596.' Later he added that in 1603 'myself at Cambridge saw the cheek-tooth of a giant in an apothecary's shop that weighed 8 lb net. Another they said was eight and one half pounds net but I saw not that. They were found in digging a gravel pit in Cambridge.' Certainly he saw something, the most likely explanation being that it was a bone or tooth of a prehistoric creature.

The couple continued to live in the Stone House, where Forman had now taken over most of the rooms. The inexperienced Anne was not, however, left to cope with running a combined household and medical practice without help, for in September they hired a new and capable servant girl, Frances Hill, who had been recommended to them by friends. There was also Forman's man, John Braddedge, whom he had to 'chastise' again that month. From the number of times he complains about his various manservants and how often he either dismissed them or they left his employment anyway, he must have been a difficult master. Of John, unlike any of the others, he leaves us a brief history.

'This boy at twelve years was put out apprentice but was stubborn and proud and self-willed and would not learn his trade but delighted in play and gambling.' Simon was sufficiently interested in Braddedge to record his subsequent history, after leaving his employment. 'He went from me to the wars in the Low Countries where he served as a lieutenant. In 1602 about the 29th April he came out of Flanders very poor and naked and after some time returned and was a soldier again in Ostend. He had begun to be bawdy and lie with wenches from sixteen years old. In 1607 he married a young woman in Flanders, a lace worker, and in 1608 he brought his wife to England, great with child, being very poor. They lodged at Lambeth and had come from the Cardinal's camp. He [John] had got a bastard by another maid he was contracted to before in Flanders; it was a boy.'[3]

September proved a busy month. Among the women who consulted Forman was Dorothy Killigrew, who was the wife of a notorious member of a highly respected family of politicians and poets. We learn that she was thirty-five and her symptoms were 'much colour, phlegm in the blood and the lungs' and that she was also pregnant. As well as a house in fashionable Canon Row in London, John and Dorothy Killigrew had a substantial dwelling in Falmouth, from which he ran a number of extremely doubtful enterprises. By consensus he was nothing but a pirate, as distinct from a privateer, and even if that were not strictly the case there is no doubt that he was closely involved with those who were. John quickly ran through all Dorothy's money, then, still finding himself in debt, set about grinding everything he could out of his unfortunate tenants. Eventually he was imprisoned for his activities, protesting in a letter to Sir Robert Cecil that he was involved only with privateers, 'men of war that were allowed in the service of her Majesty, set out and maintained at sea by great persons not Channel pirates'. The Privy Council were unconvinced and he remained in gaol until he died in 1604. The hard-pressed Dorothy stood by her man throughout.[4]

In the autumn of 1599 relatives whose menfolk were still in Ireland with the Earl of Essex came to Forman asking after their fate as rumours of disaster began to reach London. From the start of the expedition nothing had gone to plan; no sooner had Essex landed in Dublin then he began to disregard his instructions and please himself. Not only did he refuse to obey the queen's commands, but he deliberately ignored the order of the

Privy Council which was the whole purpose of the enterprise: that he should take on O'Neill's army as soon as possible and without warning, while his own troops were fresh and there was no shortage of arms and ammunition. For weeks he did nothing, his inertia finally prompting a letter from the queen to the effect that she appeared to be paying him £1,000 a day to go on a progress. It was one of a series of letters, which was not abusive but making a bitingly accurate criticism of his incompetence, his disobedience and the stark failure they resulted in, which explodes the myth that the queen was nothing more than an infatuated old woman pursuing a vain and handsome young man.[5]

The cost of the invasion was the astronomical (for the period) sum of £300,000. The personal cost was far worse, for when Essex and O'Neill finally met at the Battle of Yellow Ford, O'Neill inflicted on the English army its greatest ever defeat in Ireland. Essex lost 12,000 men, among them Dean Wood's young son David. Already smarting from Elizabeth's rebukes and aware that this was the second overseas fiasco in which he had been in command, he foolishly decided to start secret negotiations with O'Neill, who could run rings round him politically, to see if he could do a deal with him once the queen was dead. The two held a secret meeting, which was known only to the Earl of Southampton, Essex's closest confidant. Southampton, however, had taken an enormous fancy to a Captain Piers Edmund, whom he would 'kiss and fondle publicly' and dally with in his chamber 'wantonly'. During these affectionate exchanges he told his lover what Essex was up to. Edmund, frightened for his own skin, left Ireland at once, fled to London and betrayed him.

The rest, as they say, is history. Elizabeth demanded an explanation for the defeat, ordering Essex to stay in Ireland until he had saved something from the disaster. But Essex, learning that his secret was out, sailed immediately for England. He arrived in London early in the morning of 28 September to discover the queen was at Nonesuch. With a few friends he crossed the river at Lambeth, seized the nearest horses from their startled owners and set off hell for leather for the palace. Ignoring the protestations of Lord Grey of Wilton, who tried to prevent him, he pushed into the Presence Chamber, caked as he was in mud and dust, found it empty and stormed into the queen's bedchamber, where she was sitting, half-dressed, at her mirror attended by her maids. Essex fell on his knees and begged her to listen to his side of the story. Taken at a disadvantage, she sent him away to clean himself up and saw him after dinner, when she informed him that he must explain himself to the Privy Council. The council was meeting that day and a preliminary examination of Essex took place that night, after which he was sent to York House in the custody of Lord Egerton to await the findings of a special commission.

London was soon rife with rumours of troubles ahead and over the next few months Forman cast several figures, both on his own account and at the request of others, as to the possible outcome, but without coming to any conclusion. Apart from his interest in the fate of Essex, most of his concerns are of a homely nature. In spite of his marriage, his thoughts were turning more and more to the other Anne in Salisbury and on 31 October, All-Hallows Eve, he had an alarming dream about her: 'She was all in black and [had] a black cypress on her neck. She told me she lay at Roger Sharp's and there she had left her sucking child; for she gave suck and so came to seek me. We walked together, but I could not have any conference with her because of other company that was with us. It grieved me much, and so she went away I know not how; and with my grief I waked.'

At Michaelmas, though, we have a glimpse of the old Forman. He had ridden down to Gravesend on his own to visit the Webbs at their Kent property, where they entertained him with great hospitality. This he repaid by 'haleking Martha Webb fully and freely'.

After all the years of complaining about poverty, pawning rings and borrowing money off friends and family, by the New Year of 1600 he was openly boasting of how much money he was making, detailing his recent expenditure on clothes and luxuries to prove it, spending £40 on himself and £50 on his wife on clothes alone. He did not describe the dresses he ordered for her, but he had made for himself a new fine purple gown to match his other new apparel and 'my velvet cap, my velvet coat, my velvet breeches, my taffeta cloak, my hat and many other things. And [I] did let my hair and beard grow.' He also purchased another 'swatchel', a fencing sword, with its hangars (the loops which attached it to his belt) made of chased silver. 'I lent out much money on plate and jewels and had many trifles given to me.' Also, to confirm his position in his own eyes and those of others he sat to have his portrait drawn. (This is almost certainly the one of which the Royal College of Physicians has an engraving, since no other is known.)

Among his early new year visitors were, unsurprisingly, Alice Blague and Martha Webb, who must have felt she was now in a somewhat invidious position. Alice was still going to bed with Dean Wood, but also had her eye on Lord Stanwell, and came twice to ask Forman to discover if either man meant her any evil. The answer was that before the end of the month there would be trouble either for her husband or herself, but Forman who, on the whole, was truthful about the outcome of his prophesies, noted that in the event he was wrong and nothing whatsoever happened. Martha Webb wanted to know whether Walsingham cared for her and also if a 'Master Hore' fancied her. Money must have been no object to these women, for within days Alice Blague was back demanding to know if Dean Wood really loved her *only* and bringing with her a list of his other loves to discover if they might come between her and the object of her affection. Next she asked Forman if he thought she should have a child by Wood, and even if there was anything between him and her supposed best friend, Martha Webb. Simon received 26s 8d for these last two consultations and Alice promised him £5 more if he could ensure, by the use of magic, that Wood would give his heart to her alone.

On 7 January 1600, after a substantial gap, Emilia Lanier's name appeared in the casebooks, although the way Forman writes about her suggests that their on-and-off relationship had continued for at least some time after his last recorded visit. In an earlier, undated, note in Latin, he had reminded himself to cast to see how much truth there was in 'Lanier's tales of invoking spirits' and, if she had really succeeded in doing so, whether or not the spirit raised was an incubus. Also, presumably referring to their affair, he wanted to know 'whether I shall end it or no'. But by the time of her last communication there must have been a substantial cooling off, for he now cast to know 'why Mistress Lanier has sent for me; what will follow and whether she intendeth any more villainy'. He does not tell us the result and he never refers to her again.

Emilia Lanier did well enough without his advice and proved to be a tough survivor. Whether or not she really was the Dark Lady, within a few weeks of the publication of Shakespeare's Sonnets in 1611, she had a book of her own verse 'published by Richard Bowen to be sold at his shop in St. Paul's Churchyard'. It was printed by Valentine Simms, the printer of a number of the Shakespeare Quartos. Emilia, her children now grown up and her husband dead, had taken to writing poetry. She soon managed to acquire a substantial list of distinguished patrons including Queen Anne, wife to James I, and the Countesses of Kent, Cumberland, Suffolk and Dorset. The quality of the poetry rarely rises above the pedestrian, but she has a legitimate claim to be an early feminist versifier, for in several poems she set out to defend the reputations of women whom she considered history had treated unfairly, starting at the beginning with Eve and the apple and taking in other supposed villains such as Sisera, who killed Jael, Judith, who did the same for Holofernes, and Jezebel. A few lines suffice to give a flavour:

> But surely Adam cannot be excused.
> Her fault, though great, yet he was most to blame;
> What weakness offered, strength might have refused,
> Being Lord of All, the greater was his shame:
> Although the serpent's craft had her abused,
> God's Holy Word all his actions frame,
> For he was Lord and King of all the earth,
> Before poor Eve had either life or breath.

Emilia outlived Shakespeare, Simon Forman and the whole lot of them, finally dying at the age of nearly eighty after the end of the Civil War.

In February Frances Pranell was also back. She was much sought after and, as well as consulting Simon on minor medical problems, wanted to tell him all about her many suitors and ask his advice. She still hankered after Southampton in spite of the facts: not only was he married, but rumours of his love affair with Piers Edmund in Ireland were circulating at Court. In a note on 2 March Simon writes: 'I told her that she shall marry again once more before she enjoy Southampton . . . that she should stay unmarried till Midsummer be past, for it seemeth about 22 May next she will contract or marry herself to somebody. Some fret [bad] thing will fall out between Southampton and his wife. He or his wife will be in peril of death before Midsummer. She [Frances] shall do well. It seems either he or his wife will die.'[6] Again this proved to be untrue.

Beside this, in the same folio, is a letter from her written in the most fine and readable sloping hand, in which she addresses Forman as 'Father', as did a number of well-heeled young women almost as if he were their priest. On it he wrote 'this letter came this 2 March 1600':

Father, how much I think myself beholding unto you I cannot express. Notwithstanding, I do exceedingly desire to speak to you concerning the conference I lately had with you, entreating you, as ever you will pleasure me, to deal as effectually in those things then mentioned as possibly you can – that at your coming to me (which I hope you will hasten with all convenient speed) I may be assured of the event of all things. Whether they fall out sinisterly or prosperously I do not greatly care, so that I may be ascertained of the truth: the which, in regard of the great trust I repose in you, I doubt not but you will effect according to my desire. Thus, my kind considerations being remembered unto you, in haste I leave you – your loving daughter, Frances.

Beside her signature Simon wrote the word 'Howard', after which there is a postscript. 'I pray you send me word by this bearer when your best leisure will serve you to come to me, and in the meantime use such means that I may at your coming be certified of every thing at large.'

Frances was unable to make up her mind. For some time she was seriously considering Sir William Evers, he who had been so badly wounded in the border feud, but Simon saw little point in her encouraging him for 'he shall marry a widow somewhat elderly, a kind, soft, honest woman, somewhat fat and very rich. But he shall not marry Frances!' However, Evers did not give up hope and was still in the running towards the end of the year, by which time Frances had received a proposal from the Earl of Hertford. So, should she marry the earl? If she did, would she be able to give him a child? And how then should she deal with William Evers, who still wanted her?

Hertford was unattractive, had already been married twice and had a bad reputation where women were concerned, but he had two overwhelming attractions for the practical Frances: he could make her a countess and he was much older than she was and so likely to die first, leaving her free once again. She chose Hertford. It soon became common knowledge, John Chamberlain, the ubiquitous letter writer, reporting: 'Mistress Pranell is like to make a wide stride from that she was, to be Countess of Hertford; the world says they be assured already, if not married.' The wedding took place secretly and after it the prebendary of Westminster, who had officiated at it, was suspended by Archbishop Whitgift for performing it without licence or having had the banns called, and for allowing it in a place other than a proper church.[7]

Her marriage to Hertford did, however, have one casualty: one ardent suitor, Sir George Rodney of Somerset, went clean off his head with grief and as a result 'his brains were not able to bear the burden, but have played bankrupt and left him raving'. He then wrote Frances a love song in his own blood before running himself on to his sword.[8] It surprised no one that the marriage was unhappy and Frances continued to consult Simon, comforted by his forecasts that a brilliant future still lay ahead of her. In this he was proved right for on Hertford's death she made a truly spectacular match and married the Duke of Lennox.

Amid the welter of astrological questions and tales of love, marriage and adultery, Forman was also constantly treating those who needed his medical expertise for cases of scrofula, dropsy, rheumatism, bad chests, eye infections, headaches (which could be anything from eye strain to a brain tumour), mysterious stomach pains, ulcers, cancerous lumps and ordinary abscesses, troubles in the reins, stones, fevers, epilepsy, anaemia, the pox, childhood illnesses and much more. Most of his patients were grateful for his advice and ministrations and paid him well, although he continued to treat the poor for little or nothing. It was not unknown for Elizabethan physicians to find themselves faced with dissatisfied patients demanding their money back, but if his records are to be believed this happened to him only rarely. One example was Martha Webb, who came back to complain after he had treated her William for 'pains in the buttocks and hips, swelling ankles and the clap'. Martha, annoyed, questioned Simon closely as to the last complaint, though it is not clear whether this was because she had not known until then that her husband had contracted gonorrhoea or because Simon had failed to cure it.

In his notes over the years he often refers to visits to the theatre, although it was not until later, in his 'Book of Plaies', that he gave any details of what he saw. He does recount that in March 1600 he went to the playhouse to see 'the play of *Sir John Oldcastle*'. This must have been at the Rose, for it was performed by the Lord Admiral's Men and appears in the list of productions in Henslowe's diaries for that period. The text of the play, which is no masterpiece, still exists. Notoriety surrounds it, for when Shakespeare first invented the character of Falstaff he called his fat knight 'Sir John Oldcastle' which promptly brought down on his head the wrath of Lord Cobham, one of whose ancestors was a John Oldcastle who had been executed during the reign of Henry IV for supporting Owen Glendower's rebellion against the English. Shakespeare may even have known this, for the original Oldcastle, when brought to trial, admitted to having lived a life of pride, gluttony and lechery and having been cast off by the king, with whom at one time he had been very close.

Sir John Oldcastle has little to do with history and everything to do with the popularity of Falstaff and the *Henry IV* plays, which was so great that Henslowe paid a number of writers to collaborate on a project aimed at cashing in on the success of Shakespeare's creation with a similar play of their own but this time using the character's original name. The entry in the accounts for the Rose reads:

received Thomas Downton, of Philip Henslowe, to pay Mr Monday, Mr Drayton [Michael Drayton, the poet], Mr Wilson and Mr Hathway for the first part of the *Lyfe of Sir John Ouldcasstel* and in earnest of the second part for the use of the company ten pounds, I say received.

This play also upset those in high places, not least Sir Robert Cecil, who was Cobham's brother-in-law and considered Oldcastle to have been in reality a misjudged Protestant martyr. He was still incensed by the portrait of Oldcastle, thinly disguised as Shakespeare's bragging ale-swilling monster, which was a source of much glee to Essex and his followers. Essex wrote to a friend that 'Cecil's sister is married to Sir John Falstaff' and even while he was away on his fatal venture in Ireland, his wife wrote to him: 'All the news I can send you that I think will make you merry is that I read in a letter from London that Sir John Falstaff is, by his mistress Dame Pintpot, made father of a goodly miller's thumb, a boy that's all head and very little body; but this is secret.' As a result of all this Shakespeare, worried that the new play would reflect badly on him, inserted on the last page of the printed first quarto of his own *Henry IV, Part 2* the words 'For Oldcastle died a martyr and this is not the man', to distinguish it from the other play.

Forman must have gone to the performance on his own, for afterwards he picked up an Ann Sedgwick, 'alias Catlyn', whom he haleked in Aldersgate Street, 'right up against the Cock'. In the first few weeks of his marriage he admitted to bedding several women, but this did not prevent his being suspicious of his wife and seeing a lover lurking behind every door. Four days after he was with Ann Sedgwick he wrote that 'Ledsome went up to my privy unknown to me' and that afterwards he had a 'conversation' about it with his wife, during which she assured him that nothing untoward had taken place.

He remained unconvinced, but at least had the honesty to record his own inexcusable piece of behaviour. On 9 April he cast 'to know what my wife made at Bestow's when I went to the Royal Exchange and she bid the maid say she was above when I came in. And while I went up she went to call her. Because I liked not her lies and excuses, she began talking peremptory to me with howling and weeping, and would not be quiet until I gave her two or three boxes [blows on the head]. She upbraids me with her friends. It seems that she will be a whore and went out with some other intent. But as yet there is no fact done.'[9] Presumably the last sentence means that she had not slept with anyone else.

A few days afterwards news reached him that his old love, Anne Walworth, was failing fast 'of a dropsy'. The term 'dropsy' was used until well into the twentieth century to describe swelling of the limbs or abdomen, a condition which could have been caused by any number of diseases. She sent a pathetic letter to him, by John Evans of Wilton, asking for a medicine 'for her sickness, life or death' and Forman gave him an elixir made from sage, marjoram, elderbuds, ashbuds, berberis, liquorice, aniseed, aloes and juniper berries. It was to no avail and she died on 8 May. He felt her loss keenly, for, in spite of everything that had happened to both of them during the years between, he had never quite broken the emotional ties that bound them. Anne Walworth's death was not the only one that touched him, for during 1600 he lost first his brother John and then, in December, Robert, who had been closest to him. It was time to take stock.

Throughout 1600 he was busy writing his own 'books' and making copies of others. 'I wrote out two books of *De Arte Memoratus* of Apollonius Niger, drawn with gold, of the seven liberal sciences and also copied out the four books of *Stenographia* and divers other books.' In November he was summoned once more by the College of Physicians to attend them at their hall in Knightrider Street, but this time he felt so confident of his status and reputation that he simply refused to go 'and sent them a letter' instead, presumably setting out why he did not choose to obey.

Although he no longer feared the College, he was becoming increasingly tired of the continual battles and so decided to start looking for a substantial property south of the river, which would be outside its jurisdiction altogether, preferably a house with land attached where he could grow his own herbs. Possibly too the Stone House and Billingsgate now held too many memories.

13

An Eventful Year

It was March 1601 before the Formans found a house in Lambeth which suited Simon's purposes, so he found himself caught up, if only on the sidelines, in the dramatic events in the City which culminated in the Essex Rebellion in February. During this time he and those who sought him out turned to astrology in a feverish attempt to know the outcome.[1]

The special commission had charged Essex with being party to 'a disreputable and dishonourable treaty with the Earl of Tyrone' and he remained under house arrest, forbidden to see anyone, until his wife, dressed in black and almost straight from childbed, was granted an audience with the queen at which she begged to see her husband. Elizabeth relented and gradually Essex was also allowed other visitors. Soon crude graffiti referring to Robert Cecil appeared on walls, possibly at his foolish instigation. Worse still, a pamphlet was published referring to Shakespeare's play, *Richard II*, stressing the significance of the king's deposition, the subsequent triumph of Henry IV and emphasising for good measure that Devereux women had twice married Plantagenet princes. When this was shown to the queen, she commented acidly that she did not need to have the inference pointed out.

For months Essex's friends lobbied for his release while Elizabeth agonised over what action she should take. She had been bitterly hurt. At a wedding party for Lord Herbert at which she was present, eight of her maids of honour, wearing dresses of cloth-of-silver and carnation taffeta, danced a masque before her. Foremost in the troop was Mary Fitton, who, when asked which of the virtues she represented, replied, 'Affection.' 'Affection,' returned Elizabeth, 'affection's false!'

Eventually in June 1600, she reluctantly agreed to Essex leaving his London house so long as he did not come back to Court. He immediately pleaded to be allowed to see her again, for he was running short of money: when he had been in the queen's high favour, she had allowed him the tax revenue on all sweet wine coming into the country and the licence was now up for renewal. She refused his request, telling her courtiers that 'an unruly beast needs to be starved of its provender'. When the news of her decision reached Essex to all intents and purposes he signed his own death warrant, yelling for all to hear that 'the Queen's conditions are as crooked as her carcass'. She never forgave him and her advisers, aware that time was now on their side, waited their opportunity.

It came soon enough. By the autumn, encouraged by Southampton, Essex embarked on a plot to remove all power from the queen. This entailed organising a coup during which he would capture her, force her to dismiss his enemies, summon a new parliament and make her agree to his running the country. To this end he sent Simon's wily borderer friend Sir William Evers to Edinburgh in an attempt to gain the support of King James, with instructions to report back as soon as possible. The news that Evers had been seen at the Court in Edinburgh politicking on Essex's behalf reached London before he did. On his return Evers was immediately put under house arrest and could count himself fortunate that he was released some weeks later without any charges being brought against him. He would hardly have found himself alone as he mingled with the crowds who thronged Holyrood Palace, for the Scottish Court was now awash with English hopefuls jockeying for position, foremost among them Sir Robert Cecil's own envoys, who were busily assuring the king that their master would be indispensable when James ascended the throne of England.

Maybe Forman had some wind of what was in the air from Evers, for in January 1601, before the real trouble began, he was again referring in his notes to the omens that had preceded Essex setting off for Ireland. Towards the end of the month he was also drawing figures in an attempt to know what was likely to happen to him in the immediate future.

The coup was set for 8 February. The day before, Essex and his confederates arranged for a special performance of *Richard II* to be performed by the Lord Chamberlain's Men at the Globe, with Richard Burbage in the lead. Obviously unaware of the implications, Burbage had agreed to Essex's request, not least because the actors were offered 'forty shillings more than ordinary' to play the 'play of the deposing and killing of King Richard II'. Burbage's decision, made in all good faith, almost proved a disaster. When news of the performance reached the queen she reacted famously with the words, 'I am Richard II, know ye not that?' The players found themselves in deep trouble and were extremely fortunate they had a powerful patron to appeal on their behalf as they stared ruin in the face. In the event they were let off, but it was the nearest Shakespeare ever came to imprisonment for political reasons and his play was never performed again during Elizabeth's lifetime.

Whether it was because they learned of the rapturous response of the audience or because they had been watching the earl's every move and were ready to act, the Privy Council summoned Essex to appear before them immediately. He did not go. Early on the morning of 8 February he marched on Whitehall at the head of 300 'swordsmen', despite the attempts of older and wiser friends to prevent him. Recalling his triumphant ride through London on his way to Ireland, he had imagined the streets would be thronged with people cheering him on, many of them rushing to join him. But he had totally misjudged the situation. 'There was not,' wrote Sir Francis Bacon, 'in so populous a city where he thought himself held so dear, one man from the chiefest citizen to the meanest artificer or apprentice that armed with him.'

This time he rode through streets which were empty except for knots of worried people standing at street corners to watch his passing in silence. Only then, when it was too late, did he realise the full consequences of his folly and after pausing at the sheriff's house to change his shirt, he turned for home. By this time the queen's messengers were riding far and wide proclaiming him a traitor. Accompanied by Southampton, he took to the river and was rowed back to his house, which he barred and bolted in expectation of a siege. As darkness fell, Lord Nottingham and Sir Henry Sydney landed at the nearby water steps accompanied by a troop of soldiers and demanded that the two young earls surrender immediately. Essex replied that he would only do so if he could see the queen. Nottingham's response was to send for ordnance and gunpowder and give him an ultimatum: if they did not surrender, then Essex had an hour to get his wife, her sister and her children out of the house, after which he would blow it up. Essex and Southampton capitulated.

Rumours of rebellion and of bands of armed men had been sweeping the City since the crack of dawn and by first light Forman was casting (taking care to do so in Latin) to know, first, what the outcome would be and next, if the earl did not succeed and should be found guilty of treason, the ultimate fate his enemies had in store for him.[2] Later Forman added: 'he was taken in his house the following night and taken to the Tower'. The next day he asked the stars to know 'whether the Lord Essex will be executed: life or death'. The answer seems to suggest he might only be imprisoned.

On 18 February Frances, now Countess of Hertford, threw caution to the winds and rushed round to Simon, accompanied by her friend Frances Bevill, desperate to know 'whether Essex and Southampton will live or die'. Dissatisfied with the 'response' to his question on her behalf and aware that her real concern was for Southampton, he cast again on 20 February specifically to discover whether or not Southampton would go to the block and then, two days later, to know if 'Essex will live or die'. The answer to all these queries was 'they shall not die but live in prison'.

This was to prove only 50 per cent accurate. The two men were tried by their peers and Southampton was sent to the Tower and remained there until James came to the throne two years later. Essex was shown no such mercy. He and six of his followers were sentenced to death, the executions being carried out on 25 February. As might be expected from one who had never lacked panache, he went to his death beautifully dressed and with great dignity and courage. He was just thirty-three years old. On the morning of his execution the queen was in her chamber playing the virginals, attended by a group of courtiers including Sir Walter Ralegh. A messenger entered and on one knee informed her that the sentence had been carried out. Nobody spoke. Then the queen turned again to her instrument and took up the melody at exactly the point where she had left off. Forman noted, 'Essex was beheaded this day at 7.30 a.m.' Nothing in his stars was to warn Forman of the notoriety which he would suffer for centuries, thanks to a later decision to allow Essex's son to inherit his father's estate and marry another, more notorious, Frances Howard.

Whether the excitement of the times caused an upsurge in his sexual drive or variety increased his appetite, for whatever reason, during the early weeks of 1601 Forman was regularly having sex with his wife, bedding her maid, Frances Hill, and also embarked on a lengthy liaison with Anne Condwell, who from then on appears so regularly in the 'halek' notes that she might be said to be his mistress. On the morning of 27 January both Annes, his wife and Mistress Condwell, came and told him that they had dreamed they were pregnant by him and although he was complaining of a very sore throat and a bad cold, it did not prevent his making love again to Anne Condwell later that morning and his wife at ten p.m. the same evening.

As to his medical practice, he was continuing to attract the rich and powerful, one of whom was Lady Norris, whom he had first treated some three years earlier when she was twenty-four for what appears to have been the results of a botched abortion. She had sent for him using as an alias the name of her maid, Bridget Kingsmill. Simon wrote: 'She hath not been well a long time. She took it for childbed by some ointment or other thing that she did put into her quent, which did infect and envenom her blood. She hath a truckling now in her flesh like the stinging of nettles, and a rising blood in her lungs, periplomania, much gravel in the reins, fearfulness and trembling ... she is an enemy to herself and will not be ruled; not well in her matrix, a venomous humour so that she is often in great pain.'[3] Lady Norris had friends in high places for she was Sir Robert Cecil's niece, being the daughter of the Earl of Oxford who had married Cecil's sister. Oxford had quickly run through his fortune and Cecil's father, Lord Burleigh, had taken his daughter and granddaughter into his household to save them from penury, proudly providing the young woman with a huge dowry of £8,500. She had plenty of money, seems to have 'enjoyed' ill health and was always consulting one physician or another and taking pills and potions, but there was obviously nothing really wrong with her for she lived to a ripe old age.

Another high-born client, Gilbert Talbot, Earl of Shrewsbury, came to Forman to have his urine tested and he diagnosed 'cold phlegm, melancholy in the stomach, full of cold humours'. Talbot was married to Bess of Hardwick's daughter, a prominent Catholic recusant. A trawl through Forman's clientele shows that he had a number of well-known recusant families on his books, the Mores, Mullinses, Cornwallises, Digbys, Fortescues and Arundells.[4] This is interesting because many professional people were careful to steer clear of any involvement with Catholics, but Forman never did, possibly because he was old enough to remember attending mass as a child and also because he knew and understood the problems they faced through his involvement with Avisa Allen. The 'More' who consulted him was the grandson of the great Sir Thomas More, who was executed by Henry VIII. Cressacre More was twenty-nine the first time he came to Simon with 'pain in his stomach, much wind and is anxious'. He was given a draught to put him right.

The bedrock of Forman's practice, though, was still the ordinary people of London, the larger proportion being female. Among a number of women who consulted him in May was a 'Mistress Elizabeth Burbage', aged thirty-two, who came seeking relief for problems she was having with her pregnancy.[5] Was she wife to Richard Burbage? It has not been possible to prove either way, although she was about the right age and we know from the casebooks that he was consulted by players. Later in the year another Burbage, Humphrey, came for some medicine to purge him and a note written in the early part of 1601 records that a player, Francis George, 'was robbed by one Towne, another player; he at last confessed and made recompense though not in goods'. Thomas Towne was one of the Lord Admiral's Men and played at the Rose.[6]

Another four women consulted him that May, all on the same day. Joan Lylly, aged forty-five, was 'benumbed in her arms and shoulders and stopped up in the stomach and bowel'. Simon told her this would last ten days and gave her a purge. Mary Cock of the Worshipful Company of Clothmakers, aged twenty-six, was suffering from pain in her left breast and she told him of a woman she knew who 'had a wolfe in her breste', making it very hard with a great round lump, and that 'the pacient was in marvellous pain'. Possibly the lump had been lanced, for the person who was 'dressing' her wound had discovered 'a worme ded in her brest, longe and small, and a small taill and brod [sic] flat head'. Sara Craste, also aged twenty-six, was suffering from the green sickness and problems with her 'courses', which were irregular. Simon also gave her a purge, while Sara Burns aged thirty-four, who lived in Blackfriars, had a swollen leg, due, Simon told her, 'to an imposthume'.[7]

After weeks of searching, Forman had finally found what he considered to be a suitable property in Lambeth, but it took him some time to negotiate an acceptable lease with the owner, a Master Prat, of whom he took a dim view. The deal was concluded on 16 March, and an agreement signed for a rental of £20 a year when he received the key ten days later. One of the attractions was that the house had not only a sizeable garden but also an orchard with a wide variety of fruit trees, apples, plums, 'wards', quinces, pears and 'apricocks', which suggests it must have been very sheltered. He thought he might make a profit from selling much of the fruit, 'except for the apricocks', which he wanted for himself. The house brought with it grazing rights on the common.

As soon as he received the key, he began transferring goods and furniture over the river, but he and his wife did not move in for some time as he was having substantial work carried out on the property, for which he paid out '13s. 4d. to carpenters, five days apiece at 16d.; 3s. and 9s. [respectively] to a tiler and joiner; 2s. for 900 lath nails' and a further indecipherable sum for boards, laths and more nails. He also purchased thirty-two yards of 'dornix', heavy woollen cloth, for curtains and carpets. The cost of sending two lots of goods to Lambeth by water was 9s. Further proof that they were still in the Stone House as late as May is that he sent in a bill to the incoming tenant: '12s for twelve yards of wainscot' as well as sums to be negotiated for 'a joined door and partition and seventy-two yards of painted cloth in the two lower rooms'.[8]

In fact he kept a toehold in Stone House until midsummer before finally severing all connection with it in what was to be his final move. Scarcely had he had time to enjoy his new curtains and his orchard than the College of Physicians struck again, demanding his immediate presence in Knightrider Street. Secure now in Lambeth, he refused and on 25 June a committee of sixteen censors met without him. A secretary's report records first that the committee approved all statutes up to date and added several more dealing with punishments and morals. It then turned its attention to the matter in hand:

Among the many unlearned and unlawful practisioners lurking in many corners of this City, were protected from the ordinary course of our laws partly because of the very obscurity of the place and partly by the Privileges of that See wherein they have taken shelter, was one impostor by the name Forman who is now in the precincts of Lambeth. Here, just as if he were in harbour, he sailed with great joy, pleasure and complete safety so none of our officials could arrest him.

153

It was therefore decided that a humble letter of petition should be written to the most reverend Archbishop of Canterbury to obtain his approval in order that by these pleas, all those taking cover in the shadows might be routed from their hiding places.[9]

There follows a copy of the letter sent to Archbishop Whitgift: 'To the most Reverend, our most singular good lord, the Archbishop of Canterbury's Grace':

Maie it please your Grace to be advertised that one, Simon Forman, an Intruder to the Profession of Physick that hath of a long time in this Citie, as well as to the great prejudice of our privileges, as also to the intollerable abuse of her Majesty's subjects, been a great Practisioner in the same. Making a deceitful shew and colour to the Ignorant People, that his skill is more than Ordinary, depending upon the speculation and insight of Nativities and Astrology, thereby miserably demeaning the Innocence of such simple mynded people as resort unto him for Councell.

For redress, they told him, they had brought Forman before their committee on numerous occasions and, having made 'good and sufficienty tryall of his skill', had found him 'exceeding weak and ignorant in most absurd answers'. Therefore, under the powers vested in them they had 'utterly forbidden him' to deal in any further practice of that science in which he had little skill. Yet in spite of that they had now learned that Forman had taken himself off to Lambeth, which was under the archibishop's jurisdiction. Therefore, given the inadequacies of the man, they asked his Grace to allow them to do all possible to prevent his practising. 'And we shall be bound to pray for your Grace's long life, honourable prosperite – and so we most humbly take our leave – 25 June 1601.'[10]

Apart from showing that when they turned from reporting on their meetings in Latin to writing letters in English, both spelling and punctuation were inventive, it also proves how infuriated the censors were at being unable to prevent Simon Forman not only from practising but from daring to become popular and wealthy. Five days later the archbishop replied:

After my very heartie commendacions, Forman neither is, nor shall be countenanced by me; neither doth he deserve yt anyway at my handes. I have heard very ill of him; in so much as I held a meeting to call him by vertue of the Commission Ecclesiasticall for divers misdeameners if any man would have taken upon himself the prosecution of the cause against him. In which mynd I remain still. And therefore use your authorytie in the name of God. My officers shall give their assistaunce, or else they shall be no officers of myne. And so I commit you to the tuytion of Almighty God. From my house at Croydon the 30th June 1601.

Your assurd and loving Friend, Jo. Cantaur.[11]

Forman did not record his thoughts on the previous sessions when he had been hauled before the college authorities: all we have are brief references and complaints, particularly complaints about how his work succouring plague victims during the epidemics of 1592 and 1593 was never recognised; indeed that on their return from comparative safety in the countryside, one of the first things the physicians had done was to summon him before them to demand 'by what authority I had meddled in their precinct'. One remark during an unspecified session particularly galled him. Apparently one of the doctors, to the amusement of the rest, announced that he 'had learned his skill under a hedge', in other words he was a 'hedge doctor', an unskilled country yokel who had picked up his knowledge (or lack of it) from old wives and amateur surgeons.

Once in Lambeth he also felt sufficiently secure to admit that he no longer respected only the philosophy of Galen – which damned him even more in the eyes of the college censors – and went further, informing them that he considered them both ignorant and unenlightened 'in spite of Cambridge and Oxford both'.[12] Indeed he refers to Galen in doggerel:

> For I did judge according to
> The course of heaven and nature:
> And they did judge by the false pulse,
> And the deceitful water.

This was not strictly true because we know he did take careful note of the pulse points and examined patients' urine, though he believed many physicians read too much into 'paltry piss'.

Whitgift's suggestion that he should be brought before an ecclesiastical commission was intriguing as such an examination would have had nothing to do with medical competence but would have concentrated on his morals. He might well have found himself having to answer questions about his sexual adventures, bastard children and Sefton's slanders. In order for Whitgift to set up a formal commission it was necessary, as he told the college, to find a man 'to take upon himself the prosecution of the cause against him'. As no such person was prepared to come forward, the hearing never took place. Balked again, the College served yet another notice on Forman, only to have it ignored, and followed that up by serving him with a writ to appear in court, to which Forman promptly entered a counter charge. They had reached stalemate.

A few months after settling in Lambeth he took the opportunity of a prolonged visit by his in-laws and their friends to pay some calls out of town, from which he returned complaining of the unprofitability of the journeys, on one of which he had managed to lose his stockings, nightcap-band, garters and hose (one wonders in what situation he took them off), as well as the scabbard of his sword and an almanac. He took his bad temper out on his unfortunate servants – 'very disobedient and negligent' – and on his wife for her 'folly and negligence'.

The year ended as it had begun, with drama, albeit a more immediately personal one. Frances, Countess of Hertford, had introduced him to her husband, the earl, and his sister, Lady Mary. She had called to ask him if there was any sign of her having conceived a child and told him she was not finding life with the earl at all enjoyable, not least because, to keep her out of mischief, he regularly took her away and left her in his country house. Appeals to Lady Mary to ask the earl to let her spend more time in London had fallen on deaf ears.[13] Indeed, when she complained, her husband never hesitated to remind her of her obligations with the words 'Frank, how long is it since thou wert only married to Pranell?'

However, both earl and countess were at their fine London house when they invited Forman to a supper early one Sunday. He was on his way home, fortunately accompanied by his servant, when he was set on in the street by a 'Captain Hammond', and forced to fight for his life 'or we were both like to have been killed'. He gave no explanation as to why 'Captain

Hammond' attacked him, whether it was over a woman, an old quarrel or simply because the man was drunk, any of which was likely.

There is a single paragraph entry for 1602 in Forman's diary, after which it ends abruptly. The events chronicled, like those at the end of the previous year, are of a trivial nature: how his pigeons were eaten by rats, the expense of keeping horses, how he hit his right knee against a doorpost on his way out, notes on one or two patients and how his household had kept Christmas in Lambeth. Nothing else. It is hard to believe this was all he considered worth recording in a year which might well have ended in personal disaster, and it is a sad loss, for up to this point the diary provides an essential, if brief, guide to what was happening in his life. Nor, of even more significance, are there any more casebooks. If these do still exist their whereabouts have not been discovered, but Forman would not have stopped keeping case notes even if he no longer bothered with his diary. One strong possibility is that they were destroyed after his death, along with a number of other personal documents and letters, either by Anne Turner acting as intermediary of Frances, Countess of Essex, or by his widow on the orders of the countess. In any event from this point on Forman's life and times are chronicled in notes, often added to other jottings on topics he was writing about.

14

Strange Happenings in Plymouth

Leaving the Stone House after so many years and settling into the new one, took up much of Forman's time. The Elizabethans appear to have had an obsession with buried treasure and Forman's papers contain many a request for castings by hopefuls to see if gold or jewels were hidden under the floorboards or buried in their gardens. Sometimes the result (if vague) was sufficiently encouraging for them to rip up the parlour floor and set to with a spade, but there is no record of any booty being found. Forman himself was no exception and the move to Lambeth prompted him for some time to try and discover if there might be treasure buried there, 'to know what is hid, whether it may be found or no, of what value, whether newly hid, whole or diminished'. Like all the others, he was to be disappointed.

Living south of the river made it easier for him to visit the playhouses, the Rose, Globe and Swan all being within a stone's throw of each other, and he gives an account of a play called *Cox of Cullompton* by John Day and William Haughton. Both wrote for Henslowe and a note in Henslowe's diary records that they were paid twenty shillings each for their drama, *Cox of Collumpton or the Tragedy of John Cox*. The play was one of a popular genre, a kind of Elizabethan or Jacobean drama-documentary based around a tragic death or a real-life notorious murder, *A Woman Killed with Kindness*, *A Yorkshire Tragedy* and *The Witch of Edmonton* being prime examples.[1]

The plot suggests as much. Master Cox has three sons, Henry, Peter and John. On St Mark's Day Cox shoots his uncle in order to get his land for the family, which he succeeds in doing. Seven years later retribution strikes when Cox himself is shot by a man called Jarvis, after which Peter and John drown Henry before coming to sticky ends themselves. Simon often added his own thoughts on what he thought was the moral of a play and he does so in this case, although it seems to have little relevance to the plot as he describes it: 'Nota: Remember how Mr. Hammond's son slew his father, who begged for mercy, which was denied him. He foretold that his son should betray himself by laughing and so he did, and was executed for it.'[2]

Forman had now achieved almost all he had set out to do: he had established himself as a popular and respected physician and astrologer with a lucrative practice; he had a fine house, comfortably furnished; and he had a wife. But he was becoming increasingly concerned that there was still no child of the marriage, for on the face of it there should have been no problem. In spite of being in his forties, he had no reason to believe that he was not still fertile, his wife was young and healthy and they made love frequently. As time passed he began to consider the possibility of Joshua coming to live with them in Lambeth now that his mother was dead and to his great satisfaction, early in the summer of 1602, the boy was persuaded to do so. He was sixteen when his mother died, quite old enough to have a trade of his own, but if he had one then we are not told what it was. Nor do we know if Ralph Walworth had known all along that Joshua was not his child or had only learned of it on his wife's death.

But by far the most dramatic events of Forman's year, which were to result in serious accusations that he was either a proscribed Catholic priest or a black magician, took place outside London altogether. It was a strange interlude. That year the queen's ministers had decided that one last great effort should be made to intercept and capture a Spanish plate fleet. To that end a squadron of ships, based in Plymouth, was sent to sea under the command of Sir Richard Leveson. One of Leveson's lesser claims to fame is that he was the final protector of Mary Fitton, that red-headed contender for the Dark Lady who had danced before the queen in the role of 'Affection'. She had been passed from bed to bed around the Court, finally arriving in Leveson's bed from that of the young Earl of Pembroke.

Leveson chose as his vice-admiral no other than Forman's old friend, Sir

William Monson, who called on Forman on 26 February with news of the appointment and to have his horoscope cast. Between then and 3 March, when he left London, he visited Forman several times, anxious to know whether the venture would succeed and if he would come safely home. He arrived in Plymouth to discover that Leveson had already sailed, leaving orders that Monson should await the arrival of a Dutch squadron which was to rendezvous with Leveson at sea before the attack was made. But the Dutch contingent was late, the plate fleet was sighted before it arrived and Leveson found himself without sufficient firepower to attack the heavily armed guard ships escorting those carrying the treasure. As a result the venture, like that to the Azores, failed.

Monson did not return empty-handed, however, for he told Forman that 'he took a Hamburger and a Brazilman and sent them into Plymouth at the end of May'. He also attacked an East Indian carrack, laden with exotic goods, under the guns of the very Portuguese castle in which he had been held prisoner years earlier. According to Forman, the ship was 'worth £300,000 at least; her worst commodity was callico and pepper. He got great credit thereby, came to London 4 July and went to Court.'[3] No sooner had he done so than he was sent back to sea again, for the government, still expecting a possible Spanish landing in Ireland, ordered a number of vessels out on watch and Monson spent the early weeks of a poor summer patrolling the Spanish coast off Corunna.

The next time he docked in Plymouth, he sent word urgently to Forman in Lambeth, asking him to cast his horoscope to discover whether or not he should go back to sea yet once more 'with those eight vessels of the Queen's fleet'. Forman sent back a gloomy forecast. The first casting showed that if Monson did put to sea he would be 'in danger of being betrayed by one that goes with him'. The second was even worse, that at first he would be favoured 'of the prince but after that, treachery wrought'.

Deeply superstitious as he was, this made Monson so fearful for his safety on land and sea that he despatched an urgent messenger to Forman begging him to come to Plymouth in person, for he needed his protection and advice. Forman readily agreed. He enjoyed trips away from home and no doubt the prospect of some sea air and a few weeks away from London and its stinking summer streets and river was enticing, so he set off straight away, leaving his wife behind in Lambeth entertaining yet more of her many relatives.

Monson found accommodation for his friend over a goldsmith's shop in what is now the Barbican area of Plymouth. The shop was owned by a William Bentley, but soon after Forman moved in Bentley began to harbour suspicions about the occupation of his paying guest, in spite of his connection with Monson and appearance of wealth. (Forman had travelled to the West Country in some style, taking with him not only clothes, salves and medications, but books and some papers on which he had written various calculations; all this packed into a small wooden chest and a large bag or portmanteau.)

Monson made it known that his friend from London was a physician and astrologer and soon Simon was being consulted by local people, particularly those wanting him to cast their horoscopes. He became so popular that on several occasions clients were more or less queuing up in his room for a consultation and this, combined with the air of mystery with which he surrounded himself, started the wild rumours which soon began to circulate, which were then fuelled by the ramblings of a simple-minded lad who had seen what was going on and was convinced he had come across a Catholic priest or Jesuit conducting an illegal mass. Meanwhile, the landlord was putting it about that he had a conjuror or practitioner of black magic living over the shop.

The news spread round the docks, quaysides and ships finally reaching the ears of William Stilling (who spelled his name 'Stallenge'), the Queen's Victualler and Official of Customs in Plymouth, who wrote in a panic to Sir Robert Cecil, in his capacity as Secretary of State to the Privy Council:

From William Stallenge to Sir Robert Cecil:
On information given that on Friday last there was a Mass or the like exercises used in this town, at the house of William Bentlie, a goldsmith, whereat were present about six persons, in a chamber of the said house, taken at the request of Sir William Monson by one Simon Foarman [*sic*], whose dwelling, he says, is at Lambeth by London: on Sunday last, the Mayor sent to search the said house and in the said Foarman's chamber caused to be opened a chest and after, in his house, in my presence, a portmantey, wherein were found certain wicked books of conjuration, and some calculations [on] what shall become of Her Majesty's ships in this service, and at the end of

one of his books, the form of an oath, a copy whereof is enclosed. The Mayor has bound Foarman to appear before the judges in Exeter, but what information will be given against him I do not know for Sir William much favours him. The matter here by many is thought very dangerous and I can hardly have a good conceit thereof, and yet dare not condemn any – Plymouth 10 August 1602.[4]

According to Stilling, the persons present in Simon's chamber took an oath: 'I swear by God the Father, the Son and the Holy Ghost, three persons and one God in Trinity, and by all the powers of God and by all his Works, and by all the Holy contents of this book, and as I hope to be saved at the dreadful Day of Judgement, and by the way that my soul shall go, that I will never bewray [betray] of, or in this counsel, of words or matter important that shall be told me of, or by thee, during my life, but will be true and trusty to thee any more.' There follow a few more lines in cipher.

On receiving the letter Cecil must have written straight back to Stilling, ordering him to see to it that the dangerous Simon Forman leave Plymouth at once and that no one should have anything more to do with him, as the next piece of correspondence is from Monson himself and is dated only '1602'. It is a letter in which he gives, at some length, his own version of what took place and also, it must be said, unashamedly seeks to distance himself from his friend to ensure that no hint of scandal sticks to him – few people hoping for further preferment would risk tangling with the Secretary of State to the Privy Council.

'I received a message by Sir Richard Leveson from your Honour, that I shall not countenance a man in Plymouth suspected to be a conjuror,' he wrote. 'There was an accident happened, which I will deliver truly, and then you may judge how like I was to have been abused by the folly of the Mayor, if by mere fortune I had not prevented it.' He had, he explained, recently taken a youth into his service who had become so disturbed by the 'extremity of the calendar' (presumably a reference to the phases of the moon), that he had to be confined in a 'dark chamber'. One morning, when the rest of the servants were out, the lad managed to escape through the chamber window, and ran to a friend in the town to tell him that the previous day, at five in the afternoon, he had been present in a house where 'the supposed conjuror' had been celebrating the mass, along with six others, all disguised. The lad's friend, 'having as little wit as the mad body', immediately informed the mayor. The mayor at once sent a message to Monson demanding he produce the youth, to which Monson replied that the boy was mad, and asked the mayor to pardon any complaint made against him caused by his behaviour.

Next the mayor ordered the house where the incident was alleged to have taken place to be searched, especially the rooms of 'the suspected man'. Those searching found there two books, a 'piece of paper touching diseases', and another, reporting the success of one of the queen's ships, 'with the name of one, Stephen, unto it, a sailor that was to go on that same ship'. 'The man', hearing that his rooms had been searched, went to complain to the mayor, who promptly put in him the city gaol until he could prove where he was on the day the mass was supposed to have been said. 'Hearing by chance how my name was used,' continued Monson, ingenuously,

> I went at once to the Mayor and was shown the youth's confession. I told him how unlike it was any such thing could be, for that the time of day was against the use of Masses to be said and for mine own purgation, I protested that I had never been in that house in my life; that all the men in the fleet could witness I was aboard that day from one o'clock until eight at night; that the boy was mad could be proved by half the town, and, that he was locked up all that day, my servants and the folks of the house could testify.

When the mayor heard 'these evident proofs', he recalled that there was no such chamber in the house where the boy was supposed to have seen Monson, and realising his error,

> was sorry and would have delivered me the boy and his confession, which I refused to take, but wished that the boy be kept that night with a watch to observe his humour, whether he was mad or no, that all persons suspected to favour a Mass in the town might be examined, and that the man [Forman] which by name was reported by the boy to be there, might be offered his oath of supremacy, and enquiry might be made where he had been to church. All this was

163

done, the boy was found by his keepers to be mad, and all to proceed
out of an idle brain.

The mayor, being unused to such dramatic events, then asked Monson's
opinion as to what he should do about the man's books and papers.
Monson advised him that if they had anything to do with religion or state
affairs, then he should bind Forman over to answer it before the High
Commissioners, and, if he could find no friends to be bound for him, to
keep his money in deposit, 'which the Mayor told me was fifty shillings
found in his chest. What the books imported, I know not, but it is like to
be no great matter, for of the fifty shillings he kept twenty for the
answering of it. My countenancing him was to clear myself who, through
the Mayor's indiscretion, might have been brought to utter discredit.'
He then changes the subject. 'For such intelligence as I received by a
Portigall lately taken, and the Englishmen who brought it home the said
Portigall, I refer you to my other letter. – Sir William Monson, to my
master, from Plymouth.'[5]
So much for friendship. By this time Forman had been treating Monson,
his brother Sir Thomas, and their families for years. Reading this one
would have no idea of how long and well the two had known each other,
how dependent Monson had become on Forman, how it was on his own
urgent request that Forman had gone down to Plymouth in the first place.
He is not even mentioned by name – only as 'the man whose name was
reported by the boy'; as for the astrological and medical books, he dismisses
these with 'what the books imported I know not'. The letter also throws
light on the routine treatment for madness at that time: confinement in
the dark, the therapy inflicted on Malvolio in Shakespeare's *Twelfth Night*.
As to the rest, to be offered 'his oath of supremacy' meant that a
suspected Catholic would be forced to acknowledge on oath that the
queen, not the Pope, was the head of the Church in England (which
Forman would scarcely have found difficult), while the 'Stephen' referred
to in the papers found in Forman's 'portmantey' was his relative, the same
man who had romped on the bed with Bess Parker and had sailed with
Monson several times in the past as well as on this present occasion.
Before leaving London the previous time he had gone to sea, he had left
with Forman 'one cloak, green, a hat, a pair of breeches, etc. til he return.
If he return not, Sybil to have the cloak, his brother John the rest.'

Sadly Stephen never returned from his next voyage, for he was slain at sea on one of Monson's ships. Around the time of his death Forman had one of his dreams. 'I dreamt of Stephen that he was come from sea and brought me more tobacco. They had sailed in the dark long and could get nothing. At last they got something; when they came home Captain Watts sent to the ship for tobacco. We walked in a green church – lay by a wall and found two great cherries. He [Stephen] said they did ill to let them lie there till they did stink.'

In a second dream he found himself 'in a boat with others among the rocks on the coast of Cornwall; they came to the very turning beyond the Mount where the water ran swift and the stern of the boat touched high cliffs'. In his dream he landed 'where the houses were built close down to the water's edge, and lodged in an inn'. He awoke worried about the safety of his books and papers. There is no suggestion that he had ever been as far as Cornwall at this time, unless after fleeing from Plymouth he had decided to pay a visit to the far west before returning home, though he might have seen a drawing of St Michael's Mount which had impressed him. But it does look as if either Stephen, or some other seafarer, had described the position he found himself in his dream boat with some accuracy, for the place near the Mount where the houses were built 'close to the water's edge' is Marazion and 'the very turning beyond the Mount where the water ran swift' is either Land's End or the Lizard Point, both of which fit the description and have high cliffs.

All we know is that after these events in Plymouth Forman returned to London and took up the threads of his life again. We do not know if the Monson family continued to consult him, though Sir William's name was later to be linked with his in a far more notorious context. On the home front, matters seemed peaceful. Joshua had settled in with the family and Simon's sister Jane, now freed by the death of their mother, had moved in to help in the household, possibly another reason for the muddle over his wife's name.

Surveying what he had achieved, Forman decided that it was about time he had his own coat of arms and so set about having one drawn up, based on one of his fantasy genealogies: 'the true arms of Sir William Forman, knight, once Lord Mayor of London', whether or not this was believed being immaterial. He was not alone in hankering after a coat of arms, for it was becoming a trend for comfortably off Elizabethans, professional men and even well-established artisans, to grant themselves such honours without waiting to be knighted or ennobled. Shortly before he died in 1601, Shakespeare's father had one designed for himself. Unlike Simon Forman he did not need to invent a past city father as a forebear, for John Shakespeare, glover and tanner, had served as Stratford's 'Chamberlain' or Treasurer, while his wife, Mary Arden, was heiress to an old and highly respected family. But John Shakespeare did not live long enough to see the design finally carried through and it seems his son never felt the need for such a status symbol. Dr Simon Forman of Lambeth, however, did.

15

The Licensed Physician

Forman's growing wealth was reflected in his practice, which continued to increase right up until the time of his death. In his random notes, familiar names reflect the loyalty of those who had turned to him over many years: Nicholas Leate enquiring after a ship; Mistress Jane Flud (who slept with the letters from her many lovers under her pillow) asking if 'Sir Calisthenes Brook and Sir Thomas Gates and others' still loved her. Later she returned, her husband having died, because she had fallen in love with a Vincent Randall. Simon did not think much of either of them: 'It seems she shall marry, but not yet a great while. But in the end, with a miserable, ungodly, untoward old fellow [Randall]. It seems she desires him more than he desires her. She is not to be trusted, though she has a fair tongue, but will backbite and speak evil of her best friends. She professes virtue, loyalty, chastity – yet is full of vice, apt to be in love with many; have loved men of worth and base fearing creatures, even some of the clergy. She spends much in pride and is in debt, poor in respect. She is wavering-minded, light of condition and will overthrow her own estate.' At the end of the day, however, she fooled everyone and married an extremely wealthy knight, Sir Thomas May, who had a fine estate.[1]

Sir William Evers continued to seek advice about his health, as did the ubiquitous Blagues – only death would keep Forman from the attentions of Alice Blague. In January 1603 Dr Blague was confined to his house in Lambeth by the Lord Keeper as a result of a court case, thus freeing his

167

wife to continue with her intrigues, while adding to the Formans' income with a constant stream of requests for horoscope casting and medicines.

She called on him to discover who had stolen some of her clothing, a gown and a cloak, and was told 'he that stole it was called Arnold, a gentlemanlike fellow; he was taken abed with two wenches ...' A little while later she lost a valuable cup and was back again. Forman drew up a 'geomantical' figure for this and noted that the cup had not been stolen, merely mislaid, as it had been 'laid up by one of her servants'. Several times she asks about the outcome of her husband's litigation, while as for her health she had pains in the ribs and in the right side of her stomach for which she had to take special – and expensive – medicine every day for twenty-one days at 8s a glass. Her friend, Mistress Dove, also consulted him with a medical condition and he diagnosed 'heat in the head, melancholy and gall, and a pain in her left side likely to prove sciatica'.

He also kept up his connection with his most prestigious clients, the Careys. The Lord Chamberlain's daughter, Lady Hoby, who had been recommended by Alice Blague some time earlier when she had wanted to know if her father would live or die, returned 'with gout in her hands and feet and swelling in her joints; she is only thirty-four but the disease has been long upon her'. She also asked several times after the health of other members of her family and, a long time before it became fashionable, spent time in Bath taking the waters for gout. In turn Lady Hoby recommended Forman to a Dorothy Brereton, wife of 'Richard Brereton of Tatton'. A note records that Dorothy was married on 30 June 1596, 'between 4 p.m. and 5 p.m.' and was now thirty-five or thirty-six years old. 'Her husband deals hardly with her,' he wrote, 'and loves one Joan Richards in Wood Street. He had £200 per annum with her; now keeps her like a drudge and loves her not.' He does not say what she complained of, but, unusually, there is a piece of a letter from her 'desiring you to make the plaster for my back against Friday or Saturday if you possibly can, for I endure great pain. You may also tell this bearer how I must use the oil for hearing which you gave me, whether I must take it hot or cold.'[2]

The Earl of Essex was not the only famous man for whom Forman drew up figures and made calculations as to what the future might hold. He also endeavoured at various times to see what the fates had in store for other prominent figures, all of whom, of course, were totally unaware of his interest. There is, though, no record of his trying to read the queen's future in the stars, particularly her life expectancy, although this does not necessarily mean he did not do so only that he did not write down the result. Any astrologer found guilty of casting a horoscope for his monarch, unasked and without their express wish, which carried with it the hint of treason, was severely punished.

Yet from the late autumn of 1602 the rumours were growing that Elizabeth's health was failing; she was becoming forgetful and it was seen that she had taken to using a stick to help her when climbing stairs. It was also common knowledge that she still refused to acknowledge officially that James VI of Scotland would be her heir. The early months of 1603 passed in a strange limbo for the entire nation, as if everything was frozen. The atmosphere was one of uncertainty, indeed of very real fear, for past history had shown what happened when there was either no definite heir to the throne or only a weak one. Nor was it surprising that people were apprehensive at the prospect of change. Elizabeth had been on the throne so long, almost half a century, that life without her was almost unimaginable; but people of Simon's age or older could still recall the burnings at the stake, even in small country towns, of those who had refused to turn back to Catholicism in the reign of her half-sister Mary.

What comes across most poignantly from the last year of Elizabeth's life is how tired she had become, both mentally and physically. The bright mind was turning to melancholy, the tremendous energy that had carried her through the years draining away. The coronation ring, token of her long reign, became so tight that it had to be filed off and most of her old loves, friends and counsellors were dead. Also, she had never forgotten how, when Mary was dying in London, the trickle of those switching their allegiance to her as she waited for news in Hatfield, had become first a stream and then a river; never anyone's fool, she was fully aware of a similar flow now running north towards Edinburgh.

In January she caught a bad cold and thinking this an omen asked Dr Dee (now restored to favour) to cast her immediate horoscope. He did so and told her that she must 'beware Whitehall'. She took him at his word and on 14 January set off at once for Richmond, supposedly the warmest of her palaces, in spite of it being 'a filthy rainy and windy day'; but her health got no better and the royal physicians were called in to diagnose her condition. After examining her and conferring among themselves, they told her robustly that she was in no immediate danger and would live for several years yet. Then, in February, her favourite cousin, Kate, Countess of Nottingham, died and she was prostrated with grief. Kate's brother Robert Carey, Lord Hunsdon's son, wrote later that 'she grew worse after because she would be so', refusing all medicines. When her friends brought in Archbishop Whitgift and Sir Robert Cecil to persuade her to change her mind and take the advice of her doctors, she snapped that she knew her own constitution better than they did.

Robert Carey fared no better when he attempted to cheer her by telling her she was looking better. '"No, no, Robert," she replied, "I am not well," and sighed and sighed as I had never heard her do except when the Queen of Scots was beheaded,' he recorded later.[3] After that she deteriorated rapidly. She had lost the will to live, refusing the advice of Sir Robert Cecil that she should take to her bed, and spending her last days sitting bolt upright on cushions until she became so weak that her attendants were able to put her to bed. By this time the Privy Councillors, led by Cecil, were pleading with her to name James as her successor, finally standing at the bedside imploring her to make a sign with her hand, if she was unable to speak, that she agreed to his accession. Finally she did so. That evening she whispered that she wanted to see Archbishop Whitgift and Robert Carey, and when they came, she asked them to pray for her. The archbishop remained on his knees by her bedside for several hours until she sank into unconsciousness.

Father Weston, a Catholic priest who had been arrested and put in the Tower, wrote in his autobiography of that eerie night, when 'a strange silence descended on the whole city, not a bell rang out, not a bugle sounded'. March 24th was the eve of the Feast of the Annunciation of the Blessed Virgin. At a quarter to three her attendants found her lying peacefully, her head on her right arm. The queen was dead, long live the king. William Camden, in his *Annals of Elizabeth* wrote: 'She was a Queen who hath so long and with so great wisdom governed her kingdoms, as (to use the words of her Successor who in sincerity confessed so much) the like hath not been read or heard of, either in our own time or since the days of the Roman Emperor Augustus.'

The change was to be dramatic. The accession of James to the throne heralded an era during which just about everything was for sale, especially titles, when the monarch made no secret of his preference for pretty young male favourites, and in which the seeds were sown which would later engulf the country in civil war. For many commentators writing at the time, the country was ruled by those who knew the price of everything and the value of nothing.

The death of the queen was not the only event to cast a shadow over the early months of 1603, for by the previous November news of another major plague epidemic was reaching London. It had started in Spain, spread rapidly through France and into the Low Countries and ominously, by December, the first cases were confirmed in England, brought in, it was said, by ships docking in Gravesend, Yarmouth and Wapping.

The outbreak would become even more virulent than that of 1592–3, yet it began quietly enough with just three recorded deaths in London in December, four in January, another four in February and six in March. Once again many physicians would leave for the countryside and once again Simon would be left to tend its victims, but in the early months the College of Physicians was still functioning and its censors continued to pursue Simon, objecting to his activities and blackening his name wherever possible. He wrote to Richard Napier in a letter dated 16 March, 'I know, dear friend, since my last being with you, you long much to hear of me and of my estate.' He then continued with a description of how he was still being buffeted by storms and tempests for 'no, not any humble entreaty of my friends, no offers of peace, no gifts, no rewards, no conditions, no submissions can halt the persecution of the Doctors'.

Archbishop Whitgift had obviously given up trying to drive him out of Lambeth, but Simon had signally failed to persuade him to grant him a bishop's licence to practise medicine. He continued to Napier:

> I caused both my honourable Lord of Hertford and my Lady also to write most effectually to my Lord's [Archbishop Whitgift's] grace in my behalf to give me his licence, but it will not be. He gives me fair words and so drives me off with delays, saying the Doctors have written unto him desiring him most instantly not to take part with, not to get me any licence; for if he should, it would be much prejudice to them, to their privilege and to their proceedings – which makes his Grace cold in that he absolutely of his own clemency promised me at first.

Again I caused my Lady [Frances Hertford] to write in my behalf to the Lord Chief Justice and to Sir Francis Popham, his son, that his lordship should not take part with the Doctors against me. He answered that he knew me not nor had granted any warrant against me, but only set his hand to a general warrant of the Doctors and that 'henceforth he would be better advised'.

Forman ended by asking for 'Sandy's' prayers, with his good wishes to all the members of his family and to various friends and their wives whom he had met when visiting him and adds that '"Tronco" commends her to you'. A further postscript asked Napier to send to Mr Leate, by a trusty friend, the parchment book he had given him on astrology 'and he will send it to me. Bind it safe in something that it takes not wet.'[4]

By April, when the number of cases of plague recorded in London had still only risen to ten during that month and it was hoped that this time the city would get off lightly, Simon made a casting concerning a domestic incident which would make a rich scene for a playhouse comedy. He wanted to know what had become of 'the two pictures my wife lost out of her closet'. Apparently Mistress Forman had taken an old friend 'up into her chamber to a closet where hanged certain fine very small pictures'. She had then taken them out of the closet to show to the friend, who was so impressed with their quality that 'she would have begged them, but she would not give them away for anything'. The paintings must have been considered valuable if they were kept locked away rather than put on display for all to see. The friend was not the only person present, there was also 'a kinsman [of Anne's] standing by', who 'put them in his hose and, forgetting them, went away with them'. Obviously the pictures had to have been either miniatures or only a little larger if the 'kinsman' was able to stuff them down the front of his hose.

We then learn the name of the kinsman, for 'these pictures her cousin Chiche Parker carried away. The Monday before they [Anne and her friend] had them and looked on them; after which we could not find them. I sent to her [the friend] the Wednesday following, but she denied them absolutely. The woman had them not, but Chiche Parker had them and so she [Anne] had them again.'[5]

In May the number of plague deaths suddenly began to rise steeply and the order was given for infected corpses to go straight to the grave without benefit of church. By June this was superseded by another: that great pits should be dug in which the bodies of all plague victims must be buried immediately. At once there were wrangles over who should pay for what. In Westminster only 37s 6d was paid for the graves of 451 poor people and forty to fifty corpses had to be piled up in each pit, the dead being carried to them in barrows or carts. Bearers and drivers of these dreadful loads had to carry red 'wands' to show what they were about and those undertaking the task were, unsurprisingly, considered to be the hardest creatures in town, described as base-living and foul-mouthed.[6] As the toll of the dead mounted all bear pits and playhouses were closed, the companies of players finding themselves willy-nilly out on the road if they were to have any hope of making a living. As in 1592–3, quacks and fraudsters had a field day, with bogus advertisements on every post, and the authorities put out warnings against 'renegade Jews, thrasonical and unlettered chemists, outcast pettifoggers, dull pated base mechanics, stage players, pedlars and prittle prattling barbers', all of whom were blamed for spreading the disease. An anonymous verse records:

> Whole household and whole streets are stricken,
> The sick do die, the sound do sicken,
> And Lord have mercy on us crying,
> Ere mercy can come, that they are dying.[7]

Thomas Dekker, scurrying round the City reporting the effects of King Pest, as he had years earlier, came across plague-stricken victims dying in ditches, under walls, on the doorsteps of their houses as they attempted to get help, and told the story of a bride, dressed in all her finery, who died on her way to her wedding.

Living in London during that summer and much of the autumn was like being in a bad dream and nowhere was this more apparent than in Cheapside. That busy, noisy thoroughfare, usually thronged with buyers and sellers of a multitude of goods, where horsemen clattered by on their way both in and out of the City, and drinkers reeled in and out of the taverns, was silent as the grave. During those terrible months grass and rank weeds grew along the length of the street, rapidly becoming so thick that the few people who ventured out into it had to walk close to the stinking kennel in the middle, some chewing orange peel or smoking tobacco (both considered prophylactics) while attempting to keep to the windward of anyone coming the other away in case they were already affected.

It was at the beginning of June 1603, as the epidemic really took hold, that Forman suddenly achieved that which he had struggled and pleaded for over so many years: he was granted a licence to practise. The official recognition came not from the College of Physicians, who would never yield, but, to his greater satisfaction, from the University of Cambridge. A frail fragment of it still survives, the text in Latin and very brief.[8] The record of its granting is purely formal and merely states that the granting of the licence had taken place and that there was another such licence granted earlier in the year to a Thomas Scotson, 'also duly examined and approved'. The notice of Simon Forman's licence is accordingly abbreviated, and indicates that the person concerned had studied medicine for twenty years and was, to translate loosely, 'otherwise similarly to the last [the Scotson licence], more or less'.[9]

Various theories have been put forward as to why it was granted when it was: that some powerful patron had brought pressure to bear, which is possible, though if this was the case then the fact is not recorded; that it was in final recognition of his work with the sick during the plague of ten years earlier, prompted by the present epidemic; that Napier, with his close Cambridge connections, had brought his influence to bear on the university authorities. However it came about, Forman had two formidable sponsors in Dr Thomas Grinston, one of the late queen's physicians, who now attended on King James, and Dr William Ward of Eton and King's College. So it was with great pride and satisfaction that he rode over to Cambridge ceremoniously to receive his precious licence. The protection of so august a body now gave him a powerful weapon against any further moves the College of Physicians might make, for it allowed him to practise wherever he chose, including the City of London.

He returned from Cambridge to a city under siege – 1,396 people died in July and in August the number was almost double at 2,539. We know very little this time of who or how many victims he treated. Needless to say, Alice Blague was always in and out, desperately concerned about her health. Simon took her money, but found little wrong with her except that she was 'afflicted with melancholy and much wind. It makes her heavy, sad, faint, unlusty and solitary; and will drive her into a melancholy passion'. She took away both medicines and purges, never fell victim to the plague, survived her many minor ailments and outlived her dull husband to marry for a second time, though not to Dean Wood.

In September the death toll began to drop steadily and continued to do so until the end of the year. There is a record of a 'manservant of Master Forman's' being buried in Lambeth, but such a proper burial in the parish churchyard does not suggest that of a plague victim and the Forman household could congratulate itself on having survived without any of its members falling victim in spite of his visits to the houses of the sick. So when the blow fell it was all the more unexpected. Forman formally recorded what happened beside a carefully drawn astrological figure: 'This is the figure of the death of *Joshua* who died 8 October 1603. He died aged eighteen years, six months, twelve days and seven hours. He died of the Plague and of an imposthume in his stomach ... before his death he had red tokens in his groin and died the Saturday following.'

Joshua must have been away on a visit, possibly to his old home in Wiltshire, for Forman wrote: 'The Sunday morning he returned to London he took the Plague and died the Saturday following.' At first it had seemed he might pull through, 'then the imposthume broke and he vomited a great bellyful'. Joshua continued vomiting and 'died with his fingers in his mouth ... and was worshipfully buried at Lambeth seventy-two miles from the place in which he was born'.[10]

Forman's grief is expressed below:

> Darkness was on the face of the Deep,
> Darkness without light,
> Darkness in speaking,
> Darkness in understanding.

This is followed by something which is hard to read, possibly referring to the dark night of the soul. He then adds: 'His mother had died in 1600 on the 4th day of May and was buried the 8th day of May. She died of gripe and dropsy. He [Joshua] was fifteen years and thirty-eight days old when his mother died. He came to live with me in 1602 about Midsummer.'

While Forman struggled to come to terms with the death of his only son, the plague seems to have had little or no effect on the arrangements for the grand coronation of King James I. As he made his slow progress

175

from Scotland that autumn, he made new knights by the score, dubbing over 400 men on one occasion alone. A number of these were Simon's patients or acquaintances, including Sir Robert Lane of Horton in Northamptonshire (who afterwards required treatment for an apoplexy brought on by the occasion), junior members of Sir John Penruddock's family from Wiltshire and five members of the Roper family, descendents of Sir Thomas More. Later all such honours were found to have their price at a Court rotten with graft, in which the money needed to fund the king's extravagance was raised by the sale of honours. Knighthoods, which could be obtained for as little as £30, were only one of the ranks soon to be bought and sold and James quickly created 838 of these, while for £1,905 one could purchase the new rank of 'knight baronet'. Within a relatively short period James had dignified three dukes, a marquess, thirty-two earls, nineteen viscounts and fifty-six baronets, all for cash down, bringing in about £120,000 all told. Ben Jonson was one of several writers who found himself in trouble for mocking those buying preferment at Court, describing one such as 'a poor knight of England', one of the 'thirty-pound knights who most likely sold the title on to his page for £4'.[11]

For Simon it had proved a year of extremes. On the one hand he had finally achieved the professional recognition he had sought for so long, had consolidated his position in Lambeth and could rightfully inscribe himself 'gentleman'; while on the other he had lost the loved son of his youthful passion to King Pest and, ominously, there was still no sign of another child.

16

Tranquillity

The early 1600s ushered in a period of increasing tranquillity in Forman's life, during which he cultivated his garden and devoted himself to his practice and household. As to politics, if he sought instruction from the stars as to the outcome of another treasonable plot, that of Guy Fawkes and his fellow conspirators in 1605, he left no mention of it. It was a particularly miserable and dangerous time for Catholics, for the Gunpowder Plot had provided Cecil with the excuse to bring in even more draconian legislation against recusants, with the result that many of those in public life, terrified of being tarred with the same brush, no longer wanted anything to do with them. Yet Simon never turned his back on his Catholic patients and he continued to treat, along with Cressacre More, members of the Mullins, Cornwallis, Digby, Fortescue and Arundell families; another fact that would rebound against him posthumously.[1]

He had now turned fifty, still without a legitimate child, and possibly it was achieving his half century that turned his thoughts to mortal matters. Carefully dating it 4 January 1604, he wrote 'A Psalm for his Burial', verse after turgid verse (sixty in all), all based on the burial service in the Book of Common Prayer and ending with the devout hope that he will be granted a place with the saints at God's right hand.[2] Several of his brothers and a sister were now dead and by his own reckoning he had reached that age when, as a young man, he had declared that 'an old bodie about 50 years of age is not to be holpen but with great danger'. So in a further attempt to reserve a seat in heaven, he wrote a very long prayer, also designed to be said at his interment.[3]

Eight pages of verses follow under the heading 'Forman on the Wickedness of the Time', which begin with the statement 'there is no God as foolish men affirm in their mad mood' and continue:

Assemble now you people all
And mark well what I say
The life of man is like to grass
That withereth in a day
For man that is of woman born
Hath but short time to live.
He cometh up as doth the weed
That is cut down with sithe [scythe].

Oddly, in view of the careful notes of dates and times he had made about impregnation in the past, there is no record of the occasion in October 1604 when, having assiduously continued to 'halek' his wife, at long last she finally conceived. The child, a daughter, 'was born unto him [Simon] on the 10th day of July 1605 at forty minutes after 4 o'clock in the morning at Lambeth in the 53rd year of his age'. The Lambeth parish register records that on 27 July (unusually a full seventeen days after her birth, which suggests there may have been problems), 'the daughter of Simon Forman, gentleman', was baptised. The baby was given the name of Dorothy after her grandmother, sister of 'Sir Edward Munnings, knight, of Waldershare, near Dover', which again points to Simon having had only the one wife.

The Formans' joy in their child, however, was to be short-lived for 'she died at Candlemas at the age of six months'. Very fortunately, either at about that time or a little after, Anne Forman became pregnant again. The child was a boy, Clement, and Forman gives us the details on the same page on which he refers to 'Dorothy, who died young at halfe a year old. After this was born his [Simon's] son, Clemmonte, who was born the 27th day of October [1606], it being a Monday, in the forenoon.'[4]

Clement proved to be a sturdy child who was to live into adulthood. He was obviously the apple of his father's eye, for he later added with great pride that his small son 'could commit things to memory from two years

178

old and was so forward that by five years old he was able to read English and was full of spirit, all ayer [air], and was so full of action that he would never stand still'.[5]

In 1606 and 1607 the last three references to Simon Forman appear in the proceedings of the College of Physicians. On 4 December 1606 a meeting was called, which was attended by Dr Atkins (president) and other doctors. The main item on the agenda was 'the testimony that Dr. Dove wrote to the College testifying that a certain Swaine of Horsey Downe had given Mary Walker, a pregnant woman, a medicament which caused an abortion on the day after'. He had not appeared before the censors as ordered and was fined £5 in his absence and thereafter arrested and imprisoned. A brief sentence below this item notes that 'Dr. Moundeford and Dr. Pope complained again about the quack, Forman'.[6]

On 9 January 1607 the president and the group met specifically to censor him. A brief note records: 'Forman had been summonsed for this day but refuses and sent in his name one Master Whitfield, who informed us that owing to important matters of business he could not come to them: nor would he come at any other time, unless a public pledge were given regarding his return'.[7]

They were to have one final attempt. On 30 March 1607 the same committee met again and

> Mr. Pelham, a Professor of Medicine, came to the College on this day and laid information before us regarding the quack Forman and the means he uses to gain money. Firstly he asks the name and place of habitation of the patient. Then (as he openly confesses) he makes an effigy; thirdly, just as if he were a prophet, he foretells the disease and fate of the patient. Finally he prescribes medicaments.
>
> Among those whom Pelham knew had come to Forman was a man called Humphrey Ward who when he was suffering from arthritis was considered by Forman to be dropsical. Jacob Saterthwaite, living in Little Wood Street, brought a similar charge to the College against the same man, Forman, for when he had come to him at his home, he first asked his name and then where he was staying. Thirdly he fashioned an effigy and gave an opinion regarding the disease. He demanded ten pence from him for one medicament; for another five shillings and for two purgatives, four shillings.
>
> Forman was summonsed to appear but again refused to do so.[8]

After this the college censors gave up the battle. As for Forman, he now felt sufficiently secure of his ground not merely to ignore them when they summonsed him, but to return an impudent message in response. One wonders why the censors considered it so strange and incorrect to ask a patient for his name and address. If such a practice was then truly frowned upon, then it is all the more valuable that both Simon Forman and Richard Napier went against protocol in keeping detailed records of whom they treated, their place of origin and the outcome of the consultations. It also lends weight to the theory that there were further casebooks of Forman's which have not survived. As to the 'effigy', Forman never made any secret of the fact that he made such figures as tokens for the lovesick, mainly women, but nowhere in his case notes does he suggest that they played any part in his patients' medical treatment.

While he might have had a quiet life in most respects, his sex life continued unabated, a fact he felt worthy of record in continued 'halek notes'. In 1607 'on 31 March at 3 a.m. [I] halek Tronco'. On 3 April he did the same 'at 9 p.m.' and on '6 April at 6.15 p.m.', even though he had had a bad and tiring day. He repeated the activity the following morning before riding off to Swanthrop, near Farnham, to have a look at Swanthrop House, a very substantial property owned by Giles Paulet 'of the parish of Crondall', with whom he bargained for the lease. He does not explain why he did this, or whether the use of 'we' means his wife went with him, only that he took the property over from a William West before returning to London on 9 April. Since he had no plans to move from Lambeth it must have been either a second home or an investment.

His vigorous love-making with his wife continued: 'on April 12th at 4.10 a.m., on the 14th at 9 p.m., the 21st at 5.45 p.m. and on the 23rd at 5.30 p.m.' Again presumably this was noted in such detail in the event that, having now conceived two children, she might yet bear him another. On the last occasion it took place after he had been summonsed to appear on an unknown charge before the Lord Chief Justice and bailed on his own recognisance, from which he was discharged a week later. He gives no reason for this, but had earlier recorded that he was engaged at the time in further litigation over money lent.

Certainly he saw to it that the record of his sexual prowess was kept safe and by the summer of that year, when he was fifty-three, he was regularly 'haleking Tronco', a list which becomes repetitive, as well as a number of other women, two on the same day in July, 'Hester Sharp at 8 a.m. and Anne Wiseman at 3 p.m.', after which he went home and again made love to his wife. In September his old friend and regular lover Anne Condwell came to stay with the Formans to be cured of 'a disease in her leg', which gave him every opportunity to continue his relationship with her as well. What is meant by the entry 'then Margery found the cuckoo on her gown', made at the same time, is not explained.

Anne Forman did have some life of her own, regularly visiting her 'gossip' or friend, Mistress Holmes, at her home in Greenwich, where she also had relatives, the Twyne family. When the Twynes had a child, Forman was invited to be a godfather, attending the baptism in clothes bought especially for the occasion, 'a new doublet and hose of black tufted canvas with birds' eyes'. The honour must have pleased him, for John Twyne was a Fellow of the College of Physicians and an astrologer and wrote pamphlets on very similar subjects to Simon, with titles such as *The Wonderful Workmanship of the World*, *The Breviary of Britain* and, significantly, *A New Counsel Against the Plague*.[9]

Having bought the Lambeth house in part because of its orchard, Forman had become an enthusiastic gardener and by 1608 he was spending a good deal of time working in the garden and designing additions for it. In July he began work on a 'great garden of roses' (an odd time of year for such a task), starting with a dozen bushes, and a month later 'set in the gillyflowers in the inner garden'. He was still enthusiastic come November. 'On 29th November I set in the framboys [raspberry] trees under the west pale [fence] all along the Lambeth Marsh. 7th December, I set the willows all along towards the lane, and in the afternoon the first rose tree. 8th December, set the rest of the rose trees all along the bank towards the lane. 9th December all the other rose trees towards Davies' side, also set the filberts [hazel trees] . . . against the posts and towards the lane and the house. Also then the camomile beside the privy; and set primroses.'[10] Those using the privy would appreciate the aromatic scent of camomile. A week later he set in yet more rose bushes and two apple trees by the pale and also 'small roses and pinks' under it.

For advice and assistance in his work, he turned to the garden expert, Thomas Tusser. A man of many parts, Tusser was born at Rivenhall in

Essex, educated at Eton and was a chorister at St Paul's before taking his degree at Trinity College, Cambridge. After a brief spell as a Court musician, he became a farmer in Suffolk, where he wrote his first best-selling manual on gardening, *A Hundred Pointes of Good Husbandrie*. So successful was this that in 1573 he expanded it into *Five Hundred Pointes of Good Husbandrie*.

Much of the book is in verse:

> Dig garden, stroy mallow, now may ye at ease,
> And set as a dainty thy runcival pease.
> Go cut and set roses, choose aptly thy plot,
> The roots of the youngest are best to be got.

Tusser also published a number of other books, some of which repeated such useful homilies as:

> Who goeth a borrowing
> Goeth a sorrowing.
> Few lend (but fools)
> Their working tools.

To him we owe such phrases as 'February fill-the-dyke', 'Sweet April showers, do spring May flowers', even 'Christmas comes but once a year', and in *A Book of Housewifery* he observes with truth:

> Some respite to husbands the weather may send
> But housewives' affairs have never an end.

Tusser believed in sowing and planting at the right phases of the moon and planets. Radishes, for example, should be sown at the new moon, as should rosemary and lavender, while the herb colewort was to be sown in the old moon with the sign of the cross. When Forman set his beans in that January they had been 'watered twenty-four hours before, when the moon was full'.

Forman kept his own bees to supply the household's honey, mentioning how he had had to transfer them to a new hive. He hired a 'hand', that is a farm labourer or stockman, suggesting that he, like some of his better-off neighbours, grazed cattle on the common land of Lambeth Marsh. Standing on the north bank of the Thames today and looking across at the office buildings that stretch from Southwark Bridge to Vauxhall, as well as the great bulk of St Thomas's Hospital, it is almost impossible to imagine so rural a scene.

Forman was now considered sufficiently respectable to be invited to dine at some of the great halls of the craft guilds and he continued to attract distinguished clients and patients. In April 1608 Christopher Grimston, Surveyor of the Duchy of Lancaster, and now a neighbour of the Formans, enquired after the fate of his man, 'who was old and trusty, whom he had sent out with money to buy liveries' and who had never returned. Forman drew up a figure and told him that his man had not run away, but that something had happened to him. Grimston refused to be convinced until he discovered Forman had been right after all and that the unfortunate fellow had been robbed 'and beaten with bastinados and brought to Redcross Street like to die and the Friday after he sent a message to his master'. He was also consulted by Sir Richard Hawkins, who had been held prisoner by the Spaniards and now complained of 'rattling in the throat and spitting blood'. (It is not clear whether this is the same Hawkins who wanted to know how long his wife had been pregnant.)

There is also a little cameo scene which might be repeated in any bookshop today when Forman 'came into a stationer's shop in London and turned some books'. After spending some time reading, but not buying, 'the boy quarrelled much with me for tossing of his books and not setting them in order'.

1609 was the year of the formal colonisation of Virginia, when a fleet under the command of Sir George Summers and Thomas Gates, who was to be the official governor, was sent to reinforce the original settlement of Jamestown. But the ship carrying the two knights, the *Sea Venture*, became separated from the rest of the fleet during a hurricane and when the news reached England at the end of the year it was assumed that the vessel had foundered and that there were no survivors.

The crew had managed to run her ashore on the island of Bermuda where, 'through God's providence, she fell betwixt two rocks, that caused her to stand firme and not immediately be broken'. As a result those aboard survived. They were able to sustain themselves through the winter and build two pinnaces stout enough to take them safely to Virginia in the spring. The adventure caught the imagination of the population following the publication of the official account, written by Gates's secretary, William Strachey, who told of the myths surrounding 'the terrible lands of the Bermudas, that such tempests, thunders and other fearful objects are seen and heard about them, that they be commonly called the Devil's Islands . . .'. He goes on, however, to inform his readers that much of their reputation, such as their being inhabited by 'Devils and Wicked Spirits' is ill deserved, for the shipwrecked mariners had found the place as 'habitable and commodious as most places of the same climate and situation: insomuch as if the entrance into them were as easie as the place itself is contenting . . . Thus shall we make it appear that Truth is the daughter of Time and that men ought not to deny every thing which is not subject to their own sense.'[11]

Other survivors also published their accounts, giving the impression of an island paradise, 'the richest, healthfullest and most pleasing land as ever man set foot upon', wrote Sylvester Jordan. All of this, among much else, provided the inspiration for Shakespeare's *The Tempest*.

Before the fate of the *Sea Venture* was known, Forman was consulted by several women enquiring about the fortunes of their husbands, who were with the fleet, including an Elizabeth Whitehead. After recording her visit he notes that 'we had letters from him by ship that came thence and sent certain things home', adding, sadly, later 'but he came not home'. Jane Flud reappears again, anxious to learn the fate of her one-time lover, Sir Thomas Gates.

Forman was fascinated by the event and questioned closely both those who had survived the wreck and, when they returned home, those who had spent time in the new colony. 'There is in Virginia,' he wrote, 'a kind of fruit called maricock. They grow on the ground like a pompion and such a flower cometh out first before the fruit, as big as small cucumbers. They are full of seeds; the substance thereof is like a lemon and tasteth with a pleasant sharpness before they be ripe. Once ripe they are very sweet and luscious, very good to eat. Also a kind of plum, called a mutchumin, as big as an apricot, sweep and the pulp sweet, thick like marmalade: it has a binding quality, helps any flux of blood, red and yellow, and has three or four kernels; they grow on a low tree.'

He continued, 'The Indians do always in March boil the heart or pith of pine trees in water, strain it and drink the water – it purges both upwards and downwards', and in Bermuda 'there is a fruit called a plantain, [which] grows up like a cabbage, spreads out in bushes, and on branches grows long and crooked like cucumbers, and are a very delicious meat'.

He learned that the new town of Jamestown was 'on low, marshy ground, very unhealthful and ever in May, June, July and August they are much troubled with a kind of burning fever and swelling in their bodies and face; many die thereof . . . but at the head of the river it is much more pleasant, not so full of woods nor nothing so thick; both the ground and the country air is more pleasant, healthful and fertile'. From April to the end of August sturgeon were taken from the mouth of the river and there follows an enthusiastic account of the bird and animal life: 'snakes of divers colours, green, some red as blood, some speckled, some two yards long. In winter they have parakeets, also blackbirds with carnation pinions, birds all red as blood and in summer in the woods there are fireflies with lights in their tails like candles.'

There were lynxes, speckled white and black, as big as mastiffs, their skin worth twenty or thirty shillings, beavers, otters, grey foxes 'and also a beast called an opossum, as big as an old cat, but [with] a tail like a rat; his head is also like a rat'. Also raccoons, some grey, some black, 'of the bigness of a little dog like a spaniel; and musk rats live in the waters'.[12]

At the end of 1609 Forman was happy and contented in his world. Had he died then, or early in 1610 instead of in 1611, then the picture of the end of his life would be merely that of a busy and successful physician and astrologer, playing with his lively small son during his leisure time, happily planting roses in his garden, collecting honey from his hives and still making love to his wife – and others, whenever the opportunity arose. Despite his uncertain and troubled entry into his chosen vocation, the ambivalent criticisms of *The Terrors of the Night* and the hostility of the College of Physicians, it is likely he would have been remembered merely as an interesting man of his time, his name linked closely with that of the highly respected Richard Napier.

He could not possibly have imagined the consequences that would result from the arrival at his house one day, sometime early in 1610, of the attractive Mistress Anne Turner. No doubt he was somewhat flattered, for she was the wife of George Turner, a fashionable and successful doctor, who was very highly regarded by the College of Physicians despite being a Catholic. The College had made him a Fellow and in 1591–2, 1597 and

1606 he had been appointed to sit on the Committee of Censors, before becoming the College Treasurer in 1609. His pretty wife, noted for her blonde curls, had a somewhat dubious reputation, for it was rumoured that she was mistress to Sir Arthur Mainwaring, one of King James's £30 knights, and that it was Sir Arthur and not her elderly husband who was the father of her three children.

It was soon to transpire that Mistress Turner was not simply seeking Forman's advice on her own account: her true role was to be that of go-between for a much greater lady. Confusingly, this was another Frances Howard, but a lady born into far more exalted branch of the Howard family than the namesake and distant relative who had first consulted him when she was plain Mistress Frances Pranell. This Frances Howard, daughter to the Earl of Suffolk, was now the Countess of Essex and she would go down in history as one of the great beauties of her age; also as a notorious poisoner.

17

A Prophecy of Death

Although Anne Turner had a husband whose income ensured they were comfortably off, she had also developed a small business of her own. After 1603, with the reign of a new king, new fashions swept first through the Court, then spread among the better off, one of which was to stiffen the ruffs worn by both men and women with a yellow or creamy-coloured starch. Almost immediately Anne saw a money-making opportunity for this high-fashion accessory and within a short time she had produced and patented a starch recipe of her own. Demand for 'Anne Turner's yellow starch' grew rapidly, its popularity bringing her into contact with some of the highest nobility.

It is most likely that she was recommended to Forman by the Monson family, with whom she was on both social and business terms. Soon after her initial approach and consultation, Dr George Turner died, leaving Anne a relatively wealthy widow. Aware of at least some of his wife's involvement with Sir Arthur Mainwaring, he generously appointed him 'overseer to his will' for the benefit of his widow, as well as leaving him £10 to have a mourning ring made for himself with 'the posey *Fates junguntur Amates*'. But it seems that Sir Arthur baulked at the prospect of marrying his mistress and on one of Anne Turner's first visits to Forman after her husband's death, she asked for his assistance in the delicate matter of persuading the reluctant knight to make her his wife. To this end he gave her a 'philtrous powder', which 'wrought so violently with him that

187

through storm of rain and thunder he rode fifteen miles one dark night to her house, scarce knowing where he was till he was there'.[1] However, in spite of this, he never did marry Anne.

This new interest did not prevent Simon from following up other concerns. For years he had been a regular playgoer and in 1611 he began to collect together his thoughts on some of the productions he had seen. The result was *The Book of Plaies and Notes Thereof per Forman – for Common Policy*.[2] The 'book', as it survives, consists of four accounts of plays he saw at the Globe during the last spring of his life, although again it might well be that this is all that remains of a longer manuscript. However, it gives the reader an eerie feeling to look at the faded brown hand of someone who actually saw Shakespeare in performance in his own time.

Of the four performances, three – *Macbeth*, *Cymbeline* and *The Winter's Tale* – are undoubtedly Shakespeare's plays as we know them; the fourth, *Richard II*, is of more doubtful provenance. In each case Forman gives a detailed synopsis of the plot, followed sometimes by a note of what he considers to be the most important point to remember. From his previous writings it is possible to assume that *Macbeth* and *Cymbeline* would have been of particular interest, the first because of his fascination with the occult and the second since 'King Cimbelin' features in one of the fantasy genealogies.

He saw *Macbeth* at the Globe on 20 April 1611, a Saturday, and it made a considerable impression on him. He takes us step by step through the story, explaining how, after victory in a great battle, Macbeth meets 'three women fairies or nymphs', which suggests that in this very early production the 'witches' were not portrayed as ugly old hags, as has been common over the centuries, but as young fey creatures. Simon records in his own words their famous prophesy regarding the fate of Macbeth and how, afterwards, Banquo says, '"what, all to Macbeth and nothing to me?" "Yes," said the nymphs, "hail to thee Banquo; thou shalt beget kings yet be no king."' Oddly enough, for one so in thrall to magic and necromancy, at no time does he ever refer to the witches' spells, though legend has it that the one used during the famous cauldron scene was genuine, hence the play's reputation for bringing bad luck. Nor is there any mention of the scene in which the witches conjured up spirits for Macbeth, including those of the dead. What seems to have impressed Forman most was the staging when 'the ghost of Banquo came in and sat down in his [Macbeth's] chair behind him. He, turning about to sit down again, saw the ghost: which affronted him so, that he fell into a great passion of fear and fury, uttering many words about his murder.' He ends: 'Observe also how Macbeth's queen did rise in the night, and walked, and talked and confessed all. And the *Doctor* noted her words.'

There is no date given for the performance of *Cymbeline*, but again he records a detailed and accurate account of the plot, which stops abruptly before the end of a sentence; quite obviously there is missing material here. Not so with *The Winter's Tale*, seen on 15 May, which he obviously enjoyed a good deal. His synopsis of the plot is so accurate that it could almost be lifted and put into a programme today. He was particularly taken with Autolycus, that 'snapper-up of unconsidered trifles' and how he stole sheets which had been left hanging out to dry on hedges. 'Remember,' he wrote, 'how the rogue came in all tattered like Coll Pixie. How he cozened the poor man of all his money and, after, came to the sheep-shearing with the pedler's pack and there cozened them again of all their money.' He ends: 'Nota: Beware of trusting feigned beggars or fawning fellows.' He does not tell us who played the various roles in the three performances, but almost certainly he would have seen Richard Burbage as Macbeth and Leontes, and Robert Armin as Autolycus.

The mystery play is the fourth drama, which he saw on 20 April. It was called *Richard II*, yet nothing in Forman's very detailed description of what he witnessed remotely resembles Shakespeare's play of that name. For a start it does not open, as does Shakespeare's, with King Richard well into his reign intervening in the quarrel between Mowbray and Henry Bolingbroke, but with the much earlier Peasants' Revolt and how 'Jack Straw was stabbed by one, Walworth, mayor of London . . . so that he and his whole army were overthrown'.

The scene then moves to a plot made against the very young Richard by the 'Duke of Ireland', in league with the Duke of Gloucester and how the 'Duke of Ireland' was 'sent back again with a flea in his ear, and after was slain by the earl of Arundel in battle' and how Richard II invited both Gloucester and Arundel to a great banquet 'and so betrayed them and cut their heads off, etc'. Also in this drama John of Gaunt, far from being the great patriotic statesman of Shakespeare's play, 'privily contrived all villainy to set them about the ears'. Indeed he is portrayed as a villain who plots to become king himself. At one point he asks a soothsayer if he will ever be king and when the man answers 'no', promptly has him hanged. 'Beware by this example of noblemen,' warned Forman, 'and of their fair words and say little to them, lest they do the like by thee.'

It is unlikely that this is an earlier version of the *Richard II* we know, or even a lost preamble to it (which would make it twice its length). It is nearer in subject matter to an anonymous play, *Thomas of Woodstock*, which also opens with the Peasants' Revolt and the sacking of London and takes events up to King Richard's first marriage, although the plot of this piece does not really fit Forman's description either. One can only assume that what he saw was a different play altogether, one of a host from the period long since lost.

Forman was not only going to plays, he was now sufficiently well known to be featured in them. Ben Jonson in *Epicene or The Silent Woman*, written in 1609, gives us the first reference to Simon Forman on stage in an aside when one character tells another, 'I would say thou hadst the best philtre in the world and couldst do more than Madam Medea or Dr. Forman.' It has even been suggested that he provided the inspiration for Jonson's great comedy, *The Alchemist*, in which a trio of rogues set up in practice in a house vacated due to a plague epidemic, one of them posing as an astrologer and alchemist. We know that the play was put on at the Globe in 1610 with Richard Burbage playing the role of the trickster, Face, the accomplice of the fake alchemist.

A year later, in 1611, came Middleton's satirical and venal comedy, *A Chaste Maid in Cheapside*, which features a supposed 'doctor' famed for making infertile women pregnant. He is, in fact, a fortune hunter who has got all too many girls pregnant and is persuaded by his younger brother to put this to good use, in which guise he meets Lady Kix, who has been unable to oblige her elderly husband with an heir. 'Dr. Touchwood' is introduced as a physician who has already brought about nine pregnancies by the use of his magic potion. In the event it is the husband who is sent off on a ludicrous goose chase to drink the potion, while the 'doctor' takes the lady up to bed to give her a dose of his own medicine, which, needless to say, succeeds. It could be that this too was based on Simon Forman's reputation for success in an area other than medicine.

Jonson's final reference to Simon Forman is in *The Devil is an Ass*, written immediately after Forman's death, in which a would-be lover seeks to circumvent a jealous husband by passing himself off as a Spanish lady who concocts rare cosmetics to beautify women:

> All our women here
> That are of spirit and fashion flock unto her
> As to their president, their law, their canon.
> More than ever they did to Oracle Forman.[3]

If he was gaining a reputation on the stage, Forman also had dramas of his own. His final months are marked by politically dangerous events in which he was to be caught up unwittingly. From the very beginning he was on dangerous ground, for not only were the families involved extremely powerful, but one of the main protagonists was the close favourite, and most probably lover, of King James himself.

We simply do not now how much of the story Forman was aware of, or how truthful was the account Anne Turner gave him, but it had all begun several years earlier, long before his own involvement. Frances Howard had been promised in marriage to the young Earl of Essex within a few years of the execution of his father and when they were both still children. There was no pretence that the match was anything other than political or dynastic, in which a number of interests were involved, not least those of Sir Robert Cecil. At that stage Cecil had been ennobled, his careful secret negotiations with James before the death of Elizabeth having paid off. After being confirmed in the position of Principal Secretary of State, he was given first the title Viscount Cranborne and then elevated to become Earl of Salisbury.

In spite of achieving his ambitions, Cecil still felt insecure. The Essex faction, which had not disappeared with the execution of the late earl and to which some members of the Howard family belonged, still saw him as the principal influence behind their hero's downfall and swift execution. So in 1605, on Cecil's advice, King James restored the title to Essex's young son and Cecil calculated that by uniting the family of the Earl of Suffolk with that of the Earl of Essex, through the marriage of their children, any residual enmity between the two would be laid to rest. So it was that on 5 January 1606 the fifteen-year-old Frances was married to the fourteen-year-old earl. Although many young people of their age were considered ripe for wedlock and the girl ready for childbearing, in this instance it was decided that the two should not consummate the marriage for at least two years. The young earl therefore returned to his studies at Oxford, before going on a grand tour of the Continent, while her mother introduced the new young countess to the pleasures of the Court.

Much was written at the time and later of the venality of King James's Court, apart from the money-making awarding of titles and honours. In the last years of Elizabeth's reign the Court had already been described as 'a glittering misery, full of malice and spite', where those lured by ambition's 'puffball' found nothing lay beneath that surface glitter. Jacobean writers were even more critical of what followed. John Donne wrote:

> Here no one is from the extremity
> Of Vice, by any other reason free,
> But that the next to him, still, is worse than he . . .

An anonymous poet went further:

> The Court is fraught with bribery, with hate,
> With envy, lust, ambition and debate,
> With fawnings and fantastic imitation,
> With shameful sloth and base dissimulation.
> True virtue's almost quite exiled there.[4]

Into this hotbed the Countess of Suffolk, a lady with something of a reputation herself and rumoured to be one of Cecil's mistresses, brought her beautiful and wilful daughter. Frances Howard's face stares out at us from her portraits. The engraving of Simon van der Passe is of a conventionally good-looking young lady of the time, but the portrait attributed to William Larkin shows just how striking she really was: a huge ruff gives the appearance almost of a decapitated head, the features of the face perfect and regular, her eyes large and very knowing. A portrait of her husband points up the difference, for he clearly took after his grandfather, dour Sir Francis Walsingham, rather than his feckless and handsome father. They look an unlikely couple.

Sometime in 1609 Essex returned to reclaim his bride and from the first the marriage was a disaster. Although he professed ardent love for her, she was to swear that whatever she did, however hard she tried to please him in bed (even though she found him totally unattractive) he was unable to consummate the marriage, and she might have been telling the truth, for his second marriage also failed disastrously. Equally forcefully, Essex declared that he was not impotent and that the fault lay with his wife, who refused him intercourse.

The next years were taken up with Frances's fight, against the wishes of her family, to have her marriage annulled on the grounds of non-consummation. Eventually the commissioners who heard the case ordered that this be put to the test and that she should submit herself to examination by a panel of midwives and prove her virginity. Almost certainly by this time she had taken a lover and it is said that she agreed to submit to the examination so long as she might wear a veil. Another young woman was persuaded to take her place, the two most favoured candidates being either the daughter of Sir Thomas Monson (also Forman's patient), or Frances's own cousin, Mistress Fiennes. Plots of Jacobean tragedies are full of such substitutions, though it is less likely that such a subterfuge would succeed in real life.

But Frances was desperate, for she had fallen passionately in love with the king's favourite, Robert Carr, whose portrait shows an epicene, pretty young man. James also appears to have loved him to distraction, heaping honours on him, making him first Viscount Rochester and eventually Earl of Somerset. As a gentleman of the bedchamber one of Carr's duties was regularly to spend nights sleeping on a bed in the king's bedchamber which, not surprisingly, gave rise to endless rumour and speculation. There is much argument as to how far James went physically with his young male favourites, but the hazards of the situation in which Frances found herself as a result of her infatuation were extreme, even though the king seems to have regarded the relationship with a certain amount of forbearance at first. Essex, however, once he realised what was afoot, felt no such tolerance and in an attempt to remove his wife from temptation began carrying her off into the country for lengthy periods.

Frances was terrified that as soon as she was out of his sight, Carr would cease to reciprocate her love. She turned for advice to Anne Turner, the lively woman with hair 'like gold wires', who provided her with that important yellow starch, and it was Anne who suggested that she seek the help of a doctor who lived in Lambeth and who offered to act as intermediary. Dr Simon Forman, the countess was informed, was skilled in all matters of love.

Thus it was that he became caught up in the dangerous intrigue, supplying the Countess of Essex with love philtres, tokens bearing magical 'sigil' signs, pieces of parchment inscribed with 'magic writing' and much else. He also sent her 'jellies', though whether these were intended for Carr to keep him faithful, or Essex to ensure he remained impotent, is not clear: both were later alleged. Soon the amount of time Forman was spending with the Countess's go-between began to annoy young Mistress Forman, for, according to her, he would often remain closeted 'alone with Mistress Turner in his study for hours at a time'.[5] It might be that he turned this to his own advantage, even though there are no 'halek notes' to that effect.

As the months passed, the countess came to depend upon Forman more and more, referring to him in correspondence as 'Father', as had the other Frances Howard. From her unhappy country exile during the summer of 1611 she wrote a letter to Anne Turner asking her to pass on to Simon details of her plight, directing her to be sure to burn the missive after reading it. Her command obviously went unheeded for the letter still exists. In it she wrote: 'Sweet Turner, I am out of all hope of any good in this world, for my father, my mother and my brother say I should lie with him.' 'Him' in this context is her husband. The letter becomes increasingly confusing for she frequently refers to both Essex and Carr as 'lord'.

She continued, 'And my brother Howard was here and said he [Essex] would not come forth from this place all winter. So that all comfort is gone and, which is worst of all my Lord [Essex] hath complained that he hath not lain with me, and I would not suffer him to use me. My father and mother are angry, but I would rather die a thousand times over; for besides the sufferings, I shall lose his [Carr's] love if I lie with him.' She was terrified that Carr would have nothing more to do with her if Essex forced her into having sex with him, nor was the earl likely to oblige her by dying 'for my Lord is very well, as ever he was, so you may see in what miserable case I am'. She concluded by asking Anne Turner to send word to Forman of the position she found herself in, for 'he sent me word that all would be well, but I shall not be so happy as the lord to love me'.[6]

She also poured her heart out directly to Forman. 'Sweet Father – I must needs still crave your love, though I hope I shall have it and shall deserve better hereafter.' She reminded him of all the obstacles to her achieving her desire, but assured him of her trust in his ability to bring it about and 'send me good fortune. Also, I have need of it, for now I am a miserable woman.' He must do everything in his power to keep Carr faithful to her, but 'be careful that you name me not to anybody, for we have so many spies'. He would need all his wit if they were not to be betrayed 'for the world is against me'.

She felt sure of Forman's affection towards her and 'I hope you will do me good. And if I be ungrateful, let all mischief come to me. My Lord [Essex] is lusty and merry, and drinketh with his men, and useth me as doggedly as ever before, and all the contentment he gives me is to abuse me. I think I shall never be happy in this world, because he hinders all my good, and will ever, I think. Remember me, I beg for God's sake, and get me from this vile place. – Your assured, affectionate, loving daughter, Frances Essex.'[7]

Aware of the situation she might find herself in if her correspondence with Simon came to light, she added in a postscript: 'Give Turner warning of all things but not the Lord [Carr]. I would not have anything come out for fear of the Lord Treasurer [Sir Robert Cecil]; for so they may tell my father and mother and fill their ears full of toys.'

Later events must be viewed through the undoubted bias of the accounts in State Papers, when Forman's involvement was used by the prosecution in the subsequent trials. We have no way of knowing if he realised he was playing with fire, since all the relevant papers were destroyed, but given his personality and proclivities it is only too easy to see how he allowed himself to become enmeshed in the countess's affairs and how exciting he must have found it to have so beautiful and high-born a woman so dependent on him.

Although he did not know it, as these events were unfolding his own days were numbered. He had never lost the friendship and respect of Richard Napier and one of his last letters is a brief note to him dated 23 July 1611: 'Your loving and kind letters came unto me by Rutland, the carrier, who brought withal two cheeses and a little book of Merlin's as tokens of your kind goodwill and powerful courtesy. Touching those brazen moulds for carats of the planet Aretes [Aries], if you have them, if you can tell how to use them, you have a good thing for curing diseases as for other purposes to cast therein.' He ends with a reference to Ralph

Glaste, the cheesemonger, being robbed of plate and money worth £300 while at church and that 'son Clement salutes you'.[8]

In later years he and Napier were to gain the admiration of a younger astrologer and physician, William Lylly. Lylly was only nine years of age when Forman died and is largely remembered for producing a yearly almanac and for two works on eclipses of the sun, *The Eclipse of the Sun on 22 May 1639* and *A Short Method How to Judge the Effects of Eclipse*. His other claim to fame – which should be taken with a pinch of salt as he had a vested interest as an astrologer in 'proving' such forecasts – is his account of how, allegedly, Forman prophesied his own death on 1 September 1611, a week before it took place.

According to Lylly, Simon and his wife were sitting in their 'garden house' having supper when she jokingly asked him which of them would outlive the other, as both were in perfect health at the time:

'"Shall I bury you or no?" she demanded.

'He replied, very seriously, "oh Tronco, thou wilt bury me, but thou wilt much repent it."

'"Yea," she replied, "but how long first?"

'"I shall die ere Thursday night," he told her.

'Monday came, all was well,' Lylly continues. 'Tuesday came, he was not sick. Wednesday came, and still he was well: with which his impertinent wife did much twit him in the teeth. Thursday came, and dinner was ended, he very well. He went down to the waterside, and took a pair of oars to go to some buildings he was in hand with in Puddle Dock. Being in the middle of the Thames, he presently fell down, saying only "an impost, an impost", and so died.'[9]

Forman's death could have been due to any one of a number of things, from a burst ulcer, brought on by the effort of rowing, to appendicitis or even a heart attack. He left a fortune of some £1,200, along with substantial property, and willed to little Clement a book on herbs and their uses, while all his 'rarities, secret manuscripts, of what quality soever Dr Napier of Lindford in Buckinghamshire had, who had been a long time his scholar'.[10] Lylly's epitaph for him was that he was 'very judicious and fortunate in the treating of sickness which indeed was his masterpiece'.

18

Posthumous Notoriety

Simon Forman died on 8 September 1611. Until then he had been in good health, and only a few weeks earlier he had cast to see if a woman, referred to only as 'G. Cole', would 'love' him. The entry for the burial of 'Simon Forman, gentleman' on 12 September 1611 takes up only one line in the Lambeth parish register. He was fifty-nine years old, a respectable age by the standards of the day. But his lonely and unexpected death in the middle of the River Thames is not the end of the story, although it prevented the final outcome of his involvement with the Countess of Essex. For there is no doubt at all, had he lived, that at best he would have been called as a witness at the trials of Anne Turner and the countess, and at worst would have found himself in the equivalent of the dock beside them.

Within days of his death, Anne Turner arrived at Forman's house demanding that his widow hand over any papers, letters or other material in his study that might in any way incriminate her mistress or Viscount Rochester, so that she could destroy them. She softened this somewhat by adding that if Mistress Forman did as the Countess of Essex commanded, she would be rewarded. Possibly Anne Forman was not immediately ready to co-operate, for she later said that Anne Turner then went on to spell out what was likely to happen to her if she failed to do as she was asked: the Privy Council would doubtless order a search of her house and 'there might find such things that might hurt' not only the countess and

197

Rochester but Mistress Forman as well, with the result that it 'might then order that all the late doctor's wealth and property be seized'.[1]

Faced with such a choice, she did hand over some papers to Anne Turner, and destroyed others herself (which is a strong hint that Forman had probably kept up his records and case notes until the end). She kept back the countess's two letters, perhaps seeing them as useful insurance in case of future trouble. That being done, for the next two years or so she was left in peace and most probably assumed that she would hear no more of the matter.

The Overbury murder case has never lost its fascination and since Simon Forman's name is inextricably linked with it, it has a place here.[2] His death left the superstitious and increasingly frantic Frances Essex without an expert in the field of love potions and astrology in whom she could confide, so she turned once more to Anne Turner to find people willing to help her. She was introduced to a clutch of doubtful astrologers and a woman called Mary Woods, otherwise known as 'Cunning Mary', who claimed expertise in palmistry, general fortune telling and an ability to provide women with the husbands of their choice after ridding themselves of their first. There was also to be a second go-between: Richard Weston, who was already a member of Anne Turner's household, employed by her husband as a bailiff. Weston was sixty, of sober and upright appearance, but in the past had narrowly escaped hanging for coining, that is forging money.

Although the affair between Frances and Viscount Rochester was common knowledge, the king continued to heap wealth and preferment on his favourite, even giving him Crown lands. More sensationally, he made the young man a Privy Councillor. Then a month later Cecil died, leaving vacant the post of Secretary of State to the Privy Council, and the Court rang with the rumour that King James would appoint his favourite to the most powerful position in the land. However, it seems that even James baulked at that, for he left the post open and, after announcing that he was quite capable of dealing with the office himself, he appointed Rochester to assist him with the task, his special brief being the reading and analysis of foreign despatches. He also bestowed on him the Custody of the Signet, a post hitherto only held by the most privileged of councillors since the seal was affixed to the king's most important correspondence as well as to the patents authorising royal grants.

Not surprisingly the twenty-five-year-old viscount was soon out of his depth and, in desperation, turned for assistance to the man whom he considered his best friend, Sir Thomas Overbury. The two had first met in 1601, when Overbury was visiting Scotland, and had taken to each other immediately. The general opinion of Overbury was that while he was both clever and well read, as well as handsome, he was extremely arrogant and his manners were atrocious.[3] The friendship had grown even closer when the young Robert Carr came to London with the king in 1603. Indeed it was so close that the king's Master of Requests, Sir Roger Wilbraham, openly described Overbury as Rochester's 'bedfellow, minion and inward counsellor'.[4] This could explain the king's well-known antipathy towards him.

However, if Overbury's arrogance had made him unpopular at Court, he acquired a certain amount of fame in 1614 through the publication of his book, *Overbury's Characters*, a series of sketches each headed with a title such as 'The Courtier', 'The Lawyer', 'The Virtuous Widow' and 'The Fair and Happy Milkmaid', which was a best-seller by the standards of the day.

Rochester had confided details of his affair with Frances Essex to his friend. At first Overbury was happy to encourage it, but as the battle moved towards its legal climax, with Frances now determined to marry Rochester at all costs, he became increasingly critical, in part because he rightly believed that an affair, however passionate, would not make for a happy marriage. He was also disliked intensely by Frances's father, the Earl of Suffolk, and he feared that he could lose both his position assisting Rochester and his place at Court through Suffolk's influence. He therefore began seriously to persuade Rochester to disentangle himself from his involvement with the countess. Overbury had acquired another powerful enemy in Frances's great-uncle, the Earl of Northampton, a confirmed bachelor also close to Rochester, who addressed him in public as 'Sweet Rochester' and wrote him letters of undying devotion. So it was that Overbury found himself in the middle of a seething cauldron of emotions mixed with *realpolitik*.

Overbury's criticisms culminated in a huge and public row in March 1613, during which he threatened to break off all connections with his erstwhile friend and also demanded a pay-off of £1,500 for his part in a business deal he had successfully concluded for Rochester. Rochester was deeply unhappy at the estrangement and might well have begun to have second thoughts. At this point Frances became almost demented, terrified that Overbury might convince her lover not to go through with the marriage. She began plotting to rid herself of Overbury once and for all. One idea was that he should be challenged to a duel in which his opponent, using any means however foul, would ensure he died. She even suggested this to a man she knew bore a grudge towards Overbury, Sir David Wood. While agreeing to give him a beating if that was what she wanted, Wood told her bluntly that he would have nothing to do with an unfair fight designed to result in a man's death.

Either by chance, or through Northampton's machinations, the king, who was irritated at having Overbury around the Court, offered him an overseas posting as an ambassador to France, the Netherlands or Russia. Overbury did not want to accept for he had no desire to leave the Court and knew that such posts were badly paid and usually led to the political wilderness. He then made the fatal mistake of saying this, loudly and publicly, with the result that the king issued an official order for him to do as he was told. Foolishly Overbury (possibly egged on by Northampton and Rochester) again refused, allowing his enemies the excuse they had been waiting for and on 21 April 1613 he was arrested and confined in the Tower.

He had always been a hypochondriac and it was not surprising that he soon began to complain of illnesses. The principal doctor appointed to treat him was the bizarrely named Dr Theodore Turquet de Mayerne, one of the most fashionable doctors in London, although Overbury was also seen occasionally by others. Unlike Simon Forman, Dr Mayerne was considered eccentric even by the standards of the day. He believed that 'the bitterest medicines worked best' and prescribed bizarre potions, plasters and enemas. However, in spite of receiving regular medical treatment during the summer, Overbury became progressively weaker, culminating in an agonising bout of sickness in September to which he finally succumbed. By the middle of the month he was dead.

In no time the gossip both inside and outside the Court was that Overbury had been poisoned. After all, his death was extremely convenient, for with her most bitter critic out of the way, Frances drove the legal proceedings to their final conclusion, her marriage to Essex was declared null and she swiftly married her lover, the king conferring the title Earl of Somerset on Rochester to give him equal status with the

Howards. But the rumours would not go away and eventually the authorities were forced to look into them. It was discovered that a supposedly trustworthy gaoler in the Tower was the countess's former go-between, Richard Weston. Weston was immediately arrested, along with Anne Turner and a man called James Franklin, to be joined later by the Lieutenant of the Tower, Sir Gervase Elwes and Sir Thomas Monson (whose daughter was the most likely substitute for the countess at the examination by the midwifery panel). Finally the finger of suspicion pointed at the new Earl of Somerset, who was arrested and confined in the Tower, to be followed there later by Frances, who had been allowed to remain at home until she had given birth to their child.

There was general agreement that the means of death was white arsenic, most likely provided by James Franklin, a confidant of Anne Turner, but there was no consensus then, nor has there been since, as to how the poison was administered. Several suggestions were made at the subsequent trials: that Anne Turner put it in the salt she gave to Weston for Overbury's meals, that she or another likewise poisoned sweet tarts which she had taken in to him and, the most popular, that in his last days Overbury was given a poisoned enema.[5]

Weston came to trial and eventually went to the gallows, still refusing to admit his guilt, But it was the trial of Anne Turner which was to prove truly sensational, for it was then, four years after his death, that Simon Forman posthumously took centre stage. Once his relationship with Anne Turner became known, other interesting revelations followed, such as his close involvement with the Monson family over the years, including Sir Thomas, who was now also under arrest and who, like Anne Turner, was a Catholic recusant. Possibly, since the trouble in Plymouth in August 1602, involving both Forman and Sir William Monson, was recorded in State Papers, this was also taken into account.

Over the years there have been stories to the effect that Forman, not James Franklin, was accused of procuring the arsenic for the Countess of Essex, but this was not the case whatever the wild rumours circulating at the time. It was four years since the two had had any communication with each other and nothing we know of Forman suggests, even if he had become absolutely besotted with Frances Essex, that he would have agreed to any such thing. It would have gone against his vocation and everything in which he believed.

The trial of Anne Turner began before the Lord Chief Justice, Sir Edward Coke, on 7 November 1615. As in all trials of the period, the dice were heavily loaded against her. There was no presumption of innocence and in prominent cases acquittals were virtually unknown, for juries were conscious that verdicts of 'innocent' were looked on as implicit criticisms of the sovereign in whose name the case had been fought.[6] Anne Turner was accused of aiding and abetting Richard Weston in the poisoning of Sir Thomas Overbury. She had dressed herself with great care, wearing a ruff stiffened with her own fashionable yellow starch, and with her hair prettily arranged, on top of which she perched a smart hat. It was to do her little good, not least because Coke told her brusquely that she was not allowed to wear a hat in court.

Gradually the story began to unfold of the countess's infatuation, and her confiding in Anne Turner, who had agreed to seek out Dr Simon Forman of Lambeth, to ask his help in bewitching Carr and ensuring the impotency of her husband. When Anne Forman was summoned to give evidence, she produced the two letters quoted earlier along with some other material, telling the court that Anne Turner had often spent hours on end closeted alone with her late husband in his study and recalling how she had come to her house only days after his death demanding papers and letters.[7]

None of this had a direct bearing on the poisoning, but it was useful evidence to blacken Anne Turner's character further by proving her close relationship to Forman, who was now declared to have been no more than a necromancer, a practiser of black magic and a false caster of horoscopes. At some stage his house must have been searched, for the prosecution produced a range of strange and magical objects, which had been discovered there, to support their case.

These caused a sensation. Most obviously shocking, 'there was shown in court two pictures [figures] of black lead, a man and a woman naked, belly to belly, in bestial fashion', also 'the mould of brass from which they were made' and a black scarf full of 'white crosses' and along with it a parchment with the names of the Trinity 'written on it profanely'. There was also another parchment, to which was allegedly attached 'a little piece of the skin of a man', bearing the word 'Corpus' along with particular names of the devils Forman had conjured up to torment Lord Somerset and Sir Arthur Mainwaring should they prove unfaithful to their lady loves.[8]

Next came a doll in wax 'very sumptuously apparelled in silks and satins', which the prosecutors claimed had been used as a prop during Forman's magic 'incantations', but which one of those present said later was merely a model such as those used by dressmakers 'to teach us the fashion for ladies' tiring and apparel'. (Possibly this had belonged to Anne Forman.) Rumours of the significance and power of the objects reached such a pitch that it was said that, as everyone craned their necks to look when they were publicly exhibited in the court, there was a 'loud crack' from the scaffolding set up to provide public seating, which caused great fear and confusion, 'everyone fearing hurt as if the Devil had been present and grown angry to have his own workmanship showed by such as were not his own scholars'.[9] Simon Forman had spoken from the grave.

It took some time to calm the atmosphere so other documents could be produced. Among these was a list, discovered by Anne Forman and handed to Lord Justice Coke, of which ladies loved which gentleman at Court (some of them had consulted her husband). It is said that Coke was on the point of reading it out loud when he discovered the name of his own wife was at the top of it.

After this it scarcely mattered whether Anne Turner had been party to the Overbury poisoning or not, since her character had been comprehensively destroyed by her association with a man involved in the black arts; from then on she was treated as no better than a witch. The result was a foregone conclusion. Unsurprisingly, she went to pieces under questioning and her denials of complicity were swept away by the judge, on the grounds that 'denial is no good excuse for then every delinquent would escape'. During his supposedly impartial summing up, Coke thundered at her that she personified the seven deadly sins being 'a whore, a bawd, a sorcerer, a witch, a Papist, a felon, a murderer' and, worst of all, 'the daughter of the devil Forman'. This phrase led to later rumours that Anne Turner may have been one of Simon Forman's illegitimate children. There are absolutely no grounds for this assertion. 'Daughter of the Devil' was a term often applied to any woman accused of witchcraft.

The jury returned their inevitable verdict of guilty and Anne Turner was taken off to await execution. Faced with imminent death and the saving of her immortal soul, she allegedly made a rambling 'confession', including that she had seen strange 'jellies' in the countess's chamber, which were to be sent to Overbury, although she had not taken them to him herself. Later, when the Lieutenant of the Tower, Sir Gervase Elwes, came to trial, it was said that Anne Turner had 'confessed the act of poisoning persons and all circumstances freely', although there is no proof that she did so. Even if this were true one wonders what means were used to extract such a confession after she had denied it for so long.

Her execution took place on 14 November. Interest in the Overbury poisoning was so great that a massive crowd assembled at Tyburn to see the 'witch' hang. Once again she had dressed herself with care and when she reached the scaffold with great dignity she expressed her repentance for the sins that 'she came hither to die for' (though still not admitting to the poisoning), stating that she had also renounced her Catholicism and embraced the Protestant Church, which must certainly have been under duress. She then called on God to protect her children and knelt as the Lord's Prayer was said, after which her hands were tied with black ribbon, a black veil was put over her head and the cart on which she was standing pulled away, leaving her swinging in the wind. That evening her brother, a servant of Prince Charles, took her body away for decent burial in the churchyard of St Martin-in-the-Fields.

Later Sir Gervase Elwes followed her to the scaffold for his negligence and various other minor players suffered either death or long-term imprisonment, but not the instigator and prime suspect, or her husband, although both eventually came to trial and were found guilty. After their trials, the Earl and Countess of Somerset remained imprisoned in the Tower without any decision being made as to their fate, but as time passed the king relented towards his old favourite and they were both released. They lived exiled in the country, locked into a deeply unhappy marriage during which Carr never stopped blaming his wife for what had happened, until Frances died a lingering death of cancer of the breast and womb sixteen years later.

Did she do it? There have been some attempts since to exonerate her, but the general verdict is that she did, either directly or through others. As to those less elevated who went to their deaths for their supposed involvement, it is uncertain whether they had any real guilt in the matter or were merely unwitting tools.

The final words at the time on Simon Forman's involvement in the affair are in a lengthy poem, *Sir Thomas Overbury's Vision* by Richard Niccols, a close friend of the Howards, written in 1616. The reference proves that his long connection with Catholics had been noted by the authorities, possibly even his affair with Avisa Allen. In telling his version of the story, Niccols introduced the ghosts of both Weston and Anne Turner. Weston is made to grieve:

> Oh had I never known that Doctor's house,
> Where first of that whore's cup I did carouse,
> Where disloyalty did oft conceal,
> Rome's frightened rats, that overseas did steal ...

The suggestion is that Simon ran some kind of safe house from which Catholic spies and Jesuit priests could come and go in secret.

Next, the ghost of Anne Turner explains why she did what she did:

> I left my God t'ask counsel of the Devil,
> I knew there was no help from God in evil,
> As they go hooting onward into Hell,
> From thence to fetch some charm or magic spell.
> So over Thames, as o'er the'infernal lake,
> A wherry with its oars I oft did take,
> Who Charon-like did waft me to that strand
> Where Lambeth town to all well known doth stand.
> Where Forman was, that fiend in human shape,
> Oft there the Black Enchanter, with sad looks,
> Sat turning over his blasphemous books,
> Making strange characters in blood-red lines.
> Oft would he intreat the fiends below,
> In the sad house of endless pain and woe,
> And threaten them as if he could compel
> Those damned spirits to confirm his spell.

We do not know what effect, if any, Simon Forman's posthumous notoriety had on his wife and son, for Mistress Forman disappears from history and so does Clement. Since his father's medical books were passed to the Napier family, presumably he did not follow in his father's footsteps. In view of what had happened, his mother might well have considered it best to choose anonymity for them both.

Epilogue

Simon Forman was a man of many parts: showman, caring doctor, womaniser, credulous with regard to the occult, yet always questing after knowledge, his personality a mixture of vanity, obstinacy, humour, naïveté and enthusiasm. He is not the first and certainly will not be the last to try and reinvent himself as time passed, in his case by writing his autobiography and inventing a noble and heroic lineage; we must be grateful that so much of his diary survived to give us a far more realistic picture.

After nearly four hundred years of being written off as a charlatan, medical historians have of late begun to take Simon Forman seriously and reassess his place in the medicine of his day, not least because out of the years of struggle to become accepted as a physician he devised exemplary ways of properly recording case histories and encouraged Richard Napier to do the same. Also, even given his undoubted gift for enraging people and the misunderstandings over the status of the textbooks on which he relied, there were plenty of others also working without university qualifications and using similar methods, like Shakespeare's son-in-law, John Hall, who were not hauled up so often before the censors in Knightrider Street to be punished with fines and imprisonment or so publicly and frequently described as a quack.

Now, even Forman's astrology is treated sympathetically. As medical historian Michael Macdonald points out:

206

Consciously, astrologers at this level of expertise used figures to guide their analysis of symptomatic complaints in a manner analogous to the way doctors today employ laboratory tests like, for instance, a blood series. If a patient presents with lassitude, jaundice and weight loss these days, his physician orders blood tests that include a liver spectrum. If the liver enzymes are elevated, he might then go on to question a patient about his drinking habits and order a more specific battery of tests to determine whether he has cirrhosis or cancer of the liver or both. In a similar way, the astrologer analysed the pattern of stellar influences interactively, eliciting further information from the client when the horoscope had particularly sinister features. The range of these secondary signs was broader than it would be today, but not dissimilar.[1]

Such doctors were popular because they were in all likelihood good doctors by the standards of the time. In an age when experience was the critical factor in learning to diagnose and treat disease, astrologers had an unusual amount of experience which they were trained to organise in a systematic manner. And compared to the conventionally university-trained physicians, they were comparatively cheap, which was a further cause of friction with the College of Physicians.

In his notes in the rarely examined Cambridge manuscript, Simon Forman has left us written details of the remedies he used, almost all of which were herbally based and which, if they did not always do any good, were unlikely to do much harm. Compare these then with the appalling medicaments offered by Dr Theodore Turquet de Mayerne, the king's physician who attended Thomas Overbury. A typical example and one of his favourites is his 'balsam of bats for a good plaster'. The ingredients consist of three snakes cut into pieces, twelve bats, two puppies, a pound of earthworms washed in white wine, common oil, malago sack and bay leaves. The whole disgusting brew is then boiled up and strained and the marrow from stag and ox bones added to it, along with 'honey of dogs' nettles'. This was then applied to the backbone supposedly to cure a whole range of illnesses, few of which were actually afflictions of the back. Interestingly, when Overbury died he was found to have a huge, stinking and suppurating hole in his back covered by one of Mayerne's plasters.[2]

Macdonald also notes that all three of the physician/astrologers he has studied, Forman, Napier and Lylly, had a larger proportion of female patients than men, showing that they were particularly trusted by women, whose gynaecological and obstetric health problems, not to mention their fertility or lack of it, were a major source of misery, anxiety and, all too often, death. Another reason for the high number of women consulting Forman was their need to do so on behalf of their households, since women were the primary healers in the society of their day, regularly dealing with family sickness.

It is easy to forget, given the standard of medicine today, just how primitive it was four hundred years ago, before even the circulation of the blood had been understood; also how many patients died of infections, since it was not until comparatively late that the importance of asepsis was recognised, leading to a dramatic drop in the number of those dying of blood poisoning, gangrene and, in the case of women, puerperal fever following childbirth. As to any anaesthetic which might allow major surgical intervention, the only pain-killer was opium, and should such a drastic course be taken the subsequent blood loss most often led to death.

In Forman's own writings, honest and quirky as they are, he comes across as a doctor with a real interest in his patients and their condition. That they were never merely a way of making money, as was all too often the case, was shown in his care and concern for the victims of the plagues of 1592–3 and 1603.

But, medicine aside, Forman's papers, unlike any others that survive, bring to life a whole spectrum of society. The politics of the day are recorded in State Papers, the lives of the nobility in family archives. Dramatists like Middleton, Dekker and Jonson, as well as Shakespeare, give us a colourful picture of the times, but Simon Forman shows us real people. The sailors, merchant venturers, privateers and explorers of the time pass through the pages of his casebooks and diary, alongside soldiers of fortune, masters and their men, playwrights, poets, social climbers, knights of the realm and the odd lord and lady.

As for the women, apart from his desire to 'halek' any female who was remotely willing, he offers us a gallery of portraits. Some, the tuppenny whore 'Julia in Seething Lane' and the lady from Deptford 'bedangled with jewels' who left him 'a grasshopper', are described in a single line. Others are seen in far more detail, like Anne Young, first met as a teenager daringly pursuing him when he was an apprentice in Salisbury, who later became his mistress and bore him a son. Then there is the colourful, slatternly Alice Blague with her red hair and falling stockings, and the ambitious and calculating first Frances Howard, who became Frances Pranell, clawing herself up the matrimonial ladder until she reached the rank of Countess of Hertford and finally Duchess of Lennox. Other unforgettable characters are the half-Italian, musical tease, Emilia Lanier, the possible Dark Lady of the Sonnets, and the bouncing Bess, who larked on the bed with the boys and gave him a daughter. Most vivid and poignant of all is poor tragic, passionate, doomed Avisa Allen with her Catholic recusancy, her burden of guilt and her dying baby.

Of the many women who appear in the 'halek notes' only Anne Young and Avisa Allen appear to have truly touched his heart. Certainly not the young woman, chosen in no small part because of her family connections, whom he made his wife when he had almost given up finding anyone suitable who would accept him. Yet his 'Tronco', as he referred to her, finally gave him what he wanted most of all, a son and heir, the boy so full of life and 'ayer' that he would never sit still and who knew his letters before he was five years old.

Through the folios in the Bodleian Library and other scattered papers we follow Forman's struggles and setbacks, his diverse interests in science and mathematics, his fascination with the exploration of the New World, his love of theatre. To set against the picture of 'the devil Forman', flourished by Judge Coke, there is that of the established doctor who had discovered a new passion, gardening, and spent his spare time designing rose gardens, setting fruit trees to make an orchard and planting aromatic-smelling camomile 'near to the privy'.

Without ever intending to be, Forman was a vivid commentator on his time. From his consulting room in the Stone House in Thames Street he opens a door through which we can step out into the parish of Billingsgate and catch a glimpse of what it really was like to live and work in London at the turn of the seventeenth century.

Notes

The folio numbers referred to throughout are those originally given to the mss by the Ashmolean and are carried through into the Bodleian Library index. Full publication details of sources cited are given in the Bibliography.

FOREWORD

1 Murray Jones, 'Reading Medicine at Tudor Cambridge'.
2 Ashmol., folio 208.
3 Respectively, Stanier, *Magdalen School*; judge in his summing up at the trial of Anne Turner, proceedings of the Committee of Censors of the College of Physicians; *Religio Medici*, eds Grell and Cunningham.
4 Unless otherwise stated the direct quotes from Simon Forman are either from the diary or his brief autobiography.

1: CHILDHOOD AND APPRENTICESHIP

1 All material in this chapter comes from Forman's brief autobiography, Ashmol., folio 208, pp. 136–214, unless otherwise stated. Regarding the accuracy of the date and time of his birth, it is rare to have such information before the days of proper registration and birth certificates, unless the parents were people of power and wealth. Most often, a date of birth has to be estimated from the record of an infant's baptism, when the usual assumption is that it took place three days earlier.
2 Ashmol., folio 244.
3 Ibid.
4 *The Winter's Tale*, Act III, scene 3.

2: THE STUDENT PHYSICIAN

1 Ashmol., folio 208.
2 Ibid.
3 Rowse, *The Casebooks of Simon Forman*.
4 Forman's brief sojourn at Oxford provoked one of the few favourable comments on his subsequent career from a former Master of Magdalen, who wrote of him that 'the school's most famous pupil ... was that wayward genius, Simon Forman, who much improved himself in learning for two years'. Stanier, *Magdalen School*, pp. 108–10.
5 Ashmol., folio 608.
6 Porter, *The Greatest Benefit to Mankind*, pp. 73–80. I am indebted to this author for most of the information on the philosophies of both Galen and Paracelsus.
7 Ibid.
8 See a feature in the *Daily Telegraph*, 20 February 1998, by a leading academic, who admitted in a letter to the author that he did not know of the Cambridge material.
9 Murray Jones, 'Reading Medicine at Tudor Cambridge'.
10 Ibid.
11 Mary Edmunds, 'Simon Forman's Vade Mecum', from *The Book Collector*, Spring 1977.
12 King's College, mss. 16.

3: LOVE AND LITIGATION

1 Schoenbaum, *Shakespeare, a Documentary Life*.
2 Lane (ed.), *John Hall and His Patients*.
3 King's College, mss. 16.
4 Ibid.
5 The nineteenth-century academic, J.O. Halliwell Phillips – one of the first scholars to examine the Forman folios – had intended to pubish the autobiography and extracts from the diary for the Camden Society, but decided against it because 'the many "halek" notes rendered the material far too indelicate for conventional publication'. Instead he printed a mere handful of copies, marked 'For Private Circulation Only'. Halliwell Phillips (ed.), *The Autobiography and Personal Diary of Dr. Simon Forman*.
6 King's College, mss. 16.
7 Rowse, *The Casebooks of Simon Forman*.

4: 'WONDERFUL TROUBLESOME YEARS ...'

1 All diary entries from Ashmol., folio 208.
2 Ibid., folio 802.
3 Ibid.
4 Ibid., folio 354.
5 This Stephen should not be confused, with Stephen Mitchell. A. L. Rowse suggests that they were one and the same, describing Stephen Mitchell as Simon Forman's half-brother, but this was not the case. He was the son of Simon's half-sister, who married a man called Mitchell and while he and Simon became close over the years, he was only a child when these events took place.
6 Salgado, *The Elizabethan Underworld*.

Notes

7 *Shakespeare in the Public Record Office*, folio E179/146/354.
8 State Papers, Star Chamber 5/579/33.
9 Ibid.
10 Ashmol., folio 244.

5: MEDICAL MATTERS

1 Ashmol., folio 802.
2 Folger, mss. Ze28, Part II.
3 Rowse, *The Casebooks of Simon Forman*, p. 61.
4 I am indebted to Mary Edmund's paper, 'Simon Forman's Vade Mecum', in the *Book Collector* for making it possible for me to read the material in the Cambridge mss. and also for her translations from the Latin.
5 Salgado, *The Elizabethan Underworld*.
6 King's College, mss. 16.
7 East Anglian market gardener to author, plus Culpeper's *Herbal*.
8 Information given to the author by the Royal College of Physicians.
9 Wilson, *Plague in Shakespeare's London*.
10 Ibid.
11 Ashmol., folio 802.

6: THE TERRORS OF THE NIGHT

1 Ashmol., folio 206.
2 Ibid., folio 208.
3 Ibid., folio 354.
4 Wraight and Stern, *In Search of Christopher Marlowe*, London, 1965.
5 Ibid. A facsimile of the 'Baines note' can be found on pp. 308–9.
6 Greene, *A Groatsworth of Wit Bought with a Million of Repentance*.
7 Recusant Roll No. 2 (1593–4), Catholic Record Society.
8 Ashmol., folio 354.
9 Ibid., folio 234.

7: 'MANY BRABBLES AND BRAWLS'

1 Paper published by the Hakluyt Society, 1848.
2 Wraight and Stern, *In Search of Christopher Marlowe*.
3 Ashmol., folio 240.
4 Wraight and Stern, *In Search of Christopher Marlowe*.
5 Ashmol., folio 354.
6 Ibid., folio 206.
7 Royal College of Physicians, folio 51b.
8 Ibid., folio 55b.
9 Ibid., folio 102a.
10 The archive record is dated in the old way as 1593, but by Forman as 1594. The censors

were Drs Gilbert, Marbeck, D'Oylie, Williamson and Nowell. There are few verbatim transcripts of the actual exchanges, so the reports themselves are somewhat subjective.

11 Murray Jones, 'Reading Medicine in Tudor Cambridge'.
12 Michael Macdonald, 'The Career of Astrological Medicine in England', in *Religio Medici*, eds Grell and Cunningham.
13 Ashmol., folio 802.
14 Ibid., folio 205.
15 Rowse, *The Casebooks of Simon Forman*, p. 65.

8: DISTURBED DREAMS

1 Royal College of Physicians, vol. 2, folio 115b.
2 Ibid., vol. 2, folio 116b.
3 Ibid., vol. 2, folio 121b.
4 Ashmol., folio 234.
5 Ibid.
6 Ibid.
7 Ibid.
8 Rowse, *The Casebooks of Simon Forman*, p. 71.
9 King's College, mss. 16. Story also in diary, folio 802.
10 Ibid.
11 Ashmol., folio 234.
12 Ibid.

9: DEATH AND A DARK LADY

1 Ashmol., folio 226.
2 Ibid., folio 234.
3 Ibid.
4 Ibid., folio 226.
5 Ibid., folio 354.
6 Ibid.
7 Ibid., folio 802.
8 Ibid., folio 234.
9 Henslowe's Diaries, ed. W. W. Greg, p. 40.
10 Ashmol., folio 354.
11 Ibid., folio 384.
12 Chambers, *William Shakespeare*, ii, p. 90.
13 Ashmol., folio 195.
14 Rowse, *The Casebooks of Simon Forman*, p. 95.

10: FRIENDS AND ACQUAINTANCES

1 Ashmol., folio 802.
2 *Religio Medici*, eds Grell and Cunningham.
3 Ashmol./Napier 240, 103–111.

Notes

4 Ibid.
5 Aubrey, *Brief Lives*.
6 *Letters of John Chamberlain*, vol. I, ed. McLure.
7 Ashmol., folio 195.

11: POLITICS, PRIVATEERS AND MARRIAGE

1 Rowse, *The Casebooks of Simon Forman*, p. 98.
2 Ashmol., folio 192.
3 Ibid.
4 Ibid.
5 They are scattered throughout the folios but are particularly concentrated in Ashmol., folio 192.
6 Ibid.
7 Rowse, *The Casebooks of Simon Forman*, p. 180.
8 *Hakluyt's Voyages*, vol. 10, p. 266.
9 Ashmol., folio 219.
10 Ibid.
11 While the most likely explanation is that Forman's wife was known both as Jane and Anne, the deciphering of his handwriting is another possibility. *Reading Tudor and Stuart Handwriting* by Lionel Munby gives excellent examples and explanations of the idiosyncracies of sixteenth-century hands.

12: DOMESTICITY AND SUCCESS

1 Ashmol., folio 181.
2 Ibid., folio 802, p. 51.
3 Ibid., folio 206.
4 Salisbury mss. vol. VIII, p. 155.
5 Jenkins, *Elizabeth the Great*, p. 307.
6 Ashmol., folio 208, p. 144.
7 *Letters of John Chamberlain*, vol. I, p. 116.
8 Rowse, *The Casebooks of Simon Forman*, p. 236.
9 Ashmol., folio 236.

13: AN EVENTFUL YEAR

1 Ashmol., folio 411.
2 Ibid.
3 Ashmol., folio 195.
4 Ibid., and Rowse, *The Casebooks of Simon Forman*, p. 205.
5 Ashmol., folio 354.
6 Ibid.
7 Ibid., folio 236, p. 110; also King's College mss. 16, p. 71v.
8 Ashmol., folio 411, p. 103b.
9 Royal College of Physicians, folio 1496.

10 Ibid.
11 Ibid.
12 Ashmol., folio 802.
13 Lady Mary did write to her brother on Frances's behalf, to which he replied: 'I have been told that you greatly pity the estate of my wife. I cannot understand how my wife's estate is to be pitied, unless she does not discern her own happiness or acknowledge from whom, next to God, it came. Whatever she has been to me, I resolve to deal honourably with her.' Bath mss, IV, pp. 161–2.

14: STRANGE HAPPENINGS IN PLYMOUTH

1 Henslowe's Diaries, eds Foakes and Rickeat, pp. 41–2.
2 Ashmol., folio 235.
3 Ibid., folio 802.
4 No note of the happenings in Plymouth exists among Forman's papers. Nor is there any record of the events in the city archives as almost all the papers for that period were destroyed during air raids in the in the Second World War. The presence of Leveson and Monson in their respective capacities is, however, confirmed by Royal Naval archives. What we are left with is the official account in the Salisbury mss, vol. XII, pp. 290, 550–3.
5 Ibid.

15: THE LICENSED PHYSICIAN

1 Ashmol., folio 236.
2 Ibid., folio 219.
3 Carey, *Memoirs of Himself.*
4 Napier Correspondence, Ashmol., folio 240, pp. 103–11.
5 Ibid., folio 354.
6 Wilson, *Plague in Shakespeare's London.*
7 Ibid.
8 Ashmol., folio. 1301.
9 Dr E. S. Leedham, Cambridge University Library.
10 Ashmol., folio 240.
11 Jonson, *Eastward Ho!*, Act IV, scene 1.

16: TRANQUILLITY

1 Ashmol., folio 208, p. 255.
2 Ibid., folio 802.
3 Ibid.
4 Ibid., folio 225.
6 Royal College of Physicians, folio 109b.
7 Ibid.
8 Ibid.
9 Rowse, *The Casebooks of Simon Forman*, p. 256.

Notes

10 Ashmol., folio 240
11 Strachey, *The True Reportery of the Wracke and Redemption of Sir Thomas Gates.*
12 Ashmol., folio 802.

17: A PROPHECY OF DEATH

1 *State Trials*, ed. William Cobbett, vol. II, p. 923.
2 Ashmol., folio 208.
3 *The Devil is an Ass*, Act II, scene 8.
4 Somerset, *Unnatural Murder*, p. 32.
5 The material concerning Forman's widow in the subsequent legal proceedings comes from the Earwaker Papers (CR6/2/19) held as part of the Bramhall collection of manuscripts in Chester City Record Office. They were collected by William Davenport and consist of transcripts of national and personal papers. Unhappily, at the time of writing the relevant papers are in a parlous state and are awaiting restoration, which could be some considerable way off. So the exercepts quoted are taken from other published sources. It is impossible therefore to know if there is other material of Forman's in them.
6 *State Trials*, ed. William Cobbett, vol. II, pp 931–3.
7 Ibid.
8 Ashmol., folio 240, pp. 103–11.
9 Lylly, *Mr. William Lylly's History of His Life and Times*, pp. 22–3.
10 Ibid.

18: POSTHUMOUS NOTORIETY

1 Chester City Record Office, CR 63/2/19, folio 10.
2 Anne Somerset, *Unnatural Murder*, is the most recent; others are listed in the Bibliography.
3 Aubrey, *Brief Lives*, p. 317.
4 Somerset, *Unnatural Murder*, p. 75.
5 There is also a view that it is not beyond the bounds of possibility that Overbury died not of poison, but as a result of his appalling medical treatment, even though Mayerne and his apothecary were later exonerated from all responsibility for his death.
6 Somerset, *Unnatural Murder*, p. 75.
7 Chester City Record Office, CR 63/2/19, folio 10.
8 Ibid.
9 *State Trials*, pp. 993–4 et seg. Also Salisbury mss., vol. XXLL, p. 23.

EPILOGUE

1 Macdonald, *Religio Medici.*
2 Somerset, *Unnatural Murder*, pp. 204, 237–8.

Bibliography

FIRST SOURCES: MANUSCRIPTS

Bath Manuscript, British Museum.
The Bramhall Collection of Manuscripts, Chester City Record Office CR6/2/19, folio 10.
Folger Library Manuscript Ze28, Folger Library, Washington D.C.
Manuscript 16, King's College Library, Cambridge.
Records of the Royal College of Physicians 1593–1607.
The Salisbury Manuscripts, Volume viii.
Simon Forman, the Ashmolean folios (Ashmol.), Bodleian Library.

PAPERS

Recusant Roll no. 2 (1593–4), Catholic Record Office.
Calendar of State Papers, Proceedings of the Star Chamber, Public Record Office.
State Trials, ed. William Cobbett, 1809.

JOURNALS

Mary Edmund, 'Simon Forman's Vade Mecum', *Book Collector*, Spring 1977.

Bibliography

The Autobiography and Personal Diary of Dr. Simon Forman, ed. J.O. Halliwell-Phillips, London, 1849, marked 'for private circulation only'.

BOOKS

Aubrey, John, *Brief Lives*, Penguin, London, 1962.

Boas, F., *Marlowe and his Circle*, Oxford, 1929.

Chambers, E.K. *William Shakespeare, A Study of Facts and Problems*, London & N.Y., 1930.

Culpeper's Complete Herbal, London, 1995.

Foakes, R.A. and Ricker, R.T. (eds), *Henslowe's Diaries*, Cambridge, 1961.

Fraser, Antonia, *The Weaker Vessel*, London, 1984.

Greene, Robert, *A Groatsworth of Wit Bought with a Million of Repentence*, ed. G.B. Harrison, London, 1932.

Grell, O.P. and Cunningham, A. (eds), *Religio Medici*, Brookfield, USA, 1996.

Hakluyt's Voyages, vol. 10, ed. K.F. Hall, Glasgow, 1903.

Jenkins, Elizabeth, *Elizabeth the Great*, London, 1958.

Jonson, Ben, *The Devil is an Ass, Epicene, Eastward Ho!*

Lane, J. (ed.), *John Hall and his Patients*, Stratford-upon-Avon, 1996.

The Letters of John Chamberlain, vol.1, ed. Norman E. McLure, Philadelphia, 1939.

Lewis, B. (ed.), *The Shakespeare Documents*, vols I and II, Oxford, 1940.

Lindley, David, *The Trials of Frances Howard*, London, 1993.

Long, E.R. (ed.), *Selected Readings in Pathology*, London, 1961.

Lylly, William, *Mr. William Lylly's History of His Life and Times*, 1715.

Macdonald, M., *Religio Redici*, eds Grell and Cunningham, London, 1996.

McElwee, W., *The Murder of Sir Thomas Overbury*, London, 1952.

McKerrow, R.B. (ed.), *The Works of Thomas Nashe*, Oxford, 1958.

Munby, L., *Reading Tudor and Stuart Handwriting*, Salisbury, 1988.

Murray Jones, P., 'Reading Medicine at Tudor Cambridge', from *The History of Medical Education in Britain*, eds Vivian Nutton and Roy Porter, USA, 1995.

Nicholls, C., *A Cup of News*, London, 1984.

Porter, R., *The Greatest Benefit to Mankind – A History of Medicine*, London, 1997.

Rowse, A.L., *The Casebooks of Simon Forman*, London, 1974.

———, *The England of Elizabeth*, London, 1953.

Salgado, G., *The Elizabethan Underworld*, London, 1977.

Schoenbaum, S., *Shakespeare, a Documentary Life*, Oxford, 1977.

Shakespeare in the Public Record Office, HMSO, 1985.

Somerset, A., *Unnatural Murder*, London, 1997.

Stanier, R.S., *Magdalen School*, Oxford, 1958.

Strachey, William, *The True Reportery of the Wracke and Redemption of Sir Thomas Gates, Knight*, London, 1625. (A shortened and edited version appears as endpiece to the Arden Shakespeare edition of *The Tempest*, 1999.)

Wilson, F.P., *Plague in Shakespeare's London*, Oxford, 1927.

Wraight, A.D. and Stern, V.F., *In Search of Christopher Marlowe*, London, 1965.

Index

221

Index

Index